Words and Minds

'Using wide-ranging and fascinating language data, *Words and Minds*, with its multidisciplinary and cross-cultural approach, captures the reader's interest and holds it from beginning to end.'

Jean Peccei, Roehampton Institute

'For anyone interested in the functions of human language, *Words and Minds* should be essential reading. It provides a clear and exciting introduction to language as a vehicle for collaborative thought, and an authoritative survey of research taking this view. At the same time, it is full of original and exciting insights of its own, making it one of the most important books on discourse analysis to have been published in the last decade.'

Guy Cook, University of Reading

There is widespread interest in the everyday use of language. People want to know how to communicate well. *Words and Minds* takes a lively and accessible look at how we use language to combine our mental resources and get things done.

Examining everyday language and drawing on a wide range of research, but always with a light style, Neil Mercer provides a unified account of the relationship between thought and language. Mercer analyses real-life examples of language being used effectively, or otherwise, in many different settings, including workplaces and schools, the home, the Internet, and the courtroom, and offers practical insights into how we might improve our communication skills.

Words and Minds will appeal to anyone interested in language and the psychology of everyday life.

Neil Mercer is Professor of Language and Communications at The Open University.

Words and Minds

How we use language to think together

Neil Mercer

Routledge
Taylor & Francis Group

LONDON AND NEW YORK

First published 2000 by Routledge
11 New Fetter Lane, London EC4P 4EE

Simultaneously published in the USA and Canada
by Routledge
29 West 35th Street, New York, NY 10001

Reprinted 2003 (twice)

Routledge is an imprint of the Taylor & Francis Group

© 2000 Neil Mercer

Typeset in Times and Helvetica by Keystroke,
Jacaranda Lodge, Wolverhampton
Printed and bound in Great Britain by TJ International Ltd, Padstow, Cornwall

British Library Cataloguing in Publication Data
A catalogue record for this book is available from the British Library

Library of Congress Cataloging in Publication Data
Mercer, Neil
   Words and minds : how we use language to think together / Neil Mercer.
      p.   cm.
   Includes bibliographical references and index.
   1. Language and languages. 2. Thought and thinking. 3. Communication.
   I. Title.
P106 .M379 2000
302.2'24–dc21   00-022280

ISBN 0–415–22475–6 (hbk)
ISBN 0–415–22476–4 (pbk)

For Lyn and Anna

Contents

Figures

Preface

This book is about people communicating and thinking together, and it is the product of the process it describes. While the idea for this book emerged from my own research, carried out since the mid-1980s, its content draws substantially on the work of many other reseachers. First, there are those whose own examples of language use are included here, and whose explanations of how we use language to get things done have strongly influenced my own. I have tried, throughout the book, to acknowledge them clearly as the sources of such examples and ideas. There are also those friends and colleagues with whom I have worked closely, to the extent that I cannot claim sole ownership of any of the ideas presented here. I am thinking particularly of Douglas Barnes, Derek Edwards, Karen Littleton, Janet Maybin, Andy Northedge, Rupert Wegerif, Rib Davis and Sylvia Rojas-Drummond. However, while I gratefully acknowledge their intellectual contributions, I know that I may not do proper justice to them. Without the expert help of Pam Burns and Fiona Harris, producing the text of this book would have been much more difficult, and excellent editorial support at Routledge ensured the process of publication ran smoothly. Finally, to Lyn Dawes – fellow-researcher, constructive critic and source of constant encouragement – my gratitude is beyond expression.

I gratefully acknowledge the financial support for my research provided by the Economic and Social Research Council in grants to three projects (refs. COO232236, R000232731 and R000221868), and The Open University for providing an environment in which constructive interthinking flourishes.

For permission to reproduce transcripts and other material in the book, I am grateful to all concerned.

The publisher and I would like to thank Faber & Faber Ltd for permission to quote from 'Days' from *Collected Poems* by Philip Larkin © 1988, 1989 by the estate of Philip Larkin. Reprinted by permission of Farrar, Straus and Giroux, LLC.

Transcriptions

The chapters of the book contain many transcribed sequences of speech. Some (those which appear without any special acknowledgement) were recorded by me or come from research in which I was directly involved; the rest have been taken from the reports of other researchers. Generally speaking, the chapters are organized round these numbered sequences. To help readers, I have presented them all in the same way, with a number (relating to the chapter in which they appear, and their position in the chapter) and a title. I have presented my own transcriptions in a non-technical way and added conventional punctuation, so as to make them accessible to readers. For the same reason, I have adapted slightly several of the transcripts taken from other researchers' work, usually by simplifying the presentation of the transcriptions to make them clearer for readers in the context of this book. This means that I have only included such information about pauses, overlapping speech, pronunciation, emphasis and other non-verbal aspects of communication as I thought absolutely necessary in the circumstances. The basic transcription symbols I use are explained below. Occasionally more complex transcriptions are presented, in which case the symbols used are explained at that point. (For example, those associated with the methods of 'conversation analysis' are explained in Chapter 3, p. 57.)

Basic transcription symbols

1 When someone continues after an interruption this is shown thus:

Ellen: But we had someone appointed to the PTE . . .
Bill: Yeh
Ellen: . . . who was earning above the top of the lower scale.

2 Simultaneous speech is shown thus:

Peter: OK, then I'll [go.
Donna: [so will I.

3 Emphatic speech is shown underlined:

Hector: Even though I <u>told</u> him.

4 The location of inaudible words or passages is shown thus:

But if (. . .) knows.

5 Words which are unclear or uncertain appear in parentheses:

Alan: And (inevitably) so.

6 Gestures and other non-verbal actions are explained in italics:

Anne: Hah uh (*laughs*).
Trevor: OK (*long pause*).

Neil Mercer,
March 2000

1 Language as a tool for thinking

Much has been written about the relationship between language and thought, but one aspect of that relationship has not been given the attention I believe it deserves, despite its familiarity and importance in our lives. This is our use of language for thinking together, for collectively making sense of experience and solving problems. We do this 'interthinking' in ways which most of us take for granted but which are at the heart of human achievement. Language is a tool for carrying out joint intellectual activity, a distinctive human inheritance designed to serve the practical and social needs of individuals and communities and which each child has to learn to use effectively. Developing a better understanding of how we can use it to combine our intellectual resources has some useful, practical outcomes, particularly for education.

People use language every day to think and act together, and it is that normal, everyday use with which I am concerned here. Throughout the book, I will use examples of language to illustrate and explain the various ways in which it is used. These examples come from recordings made by me, or by other researchers, in homes, offices, workshops, schools, courtrooms and several other locations. The first, Sequence 1.1, is given below. It is part of a conversation I recorded when three people were trying to do a crossword puzzle. Joan and Mary are two retired sisters who spend a lot of time doing puzzles. At the point at which the sequence begins, they have been trying to finish one for a while, when a friend of theirs, Tony, comes to visit.

Sequence 1.1: A crossword puzzle

Mary: I bet he can help us do, with our crossword clue.
Joan: Where? (*looks for paper, then reads*) Here 'Material containing a regular pattern of small holes' eight letters blank blank blank B blank A blank D.
Mary: Regular holes. Oh we have struggled.
Joan: I thought, perhaps the base stuff that you use to make a tapestry. Cloth.
Mary: Cloth. Lace I thought, that has holes.
Joan: Braid?
Tony: Embroidery?
Joan: It won't fit braid, will it (*checks*). No. Yes it will.
(*All look at puzzle together*)
Tony: Embroidery, is there something called broid?
Mary: Broid?
Tony: Wait a minute, material, needn't not be cloth, it could be like material goods.
Mary: Construction material?
Joan: Board? Some kind of board? Chipboard?
Tony: No, what's it, pegboard!
Mary: Pegboard! (*Which is the right answer*)

Let us consider the order in which things are done in this sequence. First, Mary says that she 'bets' their guest could help with the crossword. Her remark functions as an invitation for Tony to participate in some joint problem-solving. Joan's action shows that she interprets the remark this way, as she looks for the problem and reads it to Tony. Mary and Joan also tell Tony what they have attempted and achieved so far. A crucial part of this process, then, is that the participants share relevant past experience and information and then use this 'common knowledge' as the foundation, the *context*, for the joint activity that follows. On this basis, Tony makes some suggestions of his own and the three speakers work *with* each other's ideas. Information is shared, but more than that is achieved. Using the tool of language, the three people together transform the given information into new understanding. As a result of their combined intellectual efforts, they solve the problem.

Sequence 1.1 is an ordinary, everyday example of a very important human process. We all think collectively, and teamwork of this kind is vital for many kinds of activity. The first step to understanding how we do it is to recognize that language has this special function for collective thinking – otherwise we are liable to underestimate its psychological and social significance. In our everyday lives, of course, we take this function completely for granted. We know that there are obvious benefits to be gained from joint mental activity, and organize our lives accordingly. We say that 'two heads are better than one', meaning that the mental resources of two or more people working together can achieve more than the sum of their individual contributions. But perhaps because we do take it so much for granted, the role of joint mental activity in human creativity is also often played down in explaining human achievements. In most societies of the developed world it is customary to explain success in terms of individual talent rather than collective effort, and we commonly celebrate those achievements by awarding prizes and other marks of acclaim to individual artists, scientists, entertainers, and so on. Yet few, if any, major achievements in the arts, sciences or industry have been made by isolated individuals. Almost always, significant achievement depends on communication *between* creative people. Impressionist art, the literature of the Brontës or the Lake poets, the structure of DNA, the microchip and the songs of the Beatles were all essentially the products of creative collectives. Creative explosions of literature, art, science and technology, which occur in particular places at particular times, represent more than coincidental collections of individual talent: they represent the building of communities of enquiry and practice which enable their members to achieve something greater than any of them ever could alone. Traditional and more conventional kinds of work have also depended, since time unreckoned, on the sharing and joint construction of knowledge amongst practitioners and on the induction of apprentices into the ways in which language is adapted to serve the needs of such communities of practice.

We use language to work successfully together; but of course we also know from everyday experience that joint activity does not necessarily lead to success. Two heads may be better sometimes, but we also say that 'too many cooks spoil the broth'. That is, we find that people frequently misunderstand each other, and that joint activity can generate confusion, stifle individual creativity and achieve only mediocrity. Studying how we normally use language to think together may help us to understand how effective collaboration can be more reliably achieved.

The evolution of language and thinking

It is hard to imagine how human social life could exist without some kind of language. The emergence of language, some time long ago in the prehistory of our species, made possible the kind of social existence which we take for granted. It gave us a crucial evolutionary advantage over other animals, partly because it became possible for us to share useful information with a new clarity and explicitness, within and across generations. Through the evolution of language, we also became capable of thinking constructively and analytically together. Other relatively intelligent species (such as chimpanzees and dolphins) have never developed comparable ways of sharing their mental resources, with the result that each individual animal can only learn from others by observation, imitation and taking part in joint activity; and most of the knowledge each chimpanzee or dolphin accumulates over a lifetime is lost when they die. Language is a unique evolutionary invention. Some animals, like honey-bees, have reliable ways of sharing useful information, using sign systems which have been evolutionarily designed and genetically programmed for a single, focused purpose. But language is a completely different kind of communicative system, because it is flexible, innovative and adaptable to the demands of changing circumstances. It enables people to create, share and consider new ideas and to reflect together on their actions (for example, to evaluate their joint activities using concepts like 'plans', 'intentions', 'honour' and 'debt'). Words mean what humans agree together to make them mean, new words can be created as required, and they can be combined to make an infinite variety of meanings. Language enables us to share thoughts about new experiences and organize life together in ways in which no other species can.

Explanations for why the evolutionary emergence of language was so important for the development of our species commonly focus on the use of language for sharing information accurately, so that it became possible for humans to learn from each other and co-ordinate their actions. For example, in his book *The Language Instinct*, the psycholinguist Steven Pinker writes: 'Simply by making noises with our mouths, we can reliably cause precise new combinations of ideas to arise in each other's minds.'[1] By emphasizing 'precision' in this way, however, there is a danger that the nature of language – its important differences from animal communication systems – and hence its real significance in human evolutionary development, will be misrepresented. Language has not been designed as a means for transmitting ideas in a precise, unchanged form from one individual brain to another. Of course humans use language to share and exchange information quite effectively, on the whole. Yet on a practical, everyday level, we all know that we do not reliably make people understand exactly what we mean. As Guy Browning, a journalist commentator on the world of work, points out:

> A shoal of a million fish might not be able to write Romeo and Juliet between them, but they can change direction as one in the blink of an eye. Using language, a human team leader can give an instruction to a team of six and have it interpreted in six completely different ways.[2]

Misunderstandings regularly arise, despite our best efforts, because there is rarely one unambiguous meaning to be discovered in what someone puts into words. But variations in interpretation are not always 'misunderstandings'. When we are dealing with complex, interesting presentations of ideas, variations in understanding are quite normal and sometimes are even welcomed: how otherwise could there be new interpretations of Shakespeare's plays, and why else are we interested in them? I am sure that my understanding of Pinker's book, despite the clarity of his writing, will not be exactly what he might have intended or expected, and I know that I will not make quite the same interpretation of it as other readers. I expect that many authors are frequently dismayed to discover that readers misunderstand their 'message'; but they should not necessarily take this as failure on their part. The act of reading any text relies on the interpretative efforts of a reader, as well as on the communicative efforts and intentions of the author.

As a system for transmitting specific factual information without any distortion or ambiguity, the sign system of honey-bees would probably win easily over human language every time. However, language offers something more valuable than mere information exchange. Because the meanings of words are not invariable and because understanding always involves interpretation, the act of communicating is always a joint, creative endeavour. Words can carry meanings beyond those consciously intended by speakers or writers because listeners or readers bring their own perspectives to the language they encounter. Ideas expressed imprecisely may be more intellectually stimulating for listeners or readers than simple facts. The fact that language is not always reliable for causing precise meanings to be generated in someone else's mind is a reflection of its powerful strength as a medium for creating new understanding. It is the inherent ambiguity and adaptability of language as a meaning-making system that makes the relationship between language and thinking so special.

We cannot, then, understand language use simply in terms of information transfer between individuals. Every time we talk with someone, we become involved in a collaborative endeavour in which meanings are negotiated and some common knowledge is mobilized. Joan, Mary and Tony in Sequence 1.1 can quickly get on with their problem-solving because they all know what a crossword puzzle is and how it is solved and they know that it is reasonable to take that shared knowledge for granted. Even a simple and brief encounter – someone requesting directions from someone else on the street – involves a certain tacit, negotiated agreement about what kind of event is taking place and how it is appropriate to behave. However, there is always the potential risk that a shared understanding and purpose may not be successfully negotiated. Different perspectives may not be reconciled (as in the joke about someone asking directions who is told 'Well, if I was trying to get there I wouldn't start from here'). But in almost every encounter we do not only gain and give information; the joint experience shapes what each participant thinks and says, in a dynamic, spiral process of mutually influenced change. We can see Joan, Mary and Tony doing this towards the end of the sequence as they explore the possible meanings of the word 'material'. The product of a conversation is usually the achievement of some new, joint, common knowledge. Language is designed for doing something much more interesting than transmitting information accurately from one brain to another: it allows the mental resources of individuals to combine in a collective, communicative intelligence which enables people to make better sense of the world and to devise practical ways of dealing with it.

A great deal of research has now been done on how infants learn to speak. Observational studies of young children learning their first words have revealed that they do not simply copy the language they hear around them. Instead, they seem to have a very specific, powerful ability to use what they hear to work out how their native language works, despite the fact that a good deal of what they hear may be grammatically incomplete or incorrect. This remarkable ability enables most children to become creative language users with astonishing rapidity, producing sequences of words which they may never have heard spoken but which conform to basic rules of grammar. Many linguists, psychologists and biologists use this evidence to argue that language is not simply a means of communication invented by our intelligent ancestors, but is a biological product of natural selection. That is, they suggest that our capacity for learning and using language must be an innate, instinctive ability, 'hard-wired' into the human brain,[3] and so have tried to determine whether the neurological organization of the brain reflects features common to all human languages – the so-called 'language universals'. While these kinds of questions about human origins are profoundly intriguing, investigating the living relationships between language, society and individual is no less interesting and important for understanding the human mind. Our brains may indeed be designed for acquiring language, and language may mirror some neurological features of the brain; but, in order to become effective communicators, children have to learn a particular language and understand how it is used to 'get things done' in their home community. The human capacity for using language may well be a biological feature, but languages, and the ways in which people use them, vary and change considerably across and within societies, while human brains do not. Each living language is therefore a cultural creation which has emerged from the history of generations of a community of users. Unlike young honey-bees, children will only learn how to use a native language – the local, specific version of the natural human communication system – by interacting with the people around them in the context of social events. As I will show in later chapters, culturally specific ways of using language are very important for the development of children's interthinking capabilities.

Language and the joint creation of knowledge

For centuries, people have wondered whether our thoughts are shaped by the meanings and structures of language (the question of *linguistic determinism*) and if people who grow up speaking different languages come to think in different ways (the question of *linguistic relativity*). Research on linguistic relativity has usually involved some attempt to discover whether native speakers of one language conceptualize the world in different ways from speakers of another language, in ways that reflect differences in the grammar and vocabulary of the languages involved. The still-inconclusive results of years of research and debate about this issue continue to accumulate on library shelves the world over, and I do not intend to pursue it further here. Rather than asking 'How, if at all, does acquiring a language influence the way an individual thinks?', I want to address the question 'How do we use language to make joint sense of experience?'

We are essentially social, communicative creatures who gain much of what we know from others and whose actions are shaped by our need to deal with the arguments, demands, requests, entreaties, threats and orders that others make to us and we make to them. At the practical level of everyday life, individual thinking and interpersonal communication have to be integrated. To make our ideas real for other people, we have to express them in words (or other kinds of symbolic representations, such as mathematical notation, diagrams and pictures). For our ideas to have any social impact, we must either act them out or communicate them to other people in ways which will influence the actions of those people. That is, we use language to transform individual thought into collective thought and action.

The word 'knowledge' is not only used to refer to the information held in an individual's brain (as in 'her knowledge of local history is phenomenal'); it is also used to refer to the sum of what is known to people, the shared resources available to a community or society (as in 'all branches of knowledge'). Knowledge in this second, social, shared sense exists primarily in the form of spoken and written language (and the related system of mathematical notation). Even though science is about material things and physical relationships, and is represented in technologies and artefacts, it is shared through words and formulae. Almost all of what any biologist knows about evolutionary theory, for example, will not have come from observing material evidence but from communicating, through language, with other biologists. Ask a chemist to explain the Periodic Table and they will use names for the elements which were given to them by other chemists, and which reflect the history of chemistry as embodied in chemistry texts and journals. Astronomers and physicists know about 'supernovas'; however, what they know is not just the result of looking through their telescopes but of reading and hearing how their colleagues have tried to explain the data at their disposal.

It is hard, if not impossible, to separate much of the knowledge that humans share from the words in which it is expressed. Try reflecting on your understanding of what you have just read on the previous page. Can you separate the content of what you have read from the language I have used? Indeed, if you try to formulate your own views on what you think I am saying, or clarify any disagreements you have with it, this will inevitably involve your own use of language as a tool for thinking. Dialogue stimulates thought in ways that non-interactive experience cannot. The veteran interviewer and recorder of oral histories, Studs Terkel, was once told by one of his informants: 'You know . . . until you asked me your questions, I never knew I felt that way',[4] and it is a common experience amongst teachers of science that it is only in trying to explain a theory or procedure that one appreciates the limits of one's own understanding. So, while I am not arguing that the workings of our minds are directly determined by our use of language, I *am* suggesting that, in normal human life, communicative activity and individual thinking have a continuous, dynamic influence on each other. By studying the joint creation of knowledge we may gain a better understanding of the relationship between individuals and the societies in which they live, and of the relationship between individual and collective forms of knowledge.

Vygotsky's ideas about language and thinking

In the 1920s, the Russian psychologist Lev Vygotsky made some interesting claims about the relationship between language and thought, and between individual and society. By all accounts he was an unusual man, a many-talented individual who directed plays and wrote about subjects as diverse as art, neurophysiology and Marxist theory. Despite having suffered a serious attack of tuberculosis, he took a very active role in the literary and scientific communities of Moscow. But his main work was as a psychologist, teaching at the university and specializing in the education of children with severe physical and learning disabilities. Soviet psychology at that time was a divided community. It was dominated by the stimulus–response conditioning theory of Vygotsky's fellow Russian Ivan Pavlov, which his supporters believed could become the basis for a truly scientific, objective, experimental study of behaviour. Others, rejecting Pavlov's influence, argued that psychology should be the study of thought and consciousness, pursued through introspection and reflection. Vygotsky did not align himself with either of these factions. Instead, he proposed that psychologists should investigate the relationships between thought, action, communication and culture. Inspired by Marxist ideas about the importance of the development of tools for the beginnings of human society, he suggested that it was the use of one distinctive tool – language – which had originally enabled human thinking and social behaviour to become so distinct from that of other animals.

Vygotsky's ideas were seen as radical and controversial in Russia, and his work was considered so threatening to orthodox Soviet psychology that the authorities eventually banned it; but there is now much support for his point of view. Vygotsky described language as having two main functions. As a communicative or *cultural tool* we use it for sharing and jointly developing the knowledge – the 'culture' – which enables organized human social life to exist and continue. He also suggested that quite early in childhood we begin to use language as a *psychological tool* for organizing our individual thoughts, for reasoning, planning and reviewing our actions. He came to believe that, during early childhood, a fusion of language and thinking occurs which shapes the rest of our mental development. Vygotsky claimed that it is the capacity for 'verbal thought' which most significantly distinguishes our intellect from that of other animals. Another key feature of his account of children's psychological development was the idea that the two functions of language, the cultural and the psychological, are integrated. As children hear people in their communities using language to describe experience and get things done, they pick up these cultural 'ways with words' and eventually make them their own psychological tools. If this process is successful, children gain ways of making sense of the world as they learn the communication skills for becoming active members of their communities. Vygotsky saw human individuals and their societies as being by linked by language into a historical, continuing, dynamic, interactive, spiral of change.

Vygotsky did not see the effect of his ideas on psychology and education, as he died of tuberculosis in 1933 at the age of 37. His book *Thought and Language*, published the year after his death, was banned almost immediately by the Soviet authorities. It first appeared in an English translation in 1962.[5] The book is, in any case, only a partial account of his theory and it took until the 1970s and 1980s for much more of his work to become available outside Russia and for its impact on the world of psychology to be felt.[6] Vygotsky provided relatively little evidence to support his interesting ideas, but those ideas have inspired more recent research. We now know that young children normally start behaving as communicative, social beings well before they take their first steps. Indeed, the failure of any child to do so is now taken as an indication of some physical or psychological disability. Infants in the cot respond in systematic ways to the gestures and expressions of their parents, and as soon as they learn their first words, they begin to take 'conversational turns' in interactions. Children do not learn language incidentally, separate from the practicalities of life. They learn language by using it to take part in the life of the community into which they are born. As Vygotsky put it: 'Children solve practical tasks with the help of their speech, as well as with their eyes and hands.'[7] The careful observations of Jerome Bruner and other developmental psychologists have shown how young children's individual development is shaped by their dialogues with the people around them.[8] Young children learn language, as well as much else that they need to know, through engaging in conversation with adults. As the linguist Michael Halliday has put it: 'When children learn language . . . they are learning the foundation of learning itself.'[9]

Using language to get things done

In everyday life people often contrast 'just talking' with 'getting things done'; but some of the most crucial things that ever happen to us, or that we make happen, are achieved by employing the tool of language. Wars have been ended, careers have been ruined and hearts have been broken because of what was said or written. Some people are granted particular, specific power by their society to do things with words. The formal cultural acts of marrying, naming, inaugurating and condemning to death are achieved through the use of language. By stating the words 'I now pronounce you husband and wife' a suitably qualified person *makes it so*. We all have such power to some extent. By saying 'I am sorry' on an appropriate occasion, for example, we apologize. The philosopher J.L. Austin called statements of this kind 'performatives', because saying them amounts to the performance of a specific social action.[10]

For any performative act to be valid, the context must be appropriate. But it is often hard to state precisely and unambiguously quite what an 'appropriate' context is. In 1998, the British press was quite taken for a time by an incident in which, due to the delayed arrival of a minister of the church, an unordained assistant stepped in and took the minister's role in completing a marriage ceremony. Legal and ecclesiastical experts did not seem to be able to provide a definitive view on whether the assistant's performative act had in fact sealed the knot for the somewhat distressed couple. The outcome of the event was thus a debate about what criteria make the performative act of 'marrying' valid. Cases of 'breach of promise', bribery and corruption may involve rather different kinds of disputes about the use of performatives. For example, one person may claim that a 'promise' was made, while another may deny it. Language is not only used to enable joint thinking about a problem, language use itself may create a problem to be resolved. I will return to this issue in later chapters.

With language we do not only 'inform' and 'promise': we 'accuse', 'defend', 'lie', 'deny', 'order' and 'persuade'. Language is a weapon in battles between competing explanations, theories and ideologies. Ask anyone who has experienced a conversion to a religious or political faith, and you will usually find that a conversation was crucial somewhere in the process. At a more workaday level, most of us find it impossible to live our lives without regularly becoming involved in some conflict of opinions. Most of the issues that people treat as important, from the concrete realities of domestic existence to grand theories of the universe, are things that they argue about. People used to believe that science advances by a simple process: when the results of new research are published, they simply prove or disprove current theories. If things were that simple, it would be hard to explain why scientists spend so much time challenging each other's methods and interpretations of findings. The advance of science, like any other serious business, depends on arguments being carried out between well-informed individuals who have a commitment to the pursuit of 'the truth'. The success of Darwin's theory of evolution certainly depended on its advocates providing evidence to support their claims; but the decisive turn in the ascendancy of that theory over creation-myth explanations of the arrival of our species is commonly associated with an argument: the public debate between Thomas Huxley and Bishop Samuel Wilberforce at Oxford in June 1860. And the part of Huxley's reported speech to be found in all dictionaries of quotations is not concerned with disputing evidence, but rather with the manner in which his eloquent opponent had used, or misused, the intellectual tool of language. It was spoken after Wilberforce had asked Huxley on which side of his family he claimed to be descended from an ape:

> [A] man has no reason to be ashamed of having an ape for his grandfather. If there were an ancestor whom I should feel shame in recalling it would rather be a *man* – a man of restless and versatile intellect – who, not content with an equivocal success in his own sphere of activity, plunges into scientific questions with which he has no real acquaintance, only to obscure them by an aimless rhetoric, and distract the attention of his hearers from the real point at issue by eloquent digressions and skilled appeals to religious prejudice.[11]

This effective 'put down' of rhetoric is, of course, itself a rhetorical triumph. This illustrates the fact that we cannot easily separate 'ideas' or 'evidence' from the ways in which language is used to present and discuss them. The process of argument is the way in which we establish which 'truths' we agree on.

The communal technology of language

A continuing and reliable source of revenue for publishers is the production of new dictionaries. Old ones go out of date because every living language continues to evolve to meet the needs of its speakers. The beauty of the design of language is that it can be adapted to suit particular kinds of activities and purposes. Not only can existing words change their meaning and be combined in novel ways, new words and structures can also be created as they are required. Specific kinds of activities require particular ways of talking and writing, and new types of activity are forever arising. Throughout the world, languages which have been used very effectively by generations of farmers and rural craft workers have had to change to accommodate the entry of their societies into the world of mechanized industries and international economies. New ways of communicating may well have important implications for how people use language to think together. The invention of written language, and then of print, made the sharing of ideas much more possible over distance and time; the invention of the telephone made it possible for people far apart to work intellectually together. With today's electronic communications, such as e-mail and computer conferencing, we can use written language for the dynamic interaction of minds; and language itself is adapted to enable this, as I will show in later chapters.

Vygotsky's image of language as a tool is a helpful one because it emphasizes that language is used for practical purposes. However, because language can be adapted into so many functional varieties to suit our cultural needs, the psychologist Gordon Wells has suggested that it is more appropriate to think of it as a whole tool-kit.[12] Children may have an innate ability to acquire the language of their home community, but there is no doubt that they have a lot of learning to do about how this tool-kit is used in particular ways within their community. The way in which children do this is rather similar to the way in which they learn to use other tools – by a combination of observing experts at work, receiving some guidance from them and trying out the tools for themselves. Learning how to use the functional artefacts of our society is not a matter of 'discovery learning', but rather a course of informal apprenticeship. We do not learn what tin-openers, hammers and screwdrivers are good for by finding one lying around as a strange and unknown object, experimenting with this object in isolation and eventually discovering it is good for something like knocking in nails.[13] We learn about hammers at the same time as we learn about the human *action of hammering*, by observing the tool being used by other people, by being shown how to hold and wield it, and by trying to use it ourselves to perform similar kinds of actions. Our first encounters with tools happen in a social context – as part of the 'cultural practices', as anthropologists call them, of social life – and so our understanding of the nature and function of those tools will be shaped by that social context. As I will show in later chapters, we do not learn how to use language in the abstract, we learn to use it by joining in the intellectual life of particular – local or virtual – communities.

Summary

From the work of researchers in many disciplines, we have some valuable insights into how language, thought and social activity are related. But there is something of special importance that language enables us to do, which, although vital for our everyday lives, is rarely held up for special consideration in research on language and thinking.

It is that language provides us with a means for *thinking together*, for jointly creating knowledge and understanding. The inherent, open-ended flexibility and ambiguity of language makes it qualitatively different from other animal communication systems; it is not simply a system for transmitting information, it is a system for thinking collectively. Language enables us to set up intellectual networks for making sense of experience and solving problems. We use it as a tool for creating knowledge, so that language and the knowledge we create with it are resources for individuals and communities. Language links individual thought with collective resources of knowledge and procedures for getting things done. It may be the capacity to integrate the social with the psychological which most of all characterizes human activity and distinguishes it from that of other animals. There are practical reasons for investigating how we use language to think together. It may, for example, help us to understand why joint activity is sometimes more or less effective, and may enable us to improve educational practice. But it may also simply offer us some new and interesting insights into how we live our social lives and get things done.

2 Laying the foundations

Despite what I have said in the previous chapter, my claim that we can observe and analyse people 'thinking together' might still seem a dubious one. Surely, it might be objected, 'thinking' is a process that takes place inside individuals' heads, and all that can be observed and analysed is people using language to communicate information and ideas? My first response to this objection is to say that the notion of 'communication' does not capture the special quality of the joint intellectual activity I am concerned with here. 'Communication' encourages the view of a linear process whereby people exchange ideas, think about them individually and then again exchange the products of their separate intellectual efforts. This does not do justice to the dynamic interaction of minds which language makes possible. Of course people think individually, but one might similarly claim that 'dancing' is necessarily an individual process, because basically it is a matter of a person using their brain to co-ordinate their own body movements; yet we commonly talk of people 'dancing together', because we wish to recognize the nature of the joint, co-ordinated physical activity involved. I have introduced the term 'interthinking' in order to focus attention on the joint, co-ordinated intellectual activity which people regularly accomplish using language.

The fact that we can never really know what anyone else is thinking is a problem faced by all research on human cognition. Fortunately, the problem is a lesser one for me than for some kinds of psychological researchers, who are indeed trying to study thought processes inside individual people's heads. But it is also a problem that we all face in our everyday lives; and in both research and everyday life we deal with that problem in practical ways, by using whatever information we can to infer what other people think. Our lives may well depend on how well we can do this. In science and other kinds of investigative research, we deploy the same perceptive faculties and reasoning powers that we use in everyday life to the study of a particular topic or problem – but in a more rigorous and systematic way. We can look carefully at how people use language to try to solve problems, argue about different points of view, resolve differences and create shared knowledge and understanding. We can see whether their use of language reveals some common strategies or techniques for doing so. We can also see what outcomes their efforts achieve, and we can add to what we observe by asking people for their own insights into what they do. In this chapter, I will describe some of the ways in which people use language to strive to reach joint understanding, and in doing so I will also introduce some concepts that are useful for analysing the process of thinking collectively. The first of these concepts is 'context'.

Context

The concept of 'context' is necessary for understanding how we use language to think together. This is rather unfortunate, because it is particularly difficult to produce a satisfactory definition of 'context' – and many people have tried.[1] No definition is widely accepted across the field of language studies, because anyone working in the field can always find good reasons for disagreeing with anyone else's definition. This state of affairs does not reflect an unusual state of chaos in the field, compared with other kinds of research, and it need not be an obstacle here. (Neuroscientists, psychologists and philosophers have similar problems with 'consciousness' and 'intelligence', as do physicists with 'time', but their research likewise continues.) I have my own conception of 'context', and Sequence 2.1 below will help me to begin to explain what this is. The sequence is an extract from a telephone conversation I recorded while doing some research on the language of work. How much sense can you make of it?

Sequence 2.1: The GAT job

Caller: Is Ellen there? It's Bill.
Secretary: I'll put you through.
Ellen: Hello, Bill.
Bill: Oh, hi. Just a quick, um, query. Umm. You, uh, with the GAT job.

Ellen:	Yeh.
Bill:	Umm, you know we were talking about the, the range which it's possible, the salary range?
Ellen:	Yeh.
Bill:	The two scales just join on, do they, end on? Or . . .
Ellen:	Yeh.
Bill:	. . . you know the discretionary range.
Ellen:	Yeh, well . . .
Bill:	(*interrupting*) Is that an overlap?
Ellen:	Um. Strictly speaking it isn't.
Bill:	Oh right.
Ellen:	But we had someone appointed to the PTE . . .
Bill:	Yeh.
Ellen:	. . . who was earning above the top of the lower scale, where . . .
Bill:	[Yeh.
Ellen:	[. . . she came from.
Bill:	Yeh.
Ellen:	And that was a short-term post and she was allowed to be appointed . . .
Bill:	[Aah.
Ellen:	[. . . to a discretionary point, so that might be an option.
Bill:	Well, sounds to me a good one. Let's, yeh, let's go for that.

You may have guessed that this was a conversation between two people who work in the same business; they are in fact a manager (Bill) and an administrator (Ellen) in the same university. Their work often brings them into contact, and this is one reason why they can begin the conversation with few preliminaries or extended explanations. They both know the nature of each other's job, and in their conversation can build easily on the 'common knowledge' of their shared workplace and of past conversations they have had on related topics (hence the use of expressions like 'You know we were talking about . . . ' and 'You know the discretionary range . . . '). They are continuing an earlier discussion of the point on a salary range at which an appointment could be made to a post in the university. The most obvious 'jargon' words are the acronyms (GAT and PTE), which, because they are not real English words at all, would be completely incomprehensible even to outsiders who were members of their language community. The phrase 'discretionary range' is made up of two English 'dictionary words', but the meaning of this phrase for the speakers in this conversation depends on some very specific, shared knowledge about the financial working practices of British universities. Because the speakers' past experience has prepared them well for this conversation, the 'jargon' used is certainly no problem. Indeed, using the specialized language of their professional community enables them to think together about the problem (how to find a suitable salary for a newly appointed person) and find an acceptable solution.

The specific information you probably lacked about the content and purpose of the conversation, and which you would need to make proper sense of it, was of course available to the speakers. They had no reason to make their meanings more explicit, because they were drawing on the common knowledge that they had accumulated from similar experiences and earlier conversations. That shared knowledge formed part of the *context* – the contextual foundation – that they created for their talk.

When dealing with spoken language, some researchers define 'context' in terms of the physical environment in which language is used, but that only provides some potential resources for our context-making. To return to Sequence 2.1: there are no good reasons for inferring that the furniture of Ellen and Bill's respective offices, or the telephone hardware they used to communicate, were important for the sense-making in their talk. Even in a face-to-face encounter, the context of a conversation between two people is not necessarily made up of the physical objects and events around the speakers. Present objects are potential contextual resources, but so are objects and events long gone, if speakers recall them and treat them as relevant. Today I stood near someone in the middle of a busy high street who was apparently conducting an intimate conversation on his mobile phone (I heard what he said quite clearly, as he used the usual bellowing style of mobile phone users in public places). Except for the speaker initially and briefly explaining where he was to his listener, the conversation I overheard seemed to rely not at all on the frantic urban life around the speaker for its contextual foundations, as it seemed to be concerned entirely with emotionally charged events that had taken place else-where. But then again, perhaps it did have some contextual function, in that the distant listener might be enabled to appreciate the speaker's sense of urgency in dealing with this matter by being aware of where he had felt driven to call from. The point is that what really counts as 'contextual' is a matter for participants in a conversation, and this is a problem for studying how we use language for making meaning together. For these kinds of reasons, I feel that we have to accept that 'context' is a mental phenomenon, and that it consists of *whatever information listeners (or readers) use to make sense of what is said (or written)*.

We always make sense of language by taking account of the circumstances in which we find it, and by drawing on any past experience that seems relevant. If you pick up a scrap of paper from the floor, and see there are printed words in English on it, you will use the information you have about where you found it and your knowledge of the forms that printed English takes, as well as what the words 'say', to decide what they mean. So when I found a piece of card on our living room table, bearing the words ' . . . full collection of these lovable . . . ', it made perfect sense to me as part of the packaging for one of the many toy cats that inhabit my daughter's room. I used several different kinds of information to do this contextualizing – the location in which I found it was relevant, as was my memory of a new cat having been bought the previous day. As well as the actual content of printed language, the bright colours of the print and its surround helped me to relate it to the domain of children's toys. One of the most important skills of literacy is being able to decide what kind of text you are dealing with and using this information to contextualize it. It is because written texts can be fairly reliably contextualized in this way that Michael Halliday (the founder of systemic functional linguistics) suggested that types or genres of written text are associated with particular 'contexts of use', and that literate people are able to draw relevant information about 'context of use' from the distinctive form and content of a text in order to identify particular functional types or genres of written language (for example, assembly instructions, personal letters, news articles, and so on) and so make sense of them.[2] According to systemic linguists, a text (which may be someone's contribution to a conversation, or a piece of written language) has its 'context of use' defined when it is generated, and so carries the stamp of its intended function in its form. This approach has provided many interesting and useful insights into the relationship between the features and styles of language and its communicative function.

However, to understand the process of collective thinking, we need a different notion of 'context' from that used by Halliday and other systemic linguists. One reason is that they are concerned with features of texts, rather than the processes of people's thinking, and so their notion of context does not capture the essentially dynamic, temporal nature of the human mental process of *contextualizing*. By 'context of use', systemic linguists mean something that a text carries with it, wherever it goes, as an enduring, identifying characteristic. The producer of a written text or utterance is assumed to be able to determine this completely. The text on a toy's packaging therefore reflects its writer's ideas about its 'context of use'. However, if the focus of our interest is the development of shared understanding rather than features of texts, 'context' is better thought of as a configuration of available information that people use for making sense of language in particular situations. 'Context' is created anew in every interaction between a speaker and listener or writer and reader. From this perspective, we must take account of listeners and readers as well as speakers and writers, who create meanings together. For example, our interpretation of what we hear or read can be revised by gaining new, relevant information. We may make a different sense of the same text – say, a statement on the toy cat's packaging about the limited safety of the product for use by very young children – depending on what relevant information we had available at any time. Say we read it once, and then have a conversation with a lawyer friend who explains that toy manufacturers are always advised to include on their packaging a carefully worded 'disclaimer' about their responsibility for safety, regardless of realistic levels of risk. That conversation would enable us to *recontextualize* the statement and hence reassess our understanding of its meaning and function.

My conception of 'context' is also meant to explain the way in which people can co-operate in making sense. For communication to be successful, the creation of context must be a co-operative endeavour. Two people may well begin a conversation with enough prior shared knowledge to be able to achieve some initial joint understanding without making a great deal of information explicit. But as the conversation progresses, speakers must continue to provide relevant information, to the best of their judgements of need and relevance, if new shared knowledge is to be constructed. Speakers and writers have a responsibility for providing their listeners or readers with what they need to know, or at least with clues to help them access what they need to observe or remember. In this way, conversations run on contextual tracks made of common knowledge.

Language and other systems for making context

Particularly useful insights into how language is used to get things done come from research on language use in work settings. This shows that language is not just an important tool for literate occupations like journalism or research, or in 'talk' occupations like broadcasting, counselling, teaching and the law, but also for a much broader range of activities. For example, research in Canada by the linguist Peter Medway has shown that even the construction industry relies heavily on language for getting things done. Building a house is not simply a matter of an architect drawing up plans and then handing them to the builder who converts them into three-dimensional reality. The whole process is one of explanation, interpretation and negotiation. Even the most carefully drawn plans have ambiguous interpretations, and the real world of work on a building site requires frequent redefinitions, reinterpretations and modifications of the plans 'on the hoof' as the work progresses. The talk transcribed in Sequence 2.2 below comes from an on-site recording made by Medway, of a conversation in which an architect (Joe) was negotiating with a heating consultant (Harry) over the location of a problematic piece of ducting. The ducting had turned out to be bulkier than anticipated in the design of the building, and Harry had previously suggested to Joe that this would require the ceiling of the building to be lower than planned. The conversation took place as Joe, Harry and Luc (the site supervisor) walked around the site. *(Because of noise on the site, some of the recorded speech was inaudible. Inaudible speech is marked by the symbol (. . .) and where the transcription is uncertain the words are in parentheses. These and other transcription symbols I have used throughout the book are explained in the Preface.)*

Sequence 2.2: Constructing the virtual building

Joe: OK, next.
(He looks up towards the underside of the concrete slab. Harry walks a couple of steps, pointing upwards. Joe and Luc accompany him.)
Harry: (. . .), right? (. . .) the ductwork coming down that way is supposed to (go through there).
Joe: Well as you were saying yesterday on the phone, Harry that if *(9-second pause while Joe spreads out a roll of drawings and looks at them)* if we lower this part by three inches . . .

Harry: Yes.
Joe: That will be fine, right?
Harry: This should be fine, (because) the ductwork can be penetrating through there OK (. . .)
Joe: Because this is at twenty-six hundred and this is twenty-seven seventy-five. (*These are figures in mm. for the height of the ceiling taken from the drawings*)
Harry: That's right.[3]

This is an interesting example because of the way in which the talk is related to the physical environment. As well as language, two other 'semiotic systems' (ways for making meaning) are involved. One is *gesture*, as when Harry points to part of the construction, and the second is *drawing*, represented by the set of architectural plans which Joe consults later. Language is often used in conjunction with these other meaning-making tools, which can be used to draw physical artefacts into the realm of the conversation. Although the concrete slab to which Harry points had been there, above them, when they began to speak, it was not necessarily part of the context for the conversation until he pointed to it. Many other bits of the partly constructed building also surrounded them, but they were not in any obvious sense 'contextual'. Similarly, once Joe had laid the drawings out in front of the three speakers, it became possible for him to refer to parts of the drawing by simply saying 'if we lower this part by three inches' because he knew the drawings now formed a contextual resource for the conversation. In doing this, he was making good use of what linguists call *exophoric reference* – employing words like 'that' and 'there' to refer to things which exist in the physical context of the talk. Exophoric reference is a kind of linguistic 'pointing'.

The discussion on the building site also drew on another kind of contextual resource: that of past shared experience. We can see this in Joe's reference to the telephone conversation he had had with Harry the previous day (in which Harry had suggested that the solution to their problem was to lower the ceiling). But in fact, although the proposed solution is phrased in terms of 'lowering' the ceiling, we should note that they are talking about a ceiling that does not yet exist. They are not really talking about either the edifice around them, or the graphical representation on the plans, but (as Medway puts it) a *virtual* building that they are constructing together, ahead of the real one, through their conversation.

Another resource that Joe and Harry can use to build context is the common knowledge each has gained from their individual training and work experience as a member of the construction industry. They are familiar with its problems, working practices, technical drawings – and, like Bill and Ellen in Sequence 2.1, they understand the technical terms and other ways of using language that are employed to get the job done in their community of work.

Contextual clues

From the point of view of a listener or reader, understanding will be limited by the quality and quantity of relevant knowledge we have for doing the work of contextualization. But we are very good at hunting out such relevant information. Given limited contextual resources, a listener or reader can often make quite good sense of language which contains elements with which they are quite unfamiliar. Look, for example, at the transcription below of someone talking in a radio interview. What sense can you make of it, and what clues do you use to do so?

> Mi salim eplikeson bilong mi na skul bod i konsiderim na bihain ekseptim mi na mi go long skul long fama.

To help you more, I can tell you that this is an example of an English pidgin language, the *Tok Pisin* ('talk pidgin') of Papua New Guinea. It is a transcription of part of a radio interview broadcast in 1972. The speaker is a student, who is telling the interviewer about his plans to study agriculture. Any reader who is familiar with English pidgins will no doubt have used that knowledge already to make some sense of what they read. According to the sociolinguist Suzanne Romaine who collected this example,[4] *Tok Pisin* developed in the time of the British Empire, when English began to be used as an official language in the region. First used as a means of communication between the indigenous population and their European colonizers, it eventually became the most important *lingua franca* for Papua New Guineans, who have around 750 indigenous languages between them. Like other English pidgins, its vocabulary is derived mainly from English, but its grammar reflects some features of the original local languages. The transcription shows the conventional, 'standardized' form of spelling used for *Tok Pisin* today, which represents in a fairly obvious way (for English speakers) how the words are pronounced (try speaking it out loud). Once you realize that some of the words are derived from English, and you have some idea of the theme being dealt with, you should be able to use this contextual information to make some sense of what is written there – without me telling you what any of the pidgin words actually mean. (See note 5 for some feedback on your attempt.)[5]

Making context

In everyday life – unless we are finding our feet in a new language environment – we do not usually have to search hard for relevant contextual information to 'crack the code' of what we hear or read in the way that was necessary for making sense of the pidgin example above. We will be interacting with people who speak or write more or less the same variety of language and, because they have a similar life experience, much common knowledge can be taken implicitly for granted. But another rather different reason is that both speakers and listeners (or writers and readers) take an active role in building the contextual foundations for effective communication. If we are trying to communicate with someone, we strive to make the contextual foundations adequate. What is more, as our talk with someone continues, earlier conversation provides a shared contextual basis for the talk which follows. Like the operators of some strange, dual-controlled track-laying vehicle called 'language', conversational partners build the contextual foundations for their own communication as they go along.[6] They usually do this without much consciousness or awareness. Nevertheless, the process of joint contextualizing can be done well or badly, as the next two sequences illustrate. The first, Sequence 2.3, is from a session which my colleagues and I recorded, in which a girl and boy (both aged 15) are doing a problem-solving communication activity called 'Map'.[7] In this activity, which is done in pairs, partners are both given maps of the same area of British countryside. However, while the map held by one partner is recent and accurate, the other partner has an old map which does not show some recent, significant changes to the environment. For example, only the more recent map shows that a motorway now bisects the area and that a railway has been dismantled. Pairs sit back to back and have to imagine that the partner with the old map has telephoned the other in the course of a country walk to ask for help in reaching the village of Penfold beyond the obstacle of the motorway (which is unmarked on the older map).

Sequence 2.3: Simon and Mandy and the map problem

Simon: Hello Mandy?

Mandy: Hello?

Simon: Yeh, right, I'm out in the country, um, at Chidding, in the phone box here, yeh?

Mandy: Yeh.

Simon: OK? And I was on a walk up to Penfold, to have a wander round up there, and to my horror, there was a motorway there across the footpath. Now um, can you direct me from Chidding to Penfold so I can get there please?

Mandy: You go down Waldon Road.

Simon: Oh, OK.

Mandy: Past the footpath, by Chidding Hall. And then . . .

Simon: (*interrupting*) Hold on. Chidding Hall.

Mandy: Yeh. And then you go up [the footpath

Simon: (*interrupting*)   [Hold on. Now where's Chidding Hall.

Mandy: Centre for Overseas Studies, by . . .

Simon: Pardon? (*interrupting*)

Mandy: Centre for Overseas Studies. (*'Chidding Hall', but not 'Centre for Overseas Studies', is marked on Simon's map*)

Simon: Oh right, got it.

Mandy: Then you go down a little bit more.

Simon: Yeh (*hesitantly*).

Mandy: By a, to a footpath.

Simon: A footpath. Ah, no I haven't got a footpath on here. Can you give me the co-ordinates, and I'll draw it in?

Mandy: Um, C1.

Simon: C1. Is it near the railway line?

Mandy: It's just across the road from the Booking Hall.

Simon: Where? (*sounding perplexed: the Booking Hall is marked on his older map as a railway station*)

Mandy: Booking Hall.

Simon: Um, no I can't find Bicking Hall.

The sequence is fairly typical of Mandy and Simon's talk throughout the activity. They interacted in a friendly way, Simon asked a lot of questions and Mandy provided answers. But Mandy hardly ever asked

Simon questions about what his map showed. She showed little evidence of being able to distance herself from her own perspective, based on the information provided by her map, and appreciate Simon's problem from his point of view. In response to his questions, she simply stated information that she had and repeated it when he enquired further. Whether this was for reasons of nervousness, lack of interest or a weakness in her communication skills I do not know; but Mandy's failure to take an active, collaborative role in building a contextual foundation of common knowledge meant that this pair did not do well on this problem. The next sequence shows two of their classmates also attempting to solve the same problem.

Sequence 2.4: Sue and Tracy and the map problem

Tracy: Does your, does your grid map go ABC along the bottom?
Sue: ABC, yes.
Tracy: And 1,2,3 along the side?
Sue: That's right.
Tracy: And north points upwards?
Sue: (*pause*) Yes.
Tracy: Well that's all right then.
Sue: OK. Have you got the canal?
Tracy: Canal, um.
Sue: Towpath?
Tracy: I've got the track of the old railway, which is right up the [top.
Sue: [Yeh
        well that's what I've got, because you've got the new one.
Tracy: Oh 'derelict canal' is that it?
Sue: Um (*sounding uncertain*).
Tracy: Well it might just be 'canal' on your one, if it's an old one.

Tracy and Sue went about the activity in a very different way from Simon and Mandy. Sequence 2.4 comes from quite early on in their attempt, and shows how they both set about finding out what information they had in common, and how their maps differed. By establishing that both maps used the same grid reference system, they were able to use this to build, quickly and very effectively, a shared contextual foundation for solving the problem together.

Conversational ground rules

I now want to introduce another concept for understanding how we lay the foundations for joint intellectual activity: 'conversational ground rules'. The original use of the term 'ground rules' was in sport, to refer to the fact that a particular playing field or ground might have local conventions, perhaps created to take account of its special physical features, which visiting players would need to be made aware of and accept. It is now commonly used to mean special or local conventions of behaviour in any area of life. By 'conversational ground rules' I mean *the conventions which language users employ to carry on particular kinds of conversations.*[8] Conversational ground rules are part of the context of any conversation. They consist of the knowledge, which may not be made explicit by speakers, about how to 'do' certain kinds of talking. Generally speaking, for spoken language to be used for effective communication, participants need to have this kind of shared understanding and agreement about what to do to make it happen.

Look at Sequence 2.5 below. The first speaker is an occupational counsellor and the second is one of her clients, an unemployed man. The interview is taking place in an office in a city in England, and was recorded by my colleague Jo Longman during our research on occupational counselling.[9] The participants are engaged in the joint task of filling in a 'Personal Training Plan Form', on behalf of the client, which must include a basic *curriculum vitae* for the client and end with some specific recommendations for courses of occupational training. This form will be used by the counsellor to apply for job vacancies and training courses on behalf of the client. What kinds of ground rules do you think are being followed here?

Sequence 2.5: Doing things with fish

Counsellor: You've not done any filleting, but you have worked with fish?
Client: Yeah.
Counsellor: So I need to know all the things that you've done with fish.
Client: Packing, that's one. Sorting out.
Counsellor: Sorting out, what do you mean by sorting out?
Client: Like grading with machinery doing it by (inaudible).
Counsellor: What do you do that by, size, how big they are, or weight?
Client: Weight. Barrowboy.

Counsellor: That means going down to the market and collecting the fish and taking it back. Right?
Client: Yeah. Skin the fish.
Counsellor: OK you were doing shop work in the video shop. So what does that involve?
Client: Getting up in the morning!
Counsellor: Yeah that's the hardest part for me too.

As analysts of the conversation, we can infer from what is said that both participants have access to some relevant shared knowledge. Some of this knowledge is quite specific: the counsellor says 'OK you were doing shop work in the video shop' and the client responds in a way which suggests that this allusion, with its apparently abrupt change of conversational topic, makes perfect sense to him. (Because I have access to the complete interview, I know that the client had provided this information earlier in summarizing his past employment.) But at a more general level, from the smooth flow of talk and the lack of any obvious signs of confusion on the part of each participant, it is obvious that something in their past experience has prepared both participants for the experience of the special kind of conversation they are engaged in, which is a conversation in which one person asks the other about their life in order to produce a written account. That is, both the counsellor and her client seem to have some shared understanding of how an occupational counselling interview should be carried out. (This is not inevitably the case, of course: some other clients we recorded in the same setting seemed surprised and aggrieved at the intrusive questioning of the counsellor.)

We can also see that this particular episode reveals how the speakers organize the 'thinking together' that is necessary to come up with a completed Personal Training Plan Form at the end of the interview. Almost all the sequence is made up of questions and answers – Q–A, Q–A, Q–A, and so on. The counsellor does nearly all the talking, and she is the only one who asks questions. That is, the two conversationalists act out their roles by using language differently, but do so in such complementary ways that a clear pattern emerges – their discourse takes on a distinctive structure. This structure is conventional for the kind of language activity commonly called an 'interview'; the talk can be thought of as the product of both speakers using their knowledge of the ground rules for doing interviews. The structure is, to some extent at least, the result of practical requirements. To be able to get information that is sufficiently clear and comprehensible, the counsellor has to ask for basic information ('. . . you have worked with fish?') and clarify the responses made ('. . . what do you mean by sorting out?') so that they can be recorded. On his part, the client has to describe particular working practices in words – something that he may never have had to do before. We can make some inferences about what they both now know that they did not know at the beginning. By the end of the interview, the counsellor has gained considerable new information about the occupational life history of her client, and so this is now (subject to all the vagaries of human memory and interpretation) shared, common knowledge. In accord with the ground rules of such interviews, the counsellor tells the client little about her own employment history. In Sequence 2.5, only one piece of information about the counsellor is offered to the client (in the last line).

The conversation in Sequence 2.5 runs quite smoothly because both participants know and accept the ground rules that the counsellor will ask questions about the client's work history, and that the client will provide clear enough answers to enable the counsellor to fill in a Personal Training Plan Form. For the client to start asking detailed questions about the counsellor's employment history, or for the counsellor to begin dictating what should be written on the form to the client, would constitute a breaking of the ground rules currently being applied. But imagine a situation in which the client and counsellor discover that they both used to work for the same firm, and their conversation switches into a discussion of the people who worked there and their personal characteristics. If that happened, we might expect to see changes in the structure of talk (for example, a more even spread of questioning between the speakers) as well as in the content. We could then infer from the talk that the use of the ground rules which apply to 'interviews' had been temporarily suspended by both speakers, and a different set of ground rules, which apply when people are engaged in 'informal conversation', was being used instead.

Cumulative talk

We can see an extract from an informal conversation in Sequence 2.6 below. Its structure is very different from that of Sequence 2.5 and I would like you to consider *how* it is different and *why* this might be so. I will provide you with some contextual information, in advance. The sequence is an extract from an informal conversation between two female, middle-class friends (K and C) in England (recorded by the sociolinguist Jennifer Coates). K is explaining that she is worried that her neighbour might be able to see into her house, because she saw him undressing in his living room.

Sequence 2.6: Screening trees

K: and I thought my God
C: yeh
K: if I can see him
C: he can see you
K: and I don't always just get undressed in my living room
C: (*laugh*)
K: you know I mean OK I'm sure he's not
C: peeping
K: peeping or anything
C: but he
K: but it just
C: you accidentally saw him
K: that's right
C: oh I don't blame you I think it needs screening trees round it. [10]

In this piece of talk, there are no questions and answers, and there is no argument. Instead, the speakers work together to produce a continuous stretch of mutually intelligible language ('if I can see him / he can see you / and I don't always just get undressed in my living room'). Contextual references to what they have already said, and to what they can both see as they speak, can be left implicit. So C says 'I don't blame you I think it needs screening trees round it' without needing to say what K might be 'blamed' for or what 'it' is. Coates suggests that the co-operative structure and implicit referencing of this kind of talk reflect one of its social functions, which is to establish and strengthen the solidarity and intimacy of the speakers. In my own research, I have usually called this kind of conversation *cumulative talk*, because speakers build on each other's contributions, add information of their own and in a mutually supportive, uncritical way construct shared knowledge and understanding. This kind of talk can be very usefully applied for getting joint work completed, as the next sequence shows. This is from a session which my colleagues and I recorded in a primary school classroom, where two 10-year-old girls, Katie and Anne, two friends, were working at the computer on the production of their own class newspaper. At the point at which the sequence begins, they have been working together on this task for a while and have already talked through various options for design and content. They have been engaged in the task for about an hour and a quarter and are trying to compose some text for their front page.

Sequence 2.7: Fantabuloso

Katie: Okay, so right then. What shall we write?

Anne: We can have something like those autograph columns and things like that and items, messages.

Katie: Inside these covers (*long pause*) Our fun filled . . .

Anne: That's it!

Katie: Something . . .

Anne: Something like that!

Katie: Yeah.

Anne: Inside this fabulous fun filled covers are – how can we have a fun filled cover? Let me try.

Katie: Inside these (*long pause*). Hah huh (*laughs*).

Anne: You sound happy on this. Fantabuloso (*laughs*).

Katie: Inside these inside these fant, inside these fun-filled, no inside these covers these fantastic these brilliant . . .

Anne: Brilliant.

Katie: Is it brilliant?

Anne: No.

Katie: No. Fantast fantabuloso shall we put that?

Anne: Yeah (. . .) fantabluloso.

Katie: Fan-tab-u-lo-so.

Anne: Loso. Fantabuloso.

Katie: Fantabuloso oso.

Anne: Fantabuloso <u>ho</u>![11]

In this sequence, we see Katie and Anne asking each other questions. They also make suggestions and offer some reasons for the decisions they take. They are clearly using language to think together about this task, but like the speakers in Sequence 2.6, they are doing so in a mutually supportive, cumulative way. One particularly interesting feature of their talk, however, is that we can see them talking the text of their newspaper into existence. Some of what they say is simply a comment to their partner ('You sound happy . . .', 'That's it!', 'Yeah'), but other things they say are proposals for the text itself ('Inside these . . .', 'Brilliant'). Anne first says 'Fantabuloso', and does so in a way that leaves it uncertain whether this is a comment or a proposal for the text. We can then see that this joke-word becomes shared property of the speakers. It is a part of the contextual foundation of their conversation, and so is a resource to which Katie can return shortly as they continue their search for a catchy opening phrase. Both then take up the word, establish joint agreement about its spelling, and use it together in a brief, playful celebration of their success in finding a catchy word for their headline.

'Cumulative talk' is based on ground rules which encourage joint, additive contributions to the talk and relatively uncritical acceptance of what partners say. Katie and Anne, like K and C in Sequence 2.6, are not only thinking through a problem together, they are affirming and developing a friendship. In cumulative talk we can see one way in which the social and intellectual uses of language are combined. There are other kinds of talk, based on different ground rules, which are also commonly used in joint work-based activity. People do not usually make explicit the conversational ground rules that they are using; such rules are normally assumed to be understood, as they are part of the more general contextual foundations for using language that can be drawn from the broader cultural base of every language user's experience in their community.

Creating a context for working together

Sequence 2.8 shows two other people navigating a way through a problem towards a solution. Read it and see what sense you can make of their conversation. *(Each speaker's words have been put in a column under their respective names.)*

Sequence 2.8: Negotiating some business

Speaker A	**Speaker B**
We'd like to get some state business.	I will have to work out something, Joe, where you could visit with the trustees.
Do you control Mr Gordon?	He'll go along with a lot of the things I recommend.

How do you and I develop a relationship?	I have a public relations firm . . . and I do business other than what I'm doing here.
I can give you $2,000 now, with a 50–50 split of the commission.	Keep talking.
I deal only with you. There's $4,000 a month possible on this.	We'll deal on a case by case basis. Can you handle X Insurance Company politics?
Here's $2,000. Let's shake hands on it. Do we have a deal?	We have a deal.
	There's 50 people I can send you. I have contacts in Boston.[12]

You probably guessed that this is a piece of business talk. The clues you used probably included the use of words like 'business' and 'trustees', the references to money changing hands and the classic business closing statement 'Let's shake hands on it'. However, although none of the words would in themselves be unfamiliar to you, you would be unlikely to know who the speakers, or the people they refer to ('the trustees', 'Mr Gordon') are, and what events have led up to this particular conversation in which 'the deal' is struck. You therefore may not have guessed that it shows two people involved in the clandestine business of negotiating a bribe. It comes from the research of a sociolinguist, Roger Shuy, and is a conversation between an undercover agent for the American law enforcement agency the FBI, Joe Hauser (Speaker A, who secretly recorded the talk), and a trade union official who was a target of the FBI's enquiries in an operation known as Brilab (an acronym for 'Bribery of Labor Unions').

Shuy has studied many such secretly recorded, clandestine conversations, and has offered the following analysis of the structure of an archetypal 'bribe' transaction:

Bribe event structure in actual bribe event

Phases	Speaker A	Speaker B
Problem	We'd like to get some state business	I will have to work out something, Joe, where you could visit with the trustees.
	Do you control Mr Gordon?	He'll go along with a lot of the things I recommend.

	How do you and I develop a relationship?	I have a public relations firm . . . and I do business other than what I'm doing here.
Proposal	I can give you $2,000 now, with a 50–50 split of the commission. I deal only with you. There's $4,000 a month possible on this.	Keep talking. We'll deal on a case by case basis. Can you handle X Insurance Company politics?
Completion	Here's $2,000. Let's shake hands on it. Do we have a deal?	We have a deal.
Extension		There's 50 people I can send you. I have contacts in Boston.[13]

Shuy claims that this 'phase' model can usefully be applied to all the tape-recorded data that he has seen presented by the FBI in bribery cases. Entry into each of the phases depends on the successful completion of the previous one. After some initial greetings (which might be considered to constitute a preliminary phase in themselves), a *problem* is presented by the first party. This usually amounts to a request for help. During this phase, the first party usually also checks on the other's authority and capacity to deliver. The next phase is the *proposal*, in which rewards are discussed and promises made. If things are going well, this phase may be used to build some kind of intimacy, with common acquaintances being mentioned, anecdotes told and so on. The final part of the negotiation is marked by entry into the *completion* phase, classically symbolized by the handshake and expressions like 'It's a deal'. There may then follow an *extension* phase, with future possibilities being introduced.

Shuy's method of analysis is intended as a practical one, and its use has influenced the course of some court cases and retrospectively cast doubt on the validity of the verdicts of others. As Shuy explains, for example, in a number of US bribery cases involving politicians and other public servants, it has been claimed by the state prosecution that the fact that a public servant has even engaged in a conversation with a would-be briber is sufficient to show that they are corrupt. Shuy suggests that juries are often easily persuaded by this line of argument, because people generally assume that two people talking together in reasonable tones, without explicit disagreement, must have shared values and purposes. Those accused of corruption are then convicted on the basis of what he calls 'conversational contamination'. However, he shows that a more careful analysis of events may reveal that the attempted bribery did not follow the model pattern, that the accused person did not collude in the bribe attempt, and the crucial stage of completion (in which 'the deal' is made) may never have materialized. An example is the following extract from a recorded conversation, between a US politician (Williams), accused of corruption, and an FBI agent (Farhart), masquerading as an Arab sheik seeking residence in the USA. In earlier conversation, Williams has agreed to advise the sheik on how he might best present his case to immigration, but with no suggestion of impropriety:

Farhart: I will, for your help, uh, assistance, I would like to give you . . . some money for, for permanent residence.

Williams: No. No. No. No, when I work in that kind of activity, it is purely a public, not uh, No, within my position, when I deal with law and legislation, it's not within . . . (*telephone rings, interrupting*). My only interest is to see this come together.[14]

On this occasion a proposal for a bribe may have been made, but, using the transcript, Shuy showed that the normal bribe structure of events had not been completed; and in what was said the offer was clearly rejected. However, Shuy's analysis did not save Senator Williams, who was convicted and imprisoned on this and similar tape evidence (none of which, Shuy suggests, was any more convincing about the senator's guilt than the above example). Shuy comments that many American trial judges are unwilling to admit a linguist as expert witness in court because they claim that any normal person can understand a conversation when they first hear it, and that to analyse talk in depth is to impose false levels of meaning on 'common-sense' understandings. They also resist the idea that repeated listenings to a tape may reveal to observers new, but no less 'genuine', meanings than were apparent on the first listening. The casualties of this obstinate naïvety are the victims of injustice.

Intercultural conversations

Helen Marriott has carried out research on what she calls 'intercultural business negotiations', transactions which involve people from significantly different cultural backgrounds. Some of her data come from a video-recorded conversation, in English but held in Japan, between a Japanese food importer and an Australian cheese manufacturer. The speakers were both amenable to being recorded. Sequence 2.9 is an extract from their conversation. *(J = Japanese speaker, A = Australian, [indicates simultaneous speech, and (.) a pause of noticeable length.)*

Sequence 2.9: Selling to Japan

J: And eh what your object to eh visit to me, is that eh introduce for eh this
A: We'd like to sell to Japan
J: sell to Japan
A: yeh
J: uh huh
A: or make it in Japan.
J: mm ah here yes
A: Either way, whichever is the best.
J: mm
A: Maybe make it here for um six months and eh if it's acceptable
J: ah six, six months
A: well we could send some samples from [Australia
J: [in Melbourne uh huh
A: and just test the market (.) if it's good we could then make it in Japan
J: uh huh (.) uh huh
A: with a joint venture.[15]

Marriott found that there were significant differences between the two men's behaviour in the interaction. The Japanese man often sought clarifications, and periodically offered summaries of information discussed. That is, he used strategies to check that there was *shared understanding* of matters being negotiated – something which the Australian rarely did. After the recording Marriott interviewed them to gain their views of how the transactions had gone. Both men felt that the other had not talked in the ways they would expect, given their business role. So, for example, the Japanese man commented: '. . . in

Japan maybe the salesman speak more more, more explanation about his company's and the condition of the trading.'[16] The Australian, on the other hand, felt that the brevity and non-committal nature of the Japanese man's reactions to his comments (as in the extract above) left him feeling 'that I don't really know what he's going to do. It finished a little bit unconcluded.'[17] Overall, then, it seems that the two men did not have a secure, shared set of ground rules for building a context for their work activity. The unfortunate consequence was that the two men failed to communicate effectively, and the Australian left feeling particularly dissatisfied with the outcome of the encounter. Although the Japanese speaker was very ready to admit to limitations in his use of English, Marriott suggests that this was not a major cause of misunderstanding. Instead she suggests that the different expectations held and interpretations made about the conversation by the two men reflected other, less obvious differences in their cultural backgrounds and experiences. To some extent, this may be a matter of Japanese and Australian people having different habitual conversational styles – ways of expressing intent, interest, and so on, by words and gestures vary considerably across societies. But Marriott emphasizes that explaining misunderstandings in terms of cultural experiences does not simply mean making generalized comparisons between Japanese and Australian ways of conversing. In the international business world of today other cultural factors besides national origin might be just as important for shaping speakers' ways of talking business and their interpretation of events. The Japanese man worked in a large, international organization: he had much more experience of intercultural business negotiations than the Australian, he had dealt a lot with foreign business people in Japan, and had made several work trips abroad. The Australian, on the other hand, worked for his own small firm, had travelled little, and his previous work had not involved him in these kinds of negotiations. In other words, the Japanese businessman was probably more familiar with the conversational ground rules for carrying on such a business negotiation, and so for predicting its structure and outcomes.

Even when people may agree that they are all engaged in the same kind of talk activity, such as 'dinner conversation', they may not necessarily have the same understanding of how it should be carried out. In her research on informal conversations, the sociolinguist Deborah Tannen has shown how even people of fairly similar social backgrounds may follow different ground rules, and how this can lead to some misunderstandings. For example, she analysed the conversation of a group of friends who had come together in the USA for a Thanksgiving dinner party.[18] The group consisted of two Californians (both men), three New Yorkers (two men and Tannen herself) and an English woman. Much conversation apparently took place during the meal, but when Tannen asked the guests afterwards if they had enjoyed it, she got very different responses. The New Yorkers had found it lively and satisfying, but the others evaluated it much less favourably. They had felt intimidated and pushed into the conversational sidelines by their New Yorker friends. One of the Californians commented: 'I'm amazed at how you guys talk over each other, saying the same thing at the same time. When I have a conversation there are pauses.' The other said he felt threatened by the New Yorkers' continual barrage of direct questions like 'How do you know that?' and 'How did you feel?' It appeared that what Tannen called the 'New York Jewish high-involvement' style of informal conversation was both unfamiliar and (on first encounter) unacceptable to her guests from California and England. That is, while the New Yorkers' ground rules might include those in the following list (and be justified in the ways in which I have justified them below), their guests would not expect to follow such rules (and would probably not be convinced by those justifications):

- Talk to relative strangers about personal matters (it shows that you are willing to trust them).
- Interrupt speakers if you have something urgent to contribute (it shows that you are enthused by what they have said).
- Ask people direct questions about their lives, interests, problems, and so on (it shows that you are interested in them).
- Tell anecdotes about things that have happened to you (it shows that you lead an interesting life, and will encourage other people to tell stories of their own).

Frames of reference

We often only realize that ground rules exist when someone breaks them. I remember first becoming aware of this from reading about the work of the sociologist Harold Garfinkel.[19] Garfinkel encouraged students to carry out what he called 'breaching experiments', of which an example was to go home to their parents' houses and, without saying anything in explanation, behave as if they were boarders rather than members of the family. This difficult activity offers insights into the ways in which the students felt it necessary to modify their behaviour to be lodger-like (such as by asking for permission to use the telephone, rather than simply taking its availability for granted). It is also interesting to note how relatives reacted: Garfinkel's students were asked 'Are you sick?', 'What are you being so superior about?', 'Are you out of your mind or are you just stupid?' In this way, it is possible to see beneath what Garfinkel calls 'the obstinate reality of everyday life', the taken-for-granted assumptions that underpin almost all conversations and which we use every day as foundations for the joint creation of new knowledge.

My appreciation of the importance of implicit ground rules was also helped by the cross-cultural research of the psychologist Michael Cole and his colleagues, who in the 1960s studied literacy and reasoning amongst members of a Liberian people called the Kpelle. Reasoned debate and argument were apparently common and important parts of Kpelle culture, but most of the people had not attended school. Sequence 2.10 shows what happened when Cole's team (one of whom was acting as the 'experimenter') asked a member of the Kpelle (the 'subject') to solve a reasoning problem, involving the fictitious characters of Flumo and Yakpalo.

Sequence 2.10: Flumo and Yakpalo

Experimenter: Flumo and Yakpalo always drink cane juice (rum) together. Flumo is drinking cane juice. Is Yakpalo drinking cane juice?

Subject: Flumo and Yakpalo drink cane juice together, but the time Flumo was drinking the first one Yakpalo was not there on that day.

Experimenter: But I told you that Flumo and Yakpalo always drink cane juice together. One day Flumo was drinking cane juice. Was Yakpalo drinking cane juice that day?

Subject: The day Flumo was drinking cane juice Yakpalo was not there on that day.

Experimenter: What is the reason?

Subject: The reason is that Yakpalo went to his farm that day and Flumo remained in town on that day . . . [20]

We can see that the experimenter and subject apparently reached an *impasse*, because while one of them treated the conversation as a way of presenting a formal test of logic (in which the people mentioned, and their actions, are simply vehicles for presenting the problem), the other treated it as a fictional scenario with more open possibilities. As Cole and his colleagues point out, neither was behaving irrationally; it is simply that they were not contextualizing the talk about the story of Flumo and Yakpalo in the same way. This reflects their different 'schooled' and 'unschooled' backgrounds. In other words, the experimenter and the subject did not establish a *shared frame of reference*: their talk lacked shared contextual foundations and they were not employing the same ground rules. This meant that they were not really engaged in the same kind of collective thinking activity. This reflected their different past cultural experiences of using language to represent and discuss intellectual problems.

We will all have discovered that, on some occasions, even people who are quite co-operatively and amicably involved in a conversation may misunderstand each other. An example from my own experience that puzzled me for a while was an occasion when I was watching television with an older relative, Auntie Mick. The programme we were watching was a game show (a type of programme I hate) in which the participants had to carry out daring kinds of activities, such as bungee jumping. As we watched, one particularly dislikable contestant (from my perspective) gestured wildly to the crowd and dived off in a reckless way in his bungee jump. Auntie Mick suddenly said: 'It's amazing that jerk doesn't break his neck!', to which my immediate response was 'Yes!', meaning that he certainly was a jerk and it was surprising that he survived such foolishness. It was only later that, on reflection, and taking account of her apparently uncritical enjoyment of the rest of the show, I realized that Auntie Mick was probably simply referring to the 'jerk' of the bungee rope, not to the character of the contestant. When I eventually asked her, she confirmed that this was what she had meant. Running over her sentence in my mind, I concluded that there was no obvious way, in terms of pronunciation or intonation, that these two possible meanings would necessarily sound different. Moreover, we were both familiar with the English language and the kind of television show we were watching. The misunderstanding which occurred clearly had something to do with shared contextual foundations, but was not of an obvious kind. I eventually concluded that one way of describing the basis of this trivial but intriguing misunderstanding was that – as in Cole's talk with the Kpelle – Auntie Mick and I were using different frames of reference. That is, although we could assume joint under-standing in general terms of what we were watching and discussing, we were each tacitly making very different, value-laden interpretations of the events being shown. Amazingly, but misleadingly, Auntie Mick's sentence expressed both our quite different interpretations.

Most of the time when we use language we depend heavily on the assumption that the person with whom we are interacting has a similar understanding of the words we use, what we are trying to achieve by talking and the ways in which we should use language to make it happen. That is, in casual conversations and many other spoken-language events (such as counselling sessions, interviews, sales encounters and lessons in school), we commonly assume that the people with whom we are dealing do not only share our understanding of the kind of interaction in which we are involved (what I have called the 'ground rules' for the talk), but also share other assumptions about values, purposes and ways of categorizing information which are important for building a shared frame of reference.

We may *not* make many assumptions about such shared under-standing if we decide that we are dealing with someone who is a novice to the kind of encounter taking place – for example, if a counsellor or therapist knows that a new client is unfamiliar with what happens in counselling sessions and so will be unfamiliar with the kind of dialogue involved, or a teacher knows that they are dealing with a student from abroad who may be unfamiliar with the conventions of classrooms. But research has shown that counsellors, teachers, medical staff, police officers and others who are in control of conversations often act as if the people with whom they are dealing *are* familiar with the relevant ground rules, and do not help 'novices' by making the ground rules explicit (or explaining why they are following them). That is, the controlling interviewers too often fail to take an active-enough role in building shared contextual foundations for talk. This may put less experienced, less powerful participants in the conversation at a great disadvantage, limiting the scope and potential benefits for them of the talk. Moreover, interviewers may treat any failure to follow the ground rules on the part of the interviewees as stupidity or unco-operative behaviour. This is bound to have some unfortunate consequences for how well interviews are used as a means for enabling a 'professional' and a 'client' to share information and think together through a problem, and is undoubtedly one of the reasons why processes of guidance, justice and medical consultation go awry.[21]

One example of this kind of problem concerns the way in which people feel it is appropriate to respond to direct requests for information. The linguist Diana Eades describes how, in Australian Aboriginal communities, it is normal for speakers to say 'yes' in conversations even when they do not necessarily agree with what the speaker says, because their culture's ground rules use this simply as a way of helping the interaction along. However, police officers, lawyers and other interrogators from white Australian backgrounds sometimes interpret such remarks as signs of agreement, with some disastrous consequences.[22]

In Aboriginal cultures (and in many others, for example amongst some indigenous American people), it is also apparently not considered polite to engage in very direct requests for information. Yet such requests are a familiar feature of teacher-led talk in the classrooms of 'mainstream' Australian society. As researchers like Ian Malcolm[23] have observed, this means that there is often a 'ground rules mismatch' between white Australian teachers and the young Aboriginal children in their classes, with the teachers finding the children strangely reluctant to engage in the kinds of question-and-answer sessions which the teachers take for granted as a normal feature of classroom communication. These different perceptions by teachers and students about how talk should be used in the classroom can have serious educational consequences. A teacher needs continually to gauge the existing levels of understanding of students, check that students have been able to follow what they have heard or have read, and assess the progress they are making as they carry out activities. One of the main ways in which they do this is by talking with students. Students make better progress when they engage with their teacher in thinking through problems and issues, so that difficulties and misunderstandings come to the surface and processes and procedures are talked through. In this way, education becomes a guided process of thinking with language, rather than merely a one-way transmission of information. But this process is unlikely to happen if teachers and students have not developed a joint understanding of the appropriate ground rules for talking together. I will say more about this in Chapter 6.

Summary

Most of the time, when we speak with other people, we do so on the assumption that they are making sense. We also assume that they will make matters as clear as they think is necessary for us to understand them. We look into what they say for clues to the kinds of contextual resources we should draw on, we may ask for relevant additional information, and we may offer some ourselves. If such assumptions are false, then this will often emerge in the course of any continued conversation, and we can treat this as a 'special case' and revise our behaviour to take account of it.

In trying to make sense of what someone says, we never rely only on our knowledge of the basic meanings of words, or our familiarity with the grammatical constructions they use. As listeners, we always access some additional, contextual information, using any explicit guidance or hints provided by a speaker and drawing on any remembered past experience which seems relevant. As a conversation progresses, the content of what is said provides a contextual foundation for the talk which follows.

'Context', in the sense in which I am using the term, is not something that exists independently of people. In order to combine their intellectual efforts, people have to strive to create foundations of common, contextualizing knowledge. People do this by drawing on whatever information resources they think are relevant. These contextual resources are likely to be found in such things as:

- the physical surroundings;
- the past shared experience and relationship of the speakers;
- the speakers' shared tasks or goals;
- the speakers' experience of similar kinds of conversation.

Language also can be used to create its own context, as I will show in more detail in the next chapter. While the contexts that conversationalists build can never be fully accessible to an observer, we can infer some of what is being treated as 'contextual' by noticing the references speakers make (for example, to their environment and events past and present) and how the information they put into a conversation is treated as an accumulating basis of common knowledge as their conversation unfolds over time.

I called one kind of contextual resource that enables people to communicate effectively 'conversational ground rules'. If these rules are broken or if speakers are not following the same ones, misunderstandings can occur. Nevertheless, such occasions are interesting because they bring the normally implicit ground rules to the surface. Conversations also depend on speakers adopting, or creating, a common 'frame of reference' for considering available information and defining what they are trying to achieve together. Misunderstandings in conversations often result from weaknesses in the contextual foundations for collective thinking.

3   The given and the new

We use language to make the future from the past, to build a relationship between what has been and what is to come; and we use the resources of past experience to make new, joint, knowledge and understanding. Using language, we can transform the raw material of our shared life experiences into stories which have continuity and coherence. This is a joint enterprise, in which we have to make assumptions about the amount of relevant prior experience and understanding we share with the people with whom we are communicating, and draw partners' attention to what is relevant. As I will explain, there are some common techniques for doing this which we all probably use, successfully or otherwise, most days of our lives.

In the previous chapter, I showed how we make sense of what we hear or read by drawing on the knowledge that we consider relevant to the current situation. Knowledge of shared history is a resource for building shared context, to which speakers can appeal explicitly or implicitly. Conversations between people who converse regularly can be considered to be episodes of 'long conversations' on particular themes that continue whenever they meet.[1] In each continuing episode, a great deal of 'common knowledge' can be safely assumed, or appealed to quite easily. Nevertheless, whenever we are conversing with another person we must make decisions about the extent to which we need to make explicit references to 'given' knowledge, and what new information we need to provide. If we want to be well understood, those decisions can be crucial. Just because shared past experience exists it does not mean that our communication partners will necessarily know which parts of it are relevant for making sense of what is said. We have to take calculated risks about how much 'context' to provide, because to refer explicitly to everything relevant would be impossible, and even to try would be a terrible waste of time. The philosopher H.P. Grice suggested that successful communication depends upon people being generally able to assume that conversational partners respect the 'co-operative principles' of providing information which is relevant, and providing it in appropriate amounts (not too much, not too little). Life would be difficult if we could not generally rely on these assumptions.[2]

Attempts to build context from shared history can be done well, or badly; they may or may not succeed. As the writer of this book, I have to judge what knowledge the average reader will have gained from each chapter, so that I can take this as a contextual 'given' for presenting new ideas in later chapters. (For example, I am now assuming that what I mean by 'context' is shared knowledge at this point.) But the responsibility for making context does not rest only with a speaker or writer. Any productive meeting of minds also requires the active, co-operative, contextualizing activity of listeners or readers in using given information to support and generate new, joint, understanding.

From the point of view of researching the process of collective thinking, failed attempts at drawing on past shared experience can be as interesting as successful ones. Look, for example, at Sequence 3.1: a conversation between a group of undergraduate psychology students (A, B, C and D, all women), whom researcher Liz Stokoe recorded as they began to try to put together an outline for a course essay on biological psychology.

Sequence 3.1: Writing an outline

C: Erm have we already done this.
D: No that was what we did in class.
C: Move over a bit.
D: I don't wanna move this way a bit.
B: What're we doing?
(*They write in silence for a while*)
B: What's today's date? twenty third?
?: Twenty fourth.
B: Twenty fourth, right.
C: Right, introduction.
B: Right, have you got the notes on that thing?
C: (*unclear*)

A: No what?

B: Right, what did you say what is the main body going to be?

A: Oh god.

D: Have you done the sociology essay?

A: Have you?

(*At this point they give up on this task and start to discuss a sociology assignment instead*)[3]

Here we have four people who, while sharing some relevant past experience and having a common task to fulfil, seem (on this particular occasion) unable to achieve much together. They request information from each other, but no-one seems able to provide much that is useful. The transcript also gives the impression of a group who are struggling to motivate and organize themselves. In her analysis, Stokoe points to the several failed attempts to focus the group on the task, each marked by the word 'right . . .'. We have probably all been members of such a group at some time.

In contrast, look next at the conversation of a group of people who are more successful in using their relevant shared past experience and intellectual capacities to deal with a task. Sequence 3.2 comes from a distinctive and interesting study of 'collective remembering' by the psychologists Middleton and Edwards. They asked a group of students to recall together something which they had all witnessed. It had to be something on which the researchers could, if necessary, check the accuracy of their recall. The group chose to try to recall the story of Steven Spielberg's feature film *E.T.*, and the sequence is an extract from their 35-minute recorded conversation.

Sequence 3.2: Remembering *E.T.*

Karen: well he goes to the fridge to get something to eat first doesn't he
with the dog following him

Diane: yeh that's it.

Karen: mm

Diane: and he finds him feeding the dog

John: and then and then he finds the beer

Diane: and then he finds the beer and what is it there's a link between
[Elliott and E.T. &

Karen: [Elliott's at school

John: [telepathic link

Diane: and that whatever happens to E.T. Elliott feels the same effects and E.T. got paralytic (*laughs*) and so E.T. is sort of going

Lesley: all a bit drunk

Tina: that's right I remember

Karen: Elliott is sitting at his school desk and they are doing experiments with frogs are they

Diane: and he lets all the frogs out

(*General hubbub of agreement*)

Tina: sets all the frogs out yeh

Lesley: and what's that little girl that he fancies

John: it's when he's watching E.T.'s watching television and John Wayne kisses the heroine in the film

Diane: oh so Elliott kisses [her

John: [and then Elliot kisses the little girl.[4]

In Sequence 3.2 we can see Karen, Diane and the others using some common techniques for doing this kind of collective intellectual activity. They attach *tag questions* to statements ('doesn't he'; 'what is it') to invite partners to check the accuracy of their recall. They make *explicit requests* for information and assistance ('what's that little girl he fancies'), and by making *overt agreements* ('yeh that's it'; 'that's right I remember') they confirm and support the efforts of their partners and so contribute to the development of a consensual account of the film. The whole of their talk gives an observer the impression of people doing a well-practised activity, easily and spontaneously. Collective remembering is a very common, everyday kind of joint thinking. Interacting with our friends, family and colleagues, we frequently use the resource of each other's memories to clarify past events, check our personal evaluations of them, and recall how to perform skilled operations. So normal and common is the phenomenon of remembering together, that it is remarkable that very little research, other than that described by Middleton and Edwards, has been done on it. Almost all research on memory (a topic of great popularity amongst psychologists, in the past and present) has been carried out only with isolated individuals, who are usually asked to do some strange de-contextualized laboratory task that bears little resemblance to the practical mental requirements of everyday life.[5]

Kinds of common knowledge

The episode of collective thinking represented by Sequence 3.2 was
built on the foundations of the common knowledge of the participants.
Several different kinds of common knowledge were involved. The
first and most obvious is their common experience of having watched
the film *E.T.* They all began the activity with at least a basic shared
understanding of the main topic and the purpose of their talk, and so
could create a shared frame of reference for their activity and make
sense of what was said – even if the information they went on to provide
was not always made very explicit. The second kind of common
knowledge on which their talk drew was past experience of doing
'collective remembering', because this is a common human pursuit.
They would all be likely to be familiar with an appropriate set
of conversational ground rules for carrying out this kind of joint
intellectual activity. Both these kinds of common knowledge are to
some extent apparent to us (as observers) in the content of the talk, and
they contribute to the fluency of the interaction. So, though the students
may all have seen the film on separate occasions, and may never have
engaged in collective remembering together before, they nevertheless
have a great deal of relevant cultural knowledge in common. A third
kind of common knowledge on which the students could probably draw
would be past joint activity. Being a group of students who were all
following the same course, they may have worked together before, and
so have a history of shared activity and personal relationships which are
acted out in this conversation. So this activity may, at least for some
of the participants, have been an episode of the 'long conversation' of
their personal relationships. And, as the conversation unfolded, they
had the resources of the history of their continuing joint activity on
which to draw. So when Lesley said: 'and what's that little girl that he
fancies', she was assuming, quite reasonably, that the others would
know that 'he' referred to the character Elliott rather than to E.T. The
common or given knowledge on which we draw in order to think
together may therefore be of several different kinds.

A lesson in history

In some situations, the way in which people attempt to build shared
context is particularly easy to observe, because at least one of the
participants involved gives explicit attention to this task. Look, for

example, at Sequence 3.3 recorded by colleagues of mine in a secondary school in Bangalore, India. We join the class at the start of an English literature lesson about a poem by John Keats.

Sequence 3.3: Teaching the *Ode to Autumn*

(The teacher enters, and the whole class stands up)
Teacher: Good morning children.
Children: *(in unison)* Good morning Mrs Pillai.
Teacher: Sit down please. Open to 'Autumn', page 8. *(The teacher and all the children open their books)* If you remember, we put up a bulletin board outside the auditorium which was called 'The Romantic Imagination'. Did, did any of you seriously look at it?
Children: *(in rough unison)* Yes.
Teacher: What was it about?
Children: Poets.
Teacher: It was about poets, about poetry. So what we are going to do today is an <u>ode</u>, called '<u>To Autumn</u>' *(she writes this on the blackboard)*.[6]

Having completed the preliminary politenesses and got the children looking at an appropriate page of text, the teacher says: 'If you remember . . .' and goes on to describe an aspect of recent past experience in the school (the putting up of the bulletin board). She asks if the students have looked at it 'seriously', and checks that they can describe its contents ('poets'). From what she says we can tell, as can her students, that she considers the contents of this board and their consideration of it relevant to the lesson which is now about to begin. That is, she makes explicit to the students that they should use what they saw on the board as contextual foundations for the work they will do that day.

It is very common for school lessons to begin with remarks by the teacher about recent past experience, and which have this sort of contextualizing function for the continuing work of the class. Often, the teacher introduces a theme or topic from their shared past, reminds the children when exactly they dealt with it, and then explicitly requires them to provide some relevant experiential knowledge from that past experience. In this way, a teacher can help children not only perceive temporal connections, but also make logical links between what they have done (and learned) and what they are going to do next. It is not surprising that these kinds of clear references to past shared experience are so frequently made by teachers. Teachers have a professional responsibility for helping their students to build new understandings upon the foundations of their previous learning, and language is the main tool available to the teaching profession for doing this. But they may also be doing something more than helping students make overall sense of the content of their learning. By encouraging students to draw on the experience of previous activities, recall relevant information from these and offer this in the forum of a class discussion, teachers can also help students to learn how language can be used as a tool for making joint, coherent sense of experience.

Techniques for building the future from the past

I have studied teachers' talk in classrooms in several parts of the world, in different educational cultures and where a variety of languages has been used. This experience has led me to believe that, wherever they are, teachers tend to use the same basic conversational techniques for building the future on the foundations of the past. Below, I give five of these techniques.[7]

Recaps

A recap is a brief review of things that happened earlier in the previous joint experience of the class. Usually teachers do this to set the scene for the current activity. The teacher in Sequence 3.3 does this with her reference to the bulletin board.

Elicitations

An elicitation, which usually takes the form of a question, is an attempt by a teacher to obtain from students information gained in past classroom activity which is relevant to current or future activity. Here is an example of a teacher beginning a lesson with a recap and following this with an elicitation:

Teacher: Right now we talked a bit last week about the rules we use when we're working in groups and how it's important when we're working in a group of people or a team of people to do certain things. Right – who can tell me some of the rules we've got – Richard?

Recaps are not only used to stimulate memories of activities carried out days or weeks ago, they may also be used to consolidate what has just happened in a class, as in the example given in Sequence 3.4 in which a teacher *recaps* a class discussion in mid-flow, and then follows this with some *elicitations* to encourage the children to reflect on what has just been said. (The discussion is about a character in a picture book that this group of 9-year-olds, some with learning difficulties, are reading together.)

Sequence 3.4: Recaps and elicitations

Teacher: Let's go back. It's interesting isn't it? First of all, let's reflect on this a minute. First of all, some people thought, somebody thought that he was in there . . .
Pupil 1: Yeh.
Pupil 2: Yeh.
Teacher: . . . and then Anthony disagreed with that, or Katie, is it? And then we said, what part of him is in there, and you said his mind, right? So this (*points to the picture*) is his mind still, is it? And Anthony picked up a clue from the writing that made him think of the mind. What word was it, Anthony, that gave you that idea about it being in his mind?
Anthony: Well, in the writing . . .
Teacher: Yeh.
Anthony: . . . bit, 'perhaps', it said 'perhaps she kept them locked up in a dark dungeon'.
Teacher: So 'perhaps', 'perhaps'. Was that the key word for you?
Anthony: Yeh.
Teacher: 'Perhaps'. It goes on to say 'perhaps', doesn't it? (*reads from page*) 'Perhaps she fed them.' It's still all in his mind, is it?
Katie: Yeh.

In the sequence, we can see that Anthony makes an interesting observation about the use of 'perhaps', which relates to how hypothetical events can be represented in literature. As well as wanting to give Anthony some positive feedback on his comment, the teacher treats it as relevant to the education of the other children in the class, and so uses the usual techniques to draw the class's attention to what Anthony has said. In this way Anthony's remark gains authoritative backing and the point becomes a highlighted feature in the joint deliberations of the group.

Repetitions

One common way in which teachers show that they accept a student's answer to their question as appropriate is by simply repeating the answer in an affirming, conclusive way, holding the answer up, so to speak, for all the class to see. On the other hand, repeating the answer in a quizzical, questioning tone suggests that it is not appropriate, and that a good answer is still being sought.

Reformulations

Having got a response from a student, teachers often paraphrase this response, putting it back to the class in a slightly different form – perhaps in a way that they think is clearer or more relevant to the current theme.

Sequence 3.5 includes examples of a teacher using *reformulations* (in italics) and **repetitions** (in bold). This is a primary class, and they are talking about breeds of dogs.

Sequence 3.5: Reformulations and repetitions

Teacher: What does breed mean – Stephen?
Stephen: Type of dog.
Teacher: *What type of dog they are*. What else can you find out about dogs from this piece of paper – Joe?
Joe: Male or female.
Teacher: *Whether it's a male or a female* – what else can you find out – look carefully – Sally?
Sally: What it eats.
Teacher: *What it likes to eat* – what else? Eleanor?
Eleanor: If it's any good for a guard dog.
Teacher: *If it's a guard dog or not – if it's any good*. What kind of dog would make a good guard dog? Joe?
Joe: Big and fierce like an Alsatian.
Teacher: **Big and fierce like an Alsatian**. What else can you find out from this piece of paper about the dogs – Camilla?
Camilla: What it likes and dislikes.
Teacher: **What it likes and dislikes**. Well done!

Exhortations

Teachers often emphasize the value of past experience for the success of the learning activities in which students are now engaged by exhorting them to 'think' or 'remember'. For example:

> 'If you think back to the lessons you've had so far, you've got to try and remember . . .'
> 'Now the thing to do is try and remember what you already know about . . .'

Of course, teachers' use of language, as the main tool of their trade, is not only concerned with creating contextual foundations from past experience. For example, teachers use repetitions not just to create meaningful links with what students say, but also to evaluate the students' contributions and so provide some kind of feedback on their learning or the quality of their participation in the class.[8] Being an effective teacher does not depend on whether you use these techniques; as I mentioned earlier, most teachers regularly use the five techniques described above. What is important is how they are used and for what purpose. Good teachers help students see the educational wood as they lead them through the trees, and it is through teachers' effective use of language that a history of classroom experience can be transformed into a future of educational progress. Using a long string of questions simply to elicit from students discrete items of factual information that they are supposed to have learned will allow a teacher to test that learning, but is unlikely to help the development of students' conceptual understanding. However, using a series of recaps, elicitations and reformulations to draw students through a logical line of thinking can be a crucial part of a good teacher's success in supporting and guiding the development of children's educational progress. In other words, learning is more likely to occur when teachers use language to encourage and support children's use of language for thinking through what they have done. Education is likely to fail when teachers overestimate learners' abilities to make connections between the past and present, or fail to realize that what they see as an obvious connection between two experiences may not be apparent to students. And if one of the aims of education is to enable students to become better users of language as a tool for thinking, both collectively and on their own, it also is likely to fail if their classroom experience consists of little more than passively listening to a teacher's voice and answering the questions a teacher asks. Children need to be enabled to become active users of the tool of language, and this means giving them opportunities for practice in less didactic kinds of conversation. I will return to this topic in Chapter 6.

How do we make conversation flow?

Although I have been discussing examples of the way in which language is used by teachers, all speakers use similar techniques for building context and developing shared knowledge when involved in joint activities. If you listen to what is happening in a few everyday conversations, you will find people doing some or all of the following:

- referring back to shared experiences;
- eliciting information;
- offering information (which is then available as a shared resource);
- justifying ideas and proposals;
- evaluating other people's contributions;
- repeating and reformulating each other's statements.

The conversational process of thinking together does not only involve the use of particular techniques, it also depends on a remarkable human ability for making conversation flow. Every fluent, continuous and intelligible conversation is a showcase for human skills in achieving co-ordinated intellectual activity. The cues speakers use to achieve joint fluency are verbal (the content of talk and its grammatical structure) and non-verbal (tone of voice, face and hand gestures, etc.). They are often subtle, and we may not be consciously aware that we are reacting to them. The cues speakers appear to be providing, and reacting to, are often only revealed to researchers when videotaped conversations are slowed down and analysed 'frame by frame'. We are generally able to recognize them because our past social and cultural experience has prepared us for the conventional ways in which conversations unfold. I described this earlier in terms of conversational ground rules. When we enter any particular situation, we use a range of clues, some obvious and some subtle, to decide what kind of conversation we are involved in and, thus, which ground rules apply. But even once a conversation is under way, the participants have to monitor each other's behaviour regularly (though they may not be conscious of doing so), looking for information which will tell them such things as when another speaker is concluding a conversational turn, expects a particular kind of response, is trying to enter or end the conversation, and so on. One very active kind of research on how conversation is achieved as a co-ordinated social activity is known as 'conversation analysis'. It is not very easy to represent these kinds of subtle cues in transcription, and the transcripts produced by conversation analysts in order to study these kinds of things have a dauntingly technical quality. A key to transcription symbols commonly used by conversation analysts is given below.[9]

Transcription symbols used in conversational analysis

(1.0) a pause of the duration shown (in seconds)
(.)   a pause of less than 0.2 seconds
·hh   an audible intake of breath by a speaker (the more hhhs, the longer the in-breath)
:::   the speaker has stretched out the preceding sound or word
Oh   spoken with emphasis
[onset of simultaneous speech
↑   onset of a marked rising intonational shift
?   the preceding word spoken with a rising inflection (not necessarily indicating a question)

Sequence 3.6 gives an example of that kind of transcription being applied to a piece of video-recorded conversation between two friends, one of whom has asked for help in moving some furniture.

Sequence 3.6: Asking for help

Ann: Are you (1.0) (*P looks up from computer, and then back at screen*) hello sorry ·hhh are you around um (.) tomorrow?
Peter: (.05) (*Looks up*) Yeh.
Ann: Cos I was like wondering if you could like ↑ help [with the moving?
Peter: [help? yes I'm not around all day.
Ann: No not all::: day.
Peter: OK.
Ann: Just when I need to carry things out.
Peter: Well::: (1.5) the afternoon would be better.

The value of this kind of transcription technique is that it represents at least some of the subtle non-verbal cues that speakers within particular societies use for making sense of what they hear. Someone familiar with the transcription system and the everyday conversations of English speakers like Ann and Peter would quickly notice how this encounter was being acted out. The kinds of remarks and hesitations made by Ann ('sorry ·hhh are you around um') indicate that she is approaching Peter for help in an apologetic, unauthoritative manner. Likewise, Peter's long, drawn-out 'well:::' can be recognized as a sign of reluctance rather than enthusiasm for doing what is requested.

Conversation analysts have tried to describe how common types of interaction are achieved co-operatively by conversational partners. For example, what cues do listeners seem to use to tell when a speaker's turn has nearly ended, so that they can take over without rudely interrupting or leaving embarrassing silences? The answer is a combination of cues from intonation and pace, as well as the structure and content of speech. As in all research on language use, much can be learned from observations of when things go wrong – for example, when conversational fluency breaks down. Sometimes, two people may be apparently developing a shared understanding, with no apparent problems, and then suddenly one of them says something that confuses the other, the process grinds to a halt and some 'repair work' has to be done if the topic in hand is to be pursued further. One way of describing this in terms I have used earlier would be to say that the joint action of context-building, which creates minute-by-minute shared frames of reference for keeping a conversation on track, suddenly stalls. Conversation analysts have identified one such kind of 'glitch' in the smooth flow of conversational activity as what they call a 'dispreferred response'. On some occasions, a speaker responds to a question or statement with a remark which is apparently not the one sought or expected by their conversational partner. By the behaviour of that partner (signs of dismay or confusion, for example) this can be identified as a response which was 'dispreferred'. This reaction then frequently motivates an explanatory account by the person who had made the inappropriate-seeming contribution.

Conversation analysis has therefore helped explain why people offer accounts or justifications at certain points in conversations. One of my own clearest and most embarrassing recollections of making a dispreferred response and trying to repair the damage was when I was standing waiting for a meal at a conference in a university abroad, and became irritated by the apparent lack of order amongst people striving to reach the serving hatch. I remarked to the stranger next to me that it seemed we had to compete for our food. 'It's survival of the fittest, don't you think?' she said. 'Of the fattest', I said. It was only on hearing her sharp intake of breath (.hhhhh) that I looked round and saw that she was a person of some considerable size. 'Oh no,' I tried to explain, 'I didn't mean you . . .' and so on into even deeper water.

Of course, we often feel obliged to offer accounts or explanations without having made inappropriate responses. Sequence 3.7 comes from a recorded interview between an occupational guidance counsellor and his client. In this extract, the counsellor has reached the point of asking the client (a man in his late twenties, whom he had met recently) to supply some information about his school experience.

Sequence 3.7: A haircut and a shave

Counsellor: So you left school when you were sixteen?
Client: Yes.
Counsellor: That's going back to 1977. You don't look that old.
Client: I've had a haircut and a shave.
Counsellor: You've had what? (*sounding perplexed*)
Client: I've had a haircut and a shave.
Counsellor: (*laughs*) You left in '77, that's what 12 or 13 years ago now isn't it?[10]

The client tries to offer an account or explanation for his youthful appearance which the counsellor appears not to understand. This is an interesting example of someone trying to offer an explanatory account which does not work because the two speakers initially appear to lack a shared frame of reference for their exchange. By the end of the sequence, the shared frame is re-established, and the counsellor returns to the main topic of the talk.

Using 'cohesive ties' to create continuity

There is a closely related but somewhat different set of language techniques that we use to relate the 'given' to the 'new'. I have shown that one way in which we create continuity in the meanings we express in language is by referring to past shared experience. A second way I have discussed is our sensitivity to subtle clues, provided by conversational partners, about when conversational turns are available, what kinds of responses are expected, and so on. A third way in which we create continuity is by creating grammatical links between phrases or sentences, so that the meaning of a long stretch of language is achieved by the relationship between these smaller units, and not just the meaning and organization of words within them. Linguists call this feature of connected speech or writing 'cohesion'. The most obvious way we do this is by using conjunctions – 'and', 'or', 'while', 'because', etc. – but there are other more subtle techniques which may be much more effective, in some situations, for enabling people who are conversing to develop continuous lines of thought together.

Linguistic research on cohesion has often focused on the use of specific grammatical devices and the repetition and substitution of particular words. Consider, for example, this set of instructions:

> Wash and core six cooking apples. Put them into a fireproof dish.

In this example, the pronoun 'them' is used to refer a reader back to 'six cooking apples'. The words 'them' and 'six cooking apples' can be said to form a 'cohesive tie'. To be more precise, linguists would describe that kind of tie as an *anaphoric reference*, meaning that the link in the text is backwards from 'them' to the earlier phrase. But links from pronouns can also be made forwards, as follows:

> This is how to get the best results. You let the berries dry in the sun, till all the moisture has gone out of them. Then you gather them up and chop them very fine.[11]

The forward linking from 'This' to the next two sentences would be described as *cataphoric reference*. We can see some examples of these kinds of links in the following passage from a novel:

> As I watched him he adjusted himself a little, visibly. His hand took hold of hers, and as she said something low in his ear he turned toward her with a rush of emotion. I think that voice held him most, with its fluctuating, feverish warmth, because it couldn't be over-dreamed – that voice was a deathless song.
>
> They had forgotten me, but Daisy glanced up and held out her hand; Gatsby didn't know me now at all.[12]

The meaningfulness of this passage for any reader will depend on a number of different ways of establishing shared understanding with the author. First, the passage is of course part of a much longer text – the novel *The Great Gatsby* by F. Scott Fitzgerald. It is meant to be encountered by a reader in the context of the whole book, and so the author will have made decisions about what he could expect readers to know already about characters, settings and plot at any time. (If you have read that novel, your recall would no doubt be alerted by the names 'Gatsby' and 'Daisy' and so you would be able to make more sense of the passage 'out of context' than someone who knew nothing of the book.)

Within the passage itself, however, the author uses several techniques to give the text cohesion, and hence draw his reader through a sequence of events. One of the most obvious and important is the use of pronouns to create cohesive ties. The repetition of 'I' throughout maintains our link, as readers, with the voice of the narrator. The use of 'his', 'he', 'himself', 'him' and 'she', 'her', 'hers' establishes in our eyes the continuity of an event involving two people observed by a third. The personal identities of these two people (established earlier in the text of the book) are reasserted in the last sentence as the use of proper names resolves the cataphoric reference of the earlier cataphoric pronouns.

There are many other ways of creating cohesion in texts, besides the use of anaphoric and cataphoric reference, and linguists have described these in some detail. To take just two more examples: the **repetition** of words can create cohesion, as can the *substitution* of a word for another which has a closely related meaning. You can see both of these techniques being used in the following example:

> Childhood *holidays* seemed to last for ever. **Days** were long, exciting, exhausting adventures. But now the weeks of *leave* I take from work pass in no time at all, and **days** seem to run together as one.

Speakers in conversations, like writers of written texts, use cohesive devices to make sense jointly with their listeners. Cohesion in unscripted spoken language is often a less orderly affair than in written texts, but nonetheless important for communicating meanings effectively. What is more, speakers can jointly, co-operatively create cohesion in the text of their speech. Sequence 3.8 below again comes from the research of the discourse analyst Liz Stokoe, and is a piece of dialogue between three women psychology students (B, J and R) as they try to construct an outline for an essay. Some of the cohesive ties are marked by lines between words and phrases. See if you can identify any examples of *anaphoric reference*, *repetition* and *substitution*.

Sequence 3.8: Cohesive ties

B: And them erm you could put what the (experiments) were and what (who did them)

J: [Yeah

R: ([Who did them) yeah

J: some of (these) being just a quick [list

B: [yeah

J: and then going into more depth in the next (paragraph) [to each (one.)

B: [Yeah

yeah each (paragraph)

J: yeah

B: Discuss (one)

J: (essay)

B: (one) at a time

R: covers (one) of the (experiments)

B: and the results which (we) don't know do (we) so (we can't) do that (*laughter*)

J: could just put stuff down like (experiment) one two three or four

B: Mm cos (we'd) have books

J: Yeah if (we) were doing it

R: (We'd) go to the library

J: Because if (we) knew how to plan it like that now then (we'd) be able to write an (essay) like that which (we can't) [13]

At the beginning of the sequence we can see how R uses *repetition* to link her statement with B's earlier remark ('who did them'), which itself contains an *anaphoric reference* to 'experiments'. Soon after, J uses the *substitution* of 'one' for 'experiment' to make a further cohesive tie. B and R repeat 'one' to make other ties; and in the final stages, J repeats her own formulation of 'if we . . .'. It is also worth noting that in the final three remarks J and R achieve cohesion by jointly creating a single sentence – and in so doing provide a good example of the mutually supportive 'cumulative talk' that I discussed in Chapter 2.

Researchers in linguistics identify the devices used to create cohesion in order to reveal how language is organized as a cohesive text. From a more psychological perspective, the same analysis reveals the way in which speakers together offer, carry along and develop ideas. So in Sequence 3.8 we can see how the students talk to develop a joint understanding of the task, share problems that they envisage will arise in doing it and try to solve them.

By combining an analysis of cohesion with an analysis of the ways in which teachers use techniques like 'recaps', 'elaborations', and so on, to link the past with present and future activity (as described earlier), we can see even more clearly how language is used to make joint, coherent sense of experience over time. This kind of analysis can be found in the work of the Australian language researcher Pauline Gibbons. Here, from her data, is a sequence from a primary school lesson about magnets.[14]

Sequence 3.9: 'Try and get a picture in your mind of what we did last Monday'

Students' talk	Teacher's talk
Children: yes	Today, well first of all let's connect ourselves back to last lesson. Was everybody here on Monday? I think we were all here on Monday. What did we do on Monday? Marcel's thinking, so's Andre. Just think. Try and get a picture in your mind of what we did last Monday. Carlos? Carlos?

Carlos: Miss we had to go in our groups and everyone had. Some people had em things to do and we had to read each instr . . .

Other child: instruction

Carlos: instruction

OK so we were in groups. What things did we have to do? Who can help Carlos explain that? Bernice?

Bernice: Like we get, like people doing the groups like using magnets? In each group like using strings and the em . . . cr . . . em the magnets, like in the cradle?

Mmm. So you're giving me some examples of the activities. What sort of activities were they, Diana?

Diana: em like there were three activities. We were in our groups . . . And like we had to follow the instructions.

Excellent. That's exactly right. There were three different experiments or three different activities. Each group had one of the activities. We had two groups working on each activity and there were instructions that you had to do to use the magnets. What I'm going to ask you to do now instead of telling me what happened straight away, I'm going to ask you to go back into those groups, OK, for a minute or two, and I want you in your group to retell or recount what you did.

Continuity and cohesion in Sequence 3.9		
Students	**Teacher**	**Comments**
	. . . Try and get a picture in your mind of what we did last Monday. Carlos? Carlos?	*The teacher exhorts the children to recall past events, and then elicits information about past experience.*
. . . we had to go in our groups . . . Some people had . . . things to do and we had to read each . . . instruction | instruction		
	OK so we were in groups. What things did we have to do?	*The teacher reformulates the student's response and elicits more information.*
the groups like using magnets . . . em the magnets		
	So you're giving me some examples of the activities. What sort of activities were they, Diana?	*The teacher reformulates the responses and elicits more information.*
em like there were three activities. We were in our groups	Excellent. That's exactly right.	*The teacher offers positive feedback.*
	There were three different experiments or three different activities. Each group had one of the activities. We had two groups working on each activity and there were instructions that you had to do, to use the magnets.	*The teacher reformulates the students' responses and elaborates the information provided.*

As Gibbons points out, the teacher uses 'we' to emphasize that shared experience is being discussed (so she says 'we were in groups', though strictly speaking only the children were). The teacher also uses some of the familiar techniques I described earlier, such as *eliciting* information about past experience from children, appropriating what the children say and *reformulating* it in her own remarks to the class in a manner which emphasizes the points she wishes to be seen as most important. Essentially, she involves the class in a joint, extended *recap* of what they had done on Monday. I have shown the teacher's use of these techniques on p. 65. And as with the group of psychology students in Sequence 3.8, the speakers here use the cohesive device of repeating certain 'key words' to create together a coherent account of the past events in question. I have also marked such repetitions – for 'groups', 'magnets', 'instruction(s)' and 'activities'.

Features which are also particularly worth noticing in Sequence 3.9 are: the teacher reformulates what the children have called 'things to do' into the more formal and technical term 'activities', which Diana then uses along with two of the other key words; and that in her final 'summing up' speech at the end of the sequence, just before the children go off into the future of their group activities, the teacher manages to bring together all the key words.

Computers and concordances

The Russian literary scholar Mikhail Bakhtin was a contemporary of Vygotsky's in the early part of the twentieth century, though apparently they never met. Bakhtin made some interesting claims about how the relationship between 'given' and 'new' knowledge is created in language. Every utterance, he said, is always in part a response to things that have been said before, and every utterance also anticipates the responses its speaker expects. From this perspective, even monologues are part of a dialogue, in which we can hear the echoes of the voices of previous speakers or writers. The meanings of the words we use are shaped and reshaped by continual usage; and, as Bakhtin put it, we do not learn words from dictionaries, we take them from other people's mouths.[15]

Linguistic research on the ways in which word meanings are shaped by use has recently been revolutionized by the use of computers, and this has enabled Bakhtin's claims to be investigated in new ways, with some interesting results. Software packages have been developed which enable any electronic file of written language (anything from a single text to a large collection of related texts, which is known as a 'corpus') to be scanned easily for all instances of particular words. The software then offers the user two main kinds of information: the frequency of occurrence of any word in a text or corpus, and a display of all those instances in the settings of surrounding words in which they occur (the immediate linguistic context of the word in the text). These types of software are known as 'concordancers', and the results they provide are called *concordances*. This technology has usually been used by linguists to study how words gather meanings from 'the company they keep' – that is, from the influence of the meanings of other words which are used with them. (Linguists call such joint occurrences of words 'collocations'.) Concordances can reveal meanings that words have gathered in use, meanings which are not captured by literal and formal definitions, and so concordance analyses of large corpuses of natural language are now commonly used for compiling dictionaries. But other kinds of research are also made more possible by concordance analysis. For example, by analysing all the occurrences of the phrase 'days are' in an 18 million-word electronic corpus of English texts, the linguist Bill Louw found that over two-thirds of them were collocated with words like 'past', 'over' and 'gone', so that the use of 'days are' seemed associated with some sense of nostalgia or lost time. Below is a tiny part of the concordance analysis he made.[16]

Part of concordance for 'days are'

1	t it yourself the prices these	**days are**	absolutely astronomica
2	ite 'The world is wide, no two	**days are**	alike, not even two ho
3	ays are gone whenel. But those	**days are**	almost twenty years go
4	glass extinction when the grey	**days are**	done but who are reaso
5	o men for unequal pay. But the	**days are**	gone whenel. But those
6	or do I. The big beer drinking	**days are**	gone. They drank becau
7	nd cry for peace. My political	**days are**	good and over. I'm not

However, Louw found no such associations for 'day is', nor for other similar time statements (such as 'weeks are'). Louw argues that, although this kind of subtle connotation of a word like 'days' is not one that most of us would be conscious of, it is an effective resource for creative writing because English speakers will at some level be sensitive to this meaning. He points out, for example, how this implication of sad regret is used in Philip Larkin's poem *Days:*[17]

> *Days*
> What are days for?
> Days are where we live.
> They come, they wake us
> Time and time over.
> They are to be happy in:
> Where can we live but days?
> Ah, solving that question
> Brings the priest and the doctor
> In their long coats
> Running over the fields.

Here the poet plays, deliberately, with our shared, half-realized understandings of the meaning of 'days'. We know 'days' represents literally a measure of time, and for us all 'days' repeatedly wake us from the darkness of nights. But, as Louw explains, although the phrase 'Days are where we live' might be expected to invoke happiness, we read it with the implicit, contextualizing knowledge of the nostalgic, regretful way that 'days are' is commonly used. There is therefore an irony in the first line, with a meaning brought out explicitly only in the last few lines.

Louw's research is relevant for understanding our use of language for collective thinking, in two main ways. First, it reveals one source of contextual information that people use to develop coherent, shared trains of thought. If we are active, participating members of a mainstream community of English speakers, when we hear someone using the phrase 'days are' (or any other common phrase) we will be able to draw subtle inferences about the intended meaning which reflect our shared history of experience in that community. Secondly, the computer-based analysis used by Louw can be applied to a transcription of a casual conversation, an interview or some other kind of conversation. It can reveal that certain words or phrases recur in a way that seems important for the developing meaning of what is being said as the conversation unfolds. This enables an analyst to form a kind of hypothesis about how the speakers are developing themes in their shared understanding. In the past, to test such a hypothesis an analyst had the laborious task of searching for each of those words in the transcript, jumping back and forwards between particular occurrences. Now, a concordancer provides, almost instantly, a table of all the occurrences of any word in its linguistic setting. In this way an analyst can move with ease between the summary table and the locations of words in the complete transcript. Where a lot of recorded language is involved – for example, a series of lessons or interviews, over several days – the saving in time and effort is very considerable.

With concordance software, it is therefore now much easier for researchers like myself to test our hypotheses about how topics are being carried forward and how meaning is being jointly developed through talk. Below is an example from my own research on language and literacy development in primary schools. I was interested in how whole-class, teacher-led sessions about fiction books being used in the class influenced children's discussions of the same books when they were talking together later in groups, without the teacher, and how ideas were carried through when the class reconvened as a whole next time. One set of recordings involved a teacher and her class (of 9- and 10-year-olds) talking about a book called *I'll Take You to Mrs Cole*, by Nigel Gray and Michael Forman. The basic story of this book is that a mother, exasperated by the mischievous behaviour of her son, threatens to have him 'minded' by a mysterious Mrs Cole who lives nearby. The boy fantasizes about what this person, and her household, might be like. Pictures in the book represent a mixture of real and fantastic events in his life. While reading the transcript of the whole-class session, my interest was taken by a sequence in which one child announced that he thought that there was not really a Mrs Cole – she was just an imaginary person created by the boy character's mother. He justified this by saying that his own mother threatens him with a similarly fictitious character. Sequence 3.10 shows part of this discussion, as the teacher and children looked at one illustrated page of the book together.

Sequence 3.10: I'll take you to Mrs Cole (whole class)

James: Don't think it's Mrs Cole at all – just an ordinary person making stew.

Girl: Why do you think it's someone else and not Mrs Cole?

James: Every time they get down to the end of the street she says 'I'll let you off, so come back in'.

Teacher: So do you think there isn't a Mrs Cole?
James: No – because my Mum's got an imaginary person.
Teacher: What does she say?
James: The shock man's coming.
Teacher: Is that a pleasant or an unpleasant threat then?
James: Unpleasant.

Having noticed that James introduced this idea through the use of the word 'imaginary', I decided to carry out a concordance search for that word, not only in the talk of the whole-class session but also in a discussion about the book by a group of children which took place later the same day. The group we recorded did not include James, though he had been part of the whole-class discussion when he made his remark. Would they pick up on his idea, taking 'imaginary' out of his mouth and using it to discuss the same issue? The results of my concordance analysis are given below. It showed that the word 'imaginary' was used eleven times. Three of these occurrences (at lines 147, 185 and 239 in the transcript) were found in the initial whole-class session, with one of these uses being by the teacher. (The teacher's talk is shown in italics.) The children in the small group also used the word twice (290, 292), and then it was used again six times by the children and the teacher in the later whole-class session.

Concordance: occurrences of 'imaginary' (whole class and small group)

Full search for <imaginary> 11 instances found

147	my Mum's got an	**imaginary**	person. *T: What does she say?* J: The shock man's
185	my Mum has got an	**imaginary**	person. . . . *T: Hold on I know you've all got lots of*
239	*She might be just an*	***imaginary***	*person. Has anyone else any comment to make*
290	time it's like it's an	**imaginary**	person because they get to Mrs Cole's house
292	go back. I think it's an	**imaginary**	person. Look at the house – the fence is broken
313	think Mrs Cole is an	**imaginary**	person and Natasha agreed with us as well
315	*the Mum think she's*	***imaginary***	*because your Mums have imaginary people too*
316	*your Mums have*	***imaginary***	*people too – which other group would like to*
317	We thought she was	**imaginary**	because they kept on letting him off
322	We think she's	**imaginary**	because they keep on saying we'll let you off
329	Mrs Cole's place isn't	**imaginary**	because Mrs Cole lives down the street

It can be seen that 'imaginary' was most frequently collocated with 'person', in the phrase 'an imaginary person', regardless of who spoke it. In the initial session the word was being used by all the speakers to discuss the same idea – whether or not Mrs Cole was 'real'. In the small group, this same pattern of meanings is continued – suggesting that the group's thinking about this issue had indeed been heavily influenced by the whole-class session. When the class reconvened later, it was James, the boy who had first used the word, who introduced it again (line 313) as he reported on his own small group's discussion. As the next fragment of talk shows, the teacher picked up on this, doing a quick 'recap' of the earlier discussion about mothers employing imaginary characters to enforce discipline. And then, as the children were encouraged by the teacher to justify their claims for the imaginary status of Mrs Cole, the collocation pattern of the word shifted, so that it was used consistently in association with 'because'. So the technology of the concordancer has provided a new way to hunt for evidence about how meaning is shared and developed. It enables us to see how lines of thought are carried and developed, and how particular words can carry the history of the communication of conversational partners into their future joint activity.

Summary

When people use language in joint activity, their talk runs along contextual foundations of their own creation. Common knowledge is a resource from which speakers and listeners can build those foundations. Speakers can appeal to this knowledge explicitly or implicitly. Speakers have to make judgements, as time passes, about how much 'context' to make explicit for their listeners (as do writers for their readers). Classrooms and other educational settings provide some good examples of the techniques speakers can use to make links of meaning between the past, present and future. Teachers habitually rely heavily on certain techniques, such as *recaps* and *reformulations*, to make these links apparent to their students. This reflects teachers' special concern with offering a clarified, coherent 'story' of classroom experience so that students grasp the overall structure and purpose of what they are doing.

Cohesive devices, such as *repetition* and *anaphoric reference*, are a different kind of technique for making connected meaning as conversations or written texts unfold. The analysis of cohesion in conversation can reveal the way in which speakers carry ideas along and develop them together.

The words and structures of a language are a kind of 'given' knowledge for each new generation of a language community. But through using language in dialogue, this new generation collectively transforms the meanings of past language use into those of the future. This process of transforming the given into the new links particular conversations with the wider cultural activities of societies. The Russian literary theorist Bakhtin claimed that every utterance, even an apparent monologue, is part of a grander dialogue, with the echoes of the meanings created by earlier speakers shaping the ways in which words are used by speakers and interpreted by listeners. Computer-based 'concordance' analyses have helped reveal much more clearly how words achieve new meanings as they are used collectively by each generation to deal with life as it unfolds, and so are now used to create dictionaries which take account of this process of change. Concordancers can also be used to track the use of words through developing conversations, thus revealing how the words are functioning as embodiments of common knowledge.

4 Persuasion, control and argument

The creation of human knowledge is not simply the accumulation of facts, skills and ways of making sense of experience. It is also a process of evolution, in which alternative explanations, proposals and solutions compete for survival. As well as providing us with the tools for building common knowledge in a cumulative, co-operative activity, language also offers techniques for setting competing ideas and interests against each other, for 'arguing a case' and persuading other people that some courses of action are better than alternatives. The art of persuasive language is sometimes called 'rhetoric', a term which has its origins in the skilful argumentative use of language by ancient Greek orators. Today, we still tend to think of rhetoric in terms of the calculated, charismatic performance of individuals: political speakers, evangelists, salespeople and confidence tricksters are obvious examples. The 'magic' is assumed to lie in the monologues they perform. In this chapter, I want to take a different perspective on persuasion and argument, one that is based on dialogue rather than monologue. There certainly are people who, through technique and charisma, are particularly effective at making others believe or do what they wish. But effective arguments are those which are accepted by others, and persuasive rhetoric can only really be judged by its effects on an audience. To understand how persuasion and argument are used to get things done, we need to study social interaction.

The term 'rhetoric' has some negative connotations (as in 'empty rhetoric'): but I ask you to suspend any possible conception of persuasion and argument as inherently dubious or aberrant activities. We can be persuaded for our better interests, not merely to serve the selfish interests of the persuader. We may change our minds because a case is made reasonably and logically, rather than because we are being brainwashed. While there are many unproductive arguments, others generate some of the most creative joint thinking we ever achieve together. New directions in human thinking often emerge when opposing viewpoints clash, and new courses of human joint action emerge when some ideas win out over others. Persuasion and argumentation are natural, and potentially very valuable, aspects of how we *reason* together.

Lists and contrasts

The analysis of persuasive speech and argumentation has been given special attention in recent years with the development of research known as 'conversation analysis' and 'discourse analysis'. One of the results of that research has been to highlight certain techniques that effective orators use to draw their audiences along a particular path of meaning, and to encourage the audience's enthusiastic participation and support. For example, the pioneering research of Max Atkinson revealed that political speakers who are good at regularly eliciting applause and other forms of positive support commonly rely on certain particular techniques.[1] By analysing recordings of political speeches to see when applause occurred, and how enthusiastic it was, he found that one technique which is particularly effective is the *three-part list*. This simply consists of making a point in three related parts. Here, for instance, is a three-part list identified by Atkinson in a speech by Margaret Thatcher to the 1980 Conservative conference:

Soviet marxism is ideologically, politically and morally bankrupt.[2]

Three-part lists are not just favoured by British Conservative politicians. Research has shown that this same technique is commonly used by politicians, evangelical preachers, salespeople and other charismatic persuaders in many parts of the world.[3] Here, for example, is an extract from a speech by Malcolm X, the American 'Black Power' leader:

And I say, I'm speaking as a Black man from America, which is a racist society. No matter how much you hear it talk about democracy

it's as racist as South Africa
or as racist as Portugal,
or as racist as any other racialist society on this earth.[4]

As the conversation analyst Robin Wooffitt says, three-part lists 'are successful at eliciting applause because they project their own completion; as they are being built, they signal when they are going to end'.[5] They are a way of making a speech more cohesive, which (as I described in the previous chapter) can be important for helping listeners make overall sense of what is being said. An interesting finding is that audiences are less responsive to lists of two, or more than three, parts. The use of such deviant lists by a speaker will probably reflect their naïvety as an orator, or their disregard for rhetorical performance. (Hence the joke about the Oxbridge professor who attempted to attract his audience's flagging attention with the remark 'And fourteenthly . . .'.)

A second technique that Atkinson and others have found is effective at gaining audience attention and raising applause is the 'contrast'. This amounts to the presentation of two conflicting statements, both of which (like the elements of the three-part list) add up to make one strong point. Here, for example, is a 'contrast' in the speech of British Labour politician Alf Morris, as identified by the political rhetoric analysts Heritage and Greatbatch:

> Governments will argue that resources are not available to help disabled people. The fact is that
> *too much is spent on the munitions of war*
> *and too little is spent on the munitions of peace.*[6]

It is quite common in such contrasts for the actual phrases to be reflections of each other's structure, as they are here. This is a technique that makes them more 'poetic' – more striking and memorable.

The study of politicians giving prepared speeches to mass audiences might seem very distant from the more spontaneous and intimate kinds of use of language for collective thinking with which I have been dealing in the book so far. But, as I suggested earlier, dialogues can take many forms. Techniques like three-part lists and contrasts are designed for interactions between a speaker and an audience, and are used to try to achieve an interpersonal rapport, to establish shared frames of reference. As ways of using language, they are also part of the shared understanding that orators and their audiences have about the 'ground rules' of the event in which they are engaged, even if that understanding is quite implicit. The successful charismatic orator uses language to create an intersubjectivity in which their audience is willingly (and even enthusiastically) drawn along the orator's line of thought. And although they are found in their most obvious and striking form in public oratory, three-part lists and contrasts are used quite often in everyday conversation. This is not so surprising, because we all often share the orator's aims of persuading people that our ideas are worthwhile, that our accounts of events are true and that we are worthy partners in some joint endeavour.

Call and response

There is some variation in the ground rules for oratorical events amongst cultures. For example, Indian orators seem to rely, more than their British counterparts, on the measured repetition of key phrases throughout a speech.[7] In communities which have strong historical links with West African cultures, speakers and audiences in church and political gatherings commonly engage in what is known as *call and response*.[8] This consists of members of the audience affirming or emphasizing a speaker's remarks (for example, by shouting 'Tell it!' or 'Yes!'). An effective speaker will be one who generates strong, regular and positive responses to their 'calls'. But again, this feature of mass oratory has some common basis in how our own ideas are stimulated by hearing the words of others. We may be enabled to think about an issue in a fresh, creative way by hearing or reading what someone else thinks about it. We may even not know what our opinion is on a certain issue until we are confronted with someone else's point of view. The 'call' they make may elicit responses on our part which are negative and critical, as well as affirmatory.

An interesting kind of 'call and response' phenomenon has been pointed out by the linguist Guy Cook in his study of playful uses of language in everyday life. He noticed that graffiti sometimes appear as additions to existing texts such as notices and advertisements, as in the following examples:[9]

> Addition to a railway notice:
> **Warning: Passengers are requested not to cross the lines**
> *It takes hours to untangle them afterwards*

Addition to the dedication in a law textbook:
To my father and mother
Thanks Son, it's just what we wanted

Addition to an advertisement for a car:
If it [this car] were a lady, it would get its bottom pinched
If this lady was a car she'd run you down

Cook suggests that these kinds of graffiti are ironic, subversive responses to 'official' pieces of writing, as if the graffiti writer felt moved to undermine the impact of the authoritative text. They are a kind of dialogue between authority and rebellion. The third example, in particular, also illustrates how opinions are not just *expressed* in dialogue, they are *generated* by dialogue. As I have just indicated, the opinion that we have about a particular issue may not exist in a clear, fully fledged form prior to our engaging in some kind of dialogue about it; and even if we think it does, it is likely to be changed by being put up against a particular point of view. There are many kinds of dialogue that can stimulate our thinking in this way – a personal conversation, a discussion in a business meeting or seminar, or an e-mail exchange are obvious examples, because we respond in words to what someone has said or written, and all participants may have opportunities to contribute.

You may recall from the previous chapter that the Russian literary scholar Bakhtin suggested that every utterance is always partly a response to things that have been said before, and is designed to take account of the responses its speaker expects. By this he meant that we may be engaging in a kind of dialogue when we read a book or newspaper article, or when we hear someone talking on radio or television, because what we read or hear provokes us to formulate our own responsive point of view. The fact that in these circumstances one participant in the dialogue (the author or broadcaster) is not able to continue the exchange, may seem to make these doubtful examples of collective thinking. Nevertheless, one key element of dialogue is present: that we (the audience) react to the ideas someone expresses by responding to what the initiator of the dialogue has said. As an introspective test of the validity of this notion, read the following extract from an article by the journalist Julie Burchill:

If I want immaturity, I'll choose a gorgeous boy with no ambition and a sweet nature. But what, it seems to me, most women of my generation are getting is the worst of both worlds: the tragic, thwarted spreading body of the middle-aged man housing the spirit and soul of the surly, sulky, pre-teen brat. . . .

The trouble is, men have got it too soft these days. In the past, just the process of being alive saw to it that boys grew up PDQ; shoved into factories at 14, as my father was, deprived of sex before marriage, adulthood seemed both the natural and desirable state for any boy on the right side of adolescence. These days, educated until they say 'when', with sex on tap, there simply seems no point in growing up.[10]

Reading Burchill's remarks will probably make you feel particularly aware of being a man or a woman, young or middle-aged. You are likely to react differently to what she says depending on whether or not you feel you are in the line of her attack. You may not feel very motivated to respond to her opinions, but reading the passage may nevertheless stimulate your views about this kind of polemical writing. Any reaction you make will involve you rehearsing, reconsidering and re-presenting the relevant information at your disposal to take account of what she has said and how she has said it. Our attitudes and opinions on issues are not like pre-recorded tapes that we run each time a topic is raised. If someone raises a topic, we recast our ideas as a form of attack, or support, for their point of view. In this way, our knowledge, opinions and attitudes are shaped by our engagement in dialogue.[11]

Metaphors

One linguistic technique favoured by both orators and poets is 'metaphor'. Metaphors are categories of likeness which people use to organize the data of experience. We say that something 'is' something else, and so make the second 'thing' a category which includes the first. So if someone says 'marriage is a ship for braving the seas of adult life', they are categorizing 'marriage' as a kind of ship. By saying this, they are suggesting that it is useful to use some of our knowledge about ships to understand marriage. They might go on to say 'the ship of their marriage had eventually run aground', meaning some sense can be made of the fate of the marriage in question by employing this metaphorical image. But an important part of the way metaphors function is that a listener must interpret the likeness as figurative, not literal: we are not really meant to think that the marriage in question is a ship, but rather that it is useful to think of it *as* one.

Some metaphors are obvious plays with the literal meanings of words, such as those often found in poetry. But metaphors are such a normal and pervasive feature of our use of language that we often do not realize we are using them. It is in fact often difficult to distinguish literal and metaphorical meanings, because metaphorical uses can influence literal meanings of words. As I explained when discussing the collocation of 'days' in the previous chapter, words gather new meanings in use. If metaphors are used frequently by many people, and the use continues over a long period of time, the metaphorical meanings may become absorbed into the literal meanings of the word or expression. In conversations, we all 'raise' our voices, 'drop' proposals, 'twist arms' to get our way and 'back off' from confrontations with little sense of metaphorical use. These are 'dead metaphors' (a metaphorical category itself, as the literal meaning of 'dead' cannot be applied to a non-living object like a word).

The cognitive scientist George Lakoff has provided a wealth of interesting examples of metaphor. He considers the creation of metaphors as one aspect of the more general human tendency to categorize experience, and suggests that the roots of the 'metaphors we live by' (as Lakoff calls them) lie in our sensory perceptions, our relationship with the physical world.[12] Here, though, I am not interested in the psychological foundations of metaphors, but rather in their function for enabling people to make sense of experience *together*. We can choose our metaphors, similes and any other categories, to suit the circumstances in which we are communicating, and the people we are communicating with. In everyday conversation as well as in public oratory, metaphors are rhetorical techniques.[13]

In a valiant but unsuccessful attempt to organize opposition to the Gulf War in 1991, Lakoff circulated by international e-mail an analysis of how the conflict leading up to the declaration of war had been described in the speeches of American politicians and generals, and in reports in American newspapers.[14] He identified some common metaphorical strategies. One was to describe the countries in direct conflict as individuals in hand-to-hand combat, competing for survival. So there was talk of the USA 'delivering a knockout punch' to Iraq, and aiming to 'push Iraq out of Kuwait'. The oil supplies to the USA which were under threat were described as a 'lifeline'. Lakoff suggested that these metaphors encouraged a particular representation of the conflict which was in accord with the policies of the dominant political forces in American government, and which hid or minimized some important factors which were not easily accommodated by that view. For example, representing each country as a single individual obscured the fact that countries are made up of many groups and individuals whose interests and risks in any war would not be equivalent. In other words, the dominant metaphors prevented the case for and against a declaration of war being discussed in a reasonable manner. For these reasons, Lakoff said, 'Metaphors can kill'.[15]

The creation and use of metaphors in mass media is a fascinating aspect of how language is used for the shaping of common knowledge. As Bakhtin said, we take words from other people's mouths.[16] So one measure of whether a new metaphor 'rings true' (as the dead metaphor puts it) as a categorization of experience is the extent to which people who hear or read it start to use it themselves. In the media-rich world most of us now inhabit, new metaphorical ways of representing experience are offered regularly. Some develop a kind of special salience, becoming part of everyday discourse. For example, 'ethnic cleansing' and 'friendly fire' are metaphorical terms which have been so commonly used in media reports of international warfare that they are unlikely to need explanation to most readers. However, as I suggested earlier, the meaning of words is not fixed; metaphors can be put to use in new contexts. Their function for making sense of experience is not necessarily limited to the circumstances they were apparently coined to deal with. Perhaps both 'ethnic cleansing' and 'friendly fire' were first used as euphemisms, ways of representing acts of war as less chilling (and less blameworthy) when reported. That is, amongst their original users they may have had the function of allowing certain actions to be considered collectively in a way that minimized emotional involvement. But in the personal conversations of my everyday life, I have only ever heard them used in a condemnatory or ironic manner, with the speaker's tone, pronunciation and other non-verbal signals making this 'alternative' meaning clear to me. Here are a couple of examples I noted recently:

> (*On a campaign in a local paper to evict gypsy encampments from unauthorized sites*) 'A bit of "ethnic cleansing" always gets the front page sorted!'

(After a work meeting in which a colleague was unexpectedly the victim of a critical attack by another colleague) 'I think Emily just got caught in a bit of friendly fire aimed at the Dean.'

On hearing the first example, I took the speaker to be using the phrase to imply that the paper's campaign had some of the same dubious (im)moral basis as those pursued by the governments who first used the term 'ethnic cleansing' (which apparently came into English as a translation from Serbo-Croat in the early 1990s). The second I understood as a humorous representation of the meeting as a battle between rival political camps in the management of the university. These English phrases, like words in any living language, gather nuances of meaning as they are used (as concordance analyses of the kind I described in the previous chapter would doubtless reveal). Their meanings shift over time, and between settings. We can study their function in the process of building shared perspectives on experience by looking at how they are used in context, by actual speakers and writers.

A very subtle kind of metaphorical technique has been identified by Michael Halliday and other systemic linguists, which is known as 'the grammatical metaphor'.[17] By this they mean that, by exercising some grammatical choice – say, choosing a passive rather than an active form of the verb – a speaker or writer offers a particular perspective on events. Compare, for example, these two sentences:

For reasons of economy, the emergency ward was closed.

Because the hospital managers wanted to save money, they decided to close the emergency ward.

The first sentence represents events as having no obvious agency behind them; no-one is identified as making them happen. In the second the agent is clearly identified. This can be considered a kind of metaphor because the grammar of each sentence presents the ward closure as a different kind of event – one that happened and one that someone *made* happen. In official statements, such as might be offered by a hospital management in a report, the first would be more likely to occur. Some linguists have argued that, through such subtle techniques, powerful agencies such as managements, the press and government can engineer interpretations of events so that members of the general public are less likely to be critical of the policies and actions that are being followed.[18] That is, they have suggested that, by the ways in which ideas are expressed, people can be led to think what the powerful would wish them to think. There are good reasons to take this claim seriously, because any way of reporting or explaining in words offers listeners or readers a ready-made interpretation of what took place. Fortunately, though, our interpretations of texts are not necessarily so determined, because no text, however apparently 'powerful', has only one inter-pretation. Its meaning is created in dialogue. Our willingness to agree or change our minds in response to ideas presented in speech or writing will depend partly on our perception of who is offering the ideas. Who is the speaker or writer? What values or interests do we associate with them? What authority do they hold to support those views? Do we have respect for that authority?

Also, like the linguists who first offered this analysis, any of us may learn to 'see' the rhetoric in the way events are described. Whether we do so, and whether we choose to question the version of events we are offered, will depend to some extent on our understanding of how language is used as a rhetorical tool (as well as the beliefs and values we bring to our interpretation). The knowledge resources we have for contextualizing and interpreting what we hear or read will shape our responses to 'powerful voices'.[19]

Even in ordinary, everyday conversation, we are all rhetoricians. Our presentation of views and opinions always, inevitably, reflects the pursuit of our interests through dialogue. As the discursive psychologist Derek Edwards has put it, if we accept that no description of anything is the only one that is reasonable or possible, the interesting question is then why, on any particular occasion, a speaker says the things that they do.[20] The idea that our choice of words may be determined by what we are trying to achieve is also well appreciated by good dramatists, theatre and film directors, as the playwright Rib Davis explains in his handbook for beginning scriptwriters:

> I was once present at a play rehearsal at which an excellent director was leading a detailed examination of the script. Before every line the director would turn to the relevant actor and ask, 'What do you want to achieve with this?', meaning, 'What do you think the character you are playing *wants to get* as a result of saying (or sometimes doing) this?' Sometimes the answers were easy, but

on other occasions the actors found it very difficult to say what the character was trying to achieve – what his or her agenda was – beyond, say, the straightforward requesting or sharing of information, or expression of emotion. Yet our motivations for saying things are often very complex, and there is a compelling theory that states that we want to 'get something out of' everything we say – that there are no utterances that are simply themselves. What we can be certain of is that during any conversation, each of us has a whole set of agenda items, some of them specific to that conversation and others of them semi-permanent, such as perhaps wishing to raise our own status relative to that of others. It is the simultaneous operation of a number of these agenda items which lends much of the fascination to dialogue.[21]

'At first I thought . . .' '. . . and then he said . . .'

Our choice of rhetorical techniques is likely to reflect what we are trying to achieve. In some situations, for example, we may want to convince people of our credibility when reporting surprising information. There are some common rhetorical techniques for doing this. Some good examples of this kind of rhetoric are revealed by the analysis of interviews with witnesses of dramatic events like armed hijacks, or those who claim to have had encounters with the paranormal. A common technique such witnesses use can be called: 'At first I thought . . . but then I realized'. That is, early in their account they establish their credentials as an 'ordinary observer' by saying that they at first thought that something relatively ordinary was going on, but then the force of other evidence caused them to make a more startling interpretation. Here is an example of such a witness account, reported by the sociologist Harvey Sacks:

> I was walking up towards the front of the airplane and I saw the stewardess standing facing the cabin and a fellow standing with a gun in her back. *And my first thought was he's showing her the gun, and then I realized that couldn't be, and then it turned out he was hijacking the plane.*[22]

Another common rhetorical technique is the use of *reported speech*. The conversation analyst Robin Wooffitt found this occurring frequently in witness accounts of paranormal experiences. Sequence 4.1 is one of his examples. *(The symbols used in the transcription are as explained on page 57.)*

Sequence 4.1: 'My God what is it'

tha:t night:
(1.5)
I don't know <u>what</u> time it was:
(1.3)
my husband and I both woke up:
(0.7)
with the mo:st d<u>read</u>ful (0.5) feeling of
(1.7)
·hhh well being (nyrie) smothered (0.3) but the
powerful smell, and a <u>black</u>ness (0.3) that was
that was (0.2) blacker than black I can't describe it
like anything else ·hh it was the most
penetrating (0.3) type of blackness ·hh
and there was this
(1.7)
what I assumed to be th- the shape of a man
in a cloak
(2.0)
it was the most (0.3) formidable
(1.2)
sight
(1.0)
my husband said 'my God what is it'
an' I just said 'now keep quiet and say the Lord's prayer'[23]

The occurrence and location in Sequence 4.1 of so many pauses over 0.6 seconds long (which *is* long for ordinary speech), as well as such other features as the speaker's audible and extended intakes of breath ('.hh'), are signs that this was a measured, dramatized account. We can see that the speaker does not only present us with her own reaction to the event, but also that of her husband. As Wooffitt says, by reporting her husband's words, the speaker introduces a corroborating witness – one who was no less shocked by the apparition – and so 'confirms the speaker's reliability as an accurate reporter of the event'.[24] Reporting of other people's words, especially those who perhaps have some special expertise or status, is a common rhetorical technique for supporting one's own arguments. (As you can see, I have just used it myself.) Claims about what someone else said may, of course, be unintentionally or deliberately false. But the 'recycling' of someone's words in this way is another example of how, to put it in the terms I used in Chapter 3, the 'given' is transformed into the 'new' in the long conversations that run through our lives.

Buying and selling

The pursuit of particular interests is fairly obvious in conversations concerned with buying and selling. The sequence below is a transcription of a telephone conversation I had a couple of years ago, captured by a phone-answering device. I had answered the phone at home, at about 8.30 in the evening. I reached the phone too late to switch the recording machine off.

Sequence 4.2: Selling insurance

Me: Hello, this is 22380.
Caller: Hello (*conversation is then halted by the recorded message on my phone machine*).
Me: Sorry about that, I didn't reach it in time.
Caller: Mr Mercer?
Me: Yes.
Caller: I'm speaking from Homes Insurance, we sent you a letter recently, did you get it?
Me: Uh, um, I'm not sure, uh.
Caller: We wrote to offer you a free consultation, with no obligations, on your personal finances. We are completely independent financial advisers, who can offer a wide range of insurance and investment tailor-made for our clients. Could we call and discuss this with you?
Me: Uhhh, no, no thanks, I think that we have, we don't need anything like that right now. If your letter turns up I'll read it. So thanks, cheerio (*hanging up quickly*).

In recent years, I have felt plagued by such unsolicited telephone sales calls. Despite my dislike for them, the experience has aroused my interest in how they are organized and functionally designed. One of my colleagues, the linguist Sharon Goodman, also began to make some enquiries into how telephone sales staff were trained.[25] On the basis of what we discovered, it seems certain that the example above has the following typical features:

1   As with all incoming telephone calls, I was the first speaker. Once I had spoken the caller addressed me formally by my (assumed) title and last name, in an enquiring manner that begged confirmation.
2   Once I had confirmed my identity, the caller talked quickly and fluently in a 'sing-song' way that suggested that they were either reading or performing a rehearsed script.
3   All the caller's turns ended with a question addressed to me. That is, having imparted some information, the caller then *elicited* information and a conversational turn from me.
4   I terminated the call.

For staff involved in selling insurance (and many other products) through telephone and face-to-face encounters, one of the earliest stages of their training involves becoming familiar with model 'scripts' which have been designed to enable them confidently and effectively to deliver their firm's message and persuade their potential customers to buy their product. This is one reason why so many telephone sales encounters have a similar form. Staff are also often formally prepared for dealing with the kind of objections customers might raise to the business being offered. One of the aims of the scripted techniques taught to sales staff by insurance companies and other similar enterprises is to use language to try to involve the client in a shared frame of reference, and to initiate a joint, co-operative investigation into the client's 'needs' which will end with a sale. That is, one rather subtle aspect of the rhetorical form of this kind of sales talk is that it is designed to persuade the client to engage in some joint thinking with the salesperson, and to help build the contextual foundations for doing so. This is done in one of two ways. First, the salesperson may introduce *particular* content, which will help establish an apparent basis of shared interests. Sales staff may be told to tell the prospective customer: 'Like you, I live and work here in Milton Keynes', and to begin to use the pronoun 'we' and the customer's first name at a certain stage (as in 'Well, Neil, now that we've worked out what your needs are . . .'). A second way is for sales staff to shape the *structure* of the talk to try to ensure that 'prospects' actively participate, and do so in such a way that they are co-opted to the pursuit of the seller's goals. So, in training, sales staff are told to ask questions which are likely to elicit positive responses, and to make sure that the 'prospect' is given conversational space and time to reply. Here, for example, is part of one model script used in training insurance sales staff for face-to-face selling:

Consultant: Is that all clear to you, Mr Brown?
　　　　　　[*Wait for him to reply*]
　　　　　　Are you happy so far?
Prospect: Yes.
Consultant: Good.
　　　　　　[*Remember to smile*][26]

Similar 'scripts' are often used by the fundamentalist Christian evangelists who appear at my doorstep. They usually begin by asking if I am concerned about some enduring human problem, such as crime, war or famine, and may even claim an interest in what my own possible solutions for these might be. They are likely next to ask if I believe that science really can offer solutions and explain our existence. In these ways, they encourage my active participation in establishing some shared frame of reference. Typically, as we proceed, they will highlight any possible areas where we seem to be in agreement. Inexorably, though, they lead the conversation down their own intended line of thought, which leads to the proposal that the answers to our problems are to be found in the Bible. The intersubjectivity in which they are willing to engage is limited, with boundaries which are defined in advance by their purpose in talking with me and by their commitment to their beliefs. Of course, the same can be said of my own participation in such conversations.

On the tape recording of Sequence 4.2, I initially sound hesitant and confused, while the caller sounds relatively confident and 'in command'. But I recovered some control and it was I who terminated the call. A salesperson making an unsolicited 'cold call' has no authority over a potential customer, and so the recipient can choose to have the last word. One reason I was initially unsuccessful at exercising control over the encounter was that I did not know what was going to happen when I picked up the telephone, while the salesman, in general terms, did. I had to gather together resources from past experience for contextualizing the conversation as it unfolded, while he had his usual resources to hand. The first recipients of telephone sales approaches were probably caught much more 'off balance' by such approaches than most of us would be today, because such conversations then were novel events. They would not have had past experience which would have helped them to categorize the interaction and predict how the event would unfold. For that reason, they might have been more easily drawn into some joint thinking and decision-making that they would have preferred to avoid. (I recall myself agreeing to a home visit in response to an early telephone sales pitch, and then bitterly regretting having done so and wondering why I had.) The risk of this continued use of the scripted strategy today, however, is that hearing someone speaking in a way which is obviously prepared and rehearsed is now likely to alert experienced recipients quickly to what is going on. They will recognize the encounter as involving them in a particular type or *genre* of language use (the 'cold call') and respond accordingly.

We can see that even if the insurance salesperson and I did not co-operatively pursue the same aims in Sequence 4.2, we nevertheless both drew on a substantial shared understanding of the kind of encounter in which we were engaged. Once I managed to recognize the type of encounter it was, the salesman and I then were able to conduct a normal (if unsuccessful, from the salesman's point of view) example of a telephone sales encounter. Because of my unwillingness to become involved, this conversation was hardly a striking example of the co-operative use of language as a tool for the joint construction of knowledge. Yet we did form some limited common knowledge in the process. For example, if the salesman had had the nerve to ring back the next night and realized he was talking again to me, I would expect him to say something like 'Hello Mr Mercer, this is Homes Insurance *again . . .*', because we now shared the history of our first encounter.

Something of the complexity of the ways in which language may be used as a tool for collective thinking is revealed in this example. Two people may, in the same interaction, be pursuing quite different aims or interests; the achievement of their goals may even be irreconcilable. There may be resistance by one partner to take part in the joint, co-operative construction of knowledge. But both participants may nevertheless draw on a shared understanding of relevant conversational ground rules, which enable them to interact fairly smoothly without misunderstanding. That is, speakers may be engaging in joint thinking at one level (that to do with the organization and flow of the discourse) but be acting quite unco-operatively at another level (concerned with creating a body of shared knowledge, solving a problem or establishing an agreed shared understanding about some past event). They establish a limited intersubjectivity, a guarded meeting of minds, in which their respective self-interests are still being clearly demarcated.

Courtroom conversations

Good examples of this kind of 'co-operative yet unco-operative' behaviour can be found in courtroom interrogations. Sequence 4.3, for example, is an extract from the testimony of Colonel Oliver North to the official hearings in the USA in the 1980s on the so-called 'Iran–Contra affair'. North is being interrogated by the official examiner Nields.

Sequence 4.3: North's testimony

Nields: Did you suggest to the Attorney General that maybe the diversion memorandum and the fact that there was a diversion need not ever come out?

North: Again, I don't recall that specific conversation at all, but I'm not saying it didn't happen.

Nields: You don't deny it?

North: No.

Nields: You don't deny suggesting to the Attorney General of the United States that he just figure out a way of keeping this diversion document secret?

North: I don't deny that I said it. I'm not saying I remember it either.[27]

Courtroom dialogues provide many examples of participants pursuing different individual agendas or interests while nevertheless maintaining a smooth and orderly flow of interaction based on a mutual acceptance of the appropriate ground rules. It is also often apparent that one participant (the lawyer) is attempting to persuade the other participant (the witness or accused) to make some personal knowledge explicit. The lawyer will also commonly seek to persuade the witness to agree to a particular representation of that information. For example, the next sequence comes from the cross-examination of a rape victim by a defence lawyer in an English court, as presented by the conversation analyst Steven Levinson.

Sequence 4.4: A coat or a dress?

Lawyer: Your aim that evening then was to go to the discotheque?
Witness: Yes.
Lawyer: Presumably you had dressed up for that, had you?
Witness: Yes.
Lawyer: And you were wearing make-up?
Witness: Yes.
Lawyer: Eye-shadow?
Witness: Yes.
Lawyer: Lipstick?
Witness: No I was not wearing lipstick.
Lawyer: You weren't wearing lipstick?
Witness: No.
Lawyer: Just eye-shadow, eye make-up?
Witness: Yes.
Lawyer: And powder presumably?
Witness: Foundation cream, yes.
Lawyer: You had had bronchitis had you not?
Witness: Yes.
Lawyer: You have mentioned in the course of your evidence about wearing a coat?
Witness: Yes.
Lawyer: It was not really a coat at all, was it?
Witness: Well, it is a sort of coat-dress and I bought it with trousers, as a trouser suit.
Lawyer: That is it down there isn't it, the red one?
Witness: Yes.
Lawyer: If we call that a dress, if we call that a dress you had no coat on at all had you?
Witness: No.
Lawyer: And this is January. It was quite a cold night?
Witness: Yes it was cold actually.[28]

Sequence 4.4 illustrates well that courtroom interrogations cannot, of course, be understood simply as conversations between a lawyer and a witness. (The same applies to radio interviews, chat show conversations and other public debates.) The key participants are the lawyer, the witness and the judge and jury. The main aim of the lawyer on occasions like those represented in Sequences 4.3 and 4.4 above is to draw the witness into a dialogue which will generate a particular account of events, an account which is compatible with the case the lawyer is trying to make. The lawyer is trying to present a particular kind of *argument*, but using the witness as a willing or unwilling accomplice to achieve this. Whether or not the witness changes his or her mind as a result of the interrogation is, generally speaking, of little concern to the lawyer: the people whose minds matter are the judge and jury.

To appreciate the rhetoric in Sequence 4.4, consider not only *what* the defence lawyer asks the victim of the alleged rape, but also *the order* in which the questions are asked. The lawyer first asks where the girl was going that evening; then how she had chosen to look, to present herself in public; and then about her health at the time. This is followed by a few questions about the best description of the garment she was wearing, and then an enquiry about the weather. Written like this, in a bald list, the topics in the lawyer's enquiry look disconnected, even random. While cohesive mechanisms like anaphoric reference and repetition (as discussed in Chapter 3) link together questions and answers dealing with each topic, they are not used to link the separate topics together. Some of the questions are obviously requests for information which the lawyer already has. Yet, as a surrogate juror, I am sure that you will be able to perceive a coherent argument, a plausible linkage of ideas, through this talk – and infer the lawyer's motive for generating it. As Levinson points out:

> . . . the functions of the questions here are to extract from the witness answers that build up to form a 'natural' argument for the jury. The argument . . . goes something like this: the victim was dressed to go dancing, she was heavily made up – something of a painted lady, in fact – and, despite the fact that she had been ill, she was wearing no coat on the cold winter's night. The implicit conclusion is that the girl was seeking sexual adventures.[29]

The lawyer's purpose is to persuade the jury to accept a certain frame of reference for interpreting the information they are given. This frame is constructed from several different kinds of relevant knowledge that, if the jurors have grown up in the same society, they are very likely to share with the lawyer. First, there is a knowledge of the relevant conversational ground rules for cross-examination in court, which will mean jurors treat as normal the lawyer's repeated demands for information which is already available. Second, they will also have an understanding of the usual function of such talk – to make a point, to support a case – which means that they are likely to (a) assume that the questions are relevant to this purpose and (b) search for coherence in the totality of what is said, even if the talk is not particularly cohesive. And third, they have knowledge of the content of the talk: the pursuit of sexual relationships, the function of make-up and discotheques in this pursuit, and the difficulty of establishing sometimes whether or not a sexual act took place with the consent of both partners. The story the lawyer is trying to co-opt the witness into telling will be familiar. Even if members of the jury ultimately reject the lawyer's argument, they are still likely to be drawn by what he says into thinking it through with him.

A few years ago, I was asked to look at some transcripts of recorded conversations that were being used in a murder trial. A man was accused of killing his wife, and one of the things the police believed he had done was to create an alibi by getting another woman (with whom he also had a relationship) to make some telephone calls soon after the murder, pretending to be the wife, so as to create the impression that she was still alive. I had a transcript of the police interrogating this woman about her alleged part in this crime. In the first part of the interview, the woman repeatedly denied the truth of the police claim, despite some circumstantial evidence against her (her recorded voice on a tape). The police interviewer began to adopt a new strategy, which was to suggest that the accused man was well known as a 'womanizer' and 'lady's man', and so was not worthy of her loyalty. This continued for a while, to little apparent effect until the following exchanges took place.

Sequence 4.5: Love lets you down

Interrogator: So why do you stay with him, what's in it for you?
Woman: Well, I guess I just love the guy.
Interrogator: Yeah, I know what you mean. Love's not something you can just put out with the milk bottles in the morning, is it?
Woman: No.
Interrogator: But it's doing you no good.
Woman: No.

Soon after this she confessed that she had, indeed, impersonated the murdered woman. Earlier attempts to undermine the woman's denials of her involvement had failed. I do not know if this piece of conversation was crucial for changing her mind, but we can at least look at the course of events as they unfolded in the talk. In the episode of talk given in Sequence 4.5, the police interrogator offered her resources to construct an account, a justification, for her own behaviour, which she could accept and relate to – that her actions had been influenced by the ties of love, within a relationship that she now saw did not serve her own interests. In the subsequent course of the interview, she and the police interviewer moved from telling very different stories of events to formulating a shared story. It may be that she was simply browbeaten into submission by the interrogator, though the transcript did not give me that impression. The transcript evidence suggested that she accepted the frame of reference offered by the interrogator and eventually agreed on the same narrative of events. I am not concerned here with the truth of her statements, or with her motives or those of the police interviewer, but with the fact that by talking with another person she came to account for her actions in a way which was consistent with an admission of guilt. The account that was eventually offered as a confession was a joint, social product of the talk. I do not need to know exactly what were the interviewee's and interviewer's motives or beliefs to make this claim.

There is a potential link here with the controversial therapeutic practice of helping people 'recover' lost memories from their distant past, usually associated with some traumatic event such as abuse in childhood.[30] While some therapists and counsellors have claimed that dialogue can reveal memories that have been 'repressed' because of their painful connotations, their critics have used the term 'False Memory Syndrome' to dispute the accuracy of this assisted recall. Lawsuits have hinged upon whether memories of past events are imaginary or have historical substance. In counselling dialogues of all kinds – indeed, in many kinds of professional–client interviews – both the therapist and patient/client contribute to the collective knowledge resources. Personal history and emotional evaluations are offered on the client's side, professional experience and expertise on the counsellor's – and both have interests they wish to pursue in the dialogues of their meetings. A client is likely to be seeking an acceptable explanation for the causes of their problems, and a course of action for overcoming them. The counsellor is likely to want to be able to generate a version of the client's 'case' which can be dealt with through the normal procedures available. The counselling dialogue must reconcile their interests and ways of making sense of experience if they are to achieve a mutually agreed version of relevant past events as explanations for current problems. In other words, the participants need to agree on a story of the client's life that they both find acceptable. Both bring to the therapy sessions ways of making sense of experience, which will be shared in the dialogue. The counsellor's professional knowledge may include ideas about the psychology of trauma, the kinds of stories which qualify as appropriate explanations, interview techniques and explanatory concepts for making professional sense of what the client says. To be more specific, a counsellor may be seeking 'repressed memories' and use certain established techniques for 'recovering' those memories. Any story which is constructed will, therefore, inevitably reflect these contributions of the counsellor; it will not have existed, as such, in the client's mind before that dialogue. However, a third party – perhaps one of those people ascribed a crucial role in the story that emerges from the 'long conversation' of a course of therapy, and who has not been a contributor to this interthinking process, will not necessarily have the same perspective or interests. Their personal store of relevant information of past events will not have contributed to the story (which may nevertheless be one that has for them high emotional significance). Under such circumstances, it is not surprising if some imaginative stories are constructed, or that third parties dispute them as 'false'. The fact that clients' accounts can be shaped by counsellors and therapists is widely accepted, but to attribute the creation of 'false memories' to nothing more than the dominating influence of one of the participants oversimplifies the process involved. If therapy sessions could be recorded and analysed in the ways I describe, 'recovered memories' could be revealed as a natural product of the kind of 'interthinking' which takes place in counselling dialogue. This might have some practical benefits for all concerned.

Power or control?

Language use in legal settings brings us again to the issues of power and control in the process of collective thinking. In particular kinds of situations, some people hold what seem necessarily to be more powerful roles: it may seem obvious that in conversations between lawyers and witnesses, police and suspects, employers and employees, teachers and students, the first named of each pair will be the speakers who are the most powerful and so will inevitably control the structure, content and social consequences of the talk. However, although the relative status of speakers can be important for understanding how they communicate, we should not assume that powerful people necessarily control the ways in which knowledge is shared and considered. The relationship between being what would seem to be the most powerful person and exercising control over the structure and content of a conversation cannot be reliably predicted. One reason is that language use is, as I have explained earlier, sensitive to particular situations and the contextual factors which participants treat as relevant. People who hold 'powerful positions', such as a managing director of a large international company or a government minister, may well normally exercise control with little opposition in the limited environments of their firms or departments, but cannot reliably be expected to be in control of the conversation when they are, say, arrested for drunken driving or unconventional sexual activities in a foreign country. What is more, because conversations are dynamic affairs, control often shifts even during them, perhaps because some new information arises which makes participants re-evaluate their relative status. (For example, both parties may realize that the revelation of personal information has led to an originally 'less powerful' person gaining potential control over the 'more powerful'.) And, of course, participants can use rhetorical techniques to persuade, undermine, or even wrest control from each other. In the courtroom, an experienced 'expert witness' may run rings round a lawyer.

For these reasons, if we want to understand how people exert influence in the process of jointly creating knowledge, the concept of 'control' is more useful than that of 'power'. 'Control' refers to what we can actually hear or see happening in any particular situation. And though we can identify some common and fairly reliable rhetorical techniques, we should not assume that certain ways of using language are intrinsically powerful; instead, we should judge their effectiveness for exerting control *in context*. So in the courtroom dialogues of Sequences 4.3 and 4.4, the fact that the lawyer asks all the questions, and the witnesses simply fill the 'response slots' they are offered in their exchanges, seems a clear indication that in that passage of speech the lawyer was in control of the talk. However, in classrooms, for example, students may exercise a degree of control through 'dumb insolence' – refusing to respond to requests that their teacher repeatedly makes. The sociolinguist Deborah Tannen explains this well when talking about how to interpret someone's silence during a conversation:

Silence has been seen as evidence of powerlessness, and doing most of the talking can seem synonymous with dominating. Researchers have counted numbers of words spoken, or timed how long people have talked, to demonstrate that men talk more than women and thereby dominate interactions. Undoubtedly, there is truth to this observation in some settings. But the association of volubility with dominance does not hold for all people, all settings, and all cultures . . . Imagine, for example, an interrogation in which an interrogator does little of the talking but holds much of the power.[31]

Different types of argument and discussion

Having considered techniques that people use to persuade others to share their point of view, advance their interests, or in other ways exercise control, I want now to move on to the third theme in the chapter title – argument. Several of the examples I have presented in this chapter could be described as kinds of 'argument'. The word 'argument' in English has several common meanings. One is to describe a confrontation between two (or more) people, a battle of words which may be aggressive and angry, in which people's main concerns may be self-defence and inflicting hurt rather than achieving a new and better joint understanding. A second use of the word is to describe a reasoned debate between people, an extended conversation focusing on a specific theme which aims to establish 'the truth' about some contentious issue. Many conversations may have features which fit both these conceptions of argument. Ways of talking can shift, of course, even within a conversation, and initial attempts by two people to reach a common understanding through dispassionate consideration of the evidence may end in angry dispute. A third use of 'argument' is to describe a special kind of monologue – a rhetorical presentation of evidence by one speaker or writer in support of a particular theory, explanation or course of action, which considers the 'pros and cons' and offers a considered conclusion. This meaning is most often applied to written language, but it also represents the kind of 'argument' which might be contained in the political speeches which I discussed at the beginning of the chapter. These meanings are not distinct, and neither are the ways of using language with which they are usually associated. But from the point of view of understanding the use of language for joint thinking, it is useful to distinguish between these different kinds of argument.

Let us first focus on conversation which represents the first kind of argument mentioned above. We can call this 'disputational talk'. Even when it is not an overtly angry exchange, disputational talk is characterized by an unwillingness to take on the other person's point of view, and the consistent reassertion of one's own. In its most archetypal form, it consists of 'yes it is – no it isn't' exchanges, commands and parallel assertions. It makes joint activity into a competition rather than a co-operative endeavour. Sequence 4.6 is an example of this kind of talk. It comes from a recording of two girls (aged 10) working together at the computer, writing some dialogue for cartoon characters.

Sequence 4.6: Jo and Carol in dispute

Carol: Just write in the next letter. 'Did you have a nice English lesson?' (*Jo typing on computer*)

Jo: You've got to get it on there. Yes thank you. Let's just have a look at that. 'Hi, Alan did you have a nice English lesson? Yes thank you, Yeah. Yes thank you it was fine.'

Carol: You've got to let me get some in sometimes.

Jo: You're typing.

Carol: Well you can do some, go on.

Jo: 'Yes thank you.'

Carol: (*Mumbles*)

Jo: You're typing. 'Yes thank you' 'I did, yeah, yes, thank you I did.'

Carol: You can spell that.

Jo: Why don't you do it?

Carol: No, because (you should).

To see an example of disputational talk of a more subtle and complex kind, we can return to Sequence 4.3. Again, this is a defensive, unco-operative encounter, in which the perspectives of the two participants compete with rather than complement each other.

The above examples of disputational talk contrast very obviously with the kind of discussion which in Chapter 2 I called 'cumulative talk' (illustrated by Sequences 2.6 and 2.7) in which speakers build on each other's contributions, add information of their own and in a mutually supportive, uncritical way construct together a body of shared knowledge and understanding. Sometimes, as the discourse analyst Brian Kleiner has illustrated, 'cumulative talk' can be used by partners to construct an 'argument' of the monologic, rhetorical kind to support their shared views. For example, in Sequence 4.7 three white American students are discussing a claim that 'minority group' students on scholarships get special treatment in their university.

Sequence 4.7: Unfair treatment

B: So it's just – i – their advantages just keep adding <u>up</u>! Their – their advantages totally keep adding <u>up</u>. [Their grade advantages,

C: [Yeah that's true. They do have – more time to relax because – they don't have to <u>work</u>. You know, like everyone else does to pay [off their loans.

B: [They'll be under less stress.

C: They – cause they're just getting money.

C: I feel really <u>bad</u> about this, because like we sound like <u>ra</u>cists or whatever, and I really don't think [I am.

B: [I don't think I'm being – I don't know – I really don't think I'm racist, I just think that

K: It's just a very unfair society that we're living in today.[32]

Kleiner suggests that this kind of talk enables the students not only to gather collective support for their views, but also jointly to define their argumentative stance in a way that avoids the possible, and undesirable, attribution of being 'racist'.

Both cumulative and disputational talk can be distinguished from a third type of discussion, 'exploratory talk'. This can be defined as follows:

> *Exploratory talk* is that in which partners engage critically but constructively with each other's ideas. Relevant information is offered for joint consideration. Proposals may be challenged and counter-challenged, but if so reasons are given and alternatives are offered. Agreement is sought as a basis for joint progress. Knowledge is made publicly accountable and reasoning is visible in the talk.[33]

An example of the kind of talk that has these characteristics is Sequence 4.8, given below. It is the talk of three children (aged 10) working together on a computer-based science activity called *Tracks*.[34] This offers them a simulated environment in which weights are pushed along surfaces of material with different frictional qualities (ice, grass, carpet), and in which the sizes of the weights and forces, as well as the surfaces, can be varied systematically. Prompts ask the children to make predictions and carry out experiments to test them. In the extract, they are carrying out one of these experiments.

Sequence 4.8: Luke, Nicola and Paul doing *Tracks*

Luke: So one of those . . . no, one grass, and one ice. And the weight's the same, so two again, and both things on four.

Nicola: Yes, two.

Luke: Both on four. Yes.

Nicola: Why don't you do one – oh, you have already! Now press 'ready'. The top weight will go faster.

Paul: Would it?

Luke: Yes, because it's a smooth.

Nicola: Yes. Because it's slippery, it'll go faster. Yes, it does.

Luke: Why?

Paul: Because if there was a rough surface and the bottom one was on ice.

Nicola: If there was a rough surface, there's more friction, it would slow it down.

Luke: [Yes.

Paul: [Yes.

We see Luke, Nicola and Paul all offering opinions and giving reasons to support them. They seek each other's views, use questions to elicit reasons. Relevant information is made explicit. All the children are actively involved, their reasoning is often made explicit in the talk, and they come to agreement before taking joint action. (Sequence 1.1 in Chapter 1 is also a good illustration of this kind of co-reasoning activity.) In this 'exploratory' kind of talk, reasons and explanations are made *as explicit as is necessary*, given the contextual foundations for the talk which are shared by the participants, to enable each of them to make critical evaluations and reach joint conclusions.

The three types of talk also represent different ways in which *control* is handled in a conversation. In cumulative talk, participants do not strive for control, while in disputational talk they do. In exploratory talk, control is a matter of constant negotiation, as speakers offer contributions which may, if partners are persuaded, determine the subsequent direction of collective thinking.

Arguing your case

Let us now look at another example of an argument. Sequence 4.9 below is an extract from a conversation between a mother (Amy) and her teenage daughter (Jess). It was accidentally recorded by a telephone answering machine in the room where they were talking (so the speakers were not aware that they were being recorded). The conversation is about a common issue in parent–teenager relations: money. As you read it, consider: is this 'cumulative', 'disputational' or 'exploratory' talk?

Sequence 4.9: Pocket money

Amy: How much is it going to cost you tomorrow?
Jess: Tomorrow? A couple of pounds. Nicola said just take a fiver and you probably won't have to use it all.
Amy: Well you'll have to find it.
Jess: Well what am I going to spend tonight?
Amy: I can't afford for you to go to the pub, and I'm not going to.
Jess: Yeah well I'll give you the money back once I've spoken [to Dad.
Amy: 　　　　　　　　　　　　　　　　　　　　　　　　　　　[I don't want you to spend this much money sitting in a pub drinking.
Jess: Well drinking
Amy: (*interrupting*) Fifteen pounds you've spent already and you'll spend another five pounds.
Jess: I haven't spent fifteen pounds Mum. OK just give me a pound then.
Amy: What for?
Jess: (*Exasperated sigh*) God you don't listen at all.

This conversation draws heavily on the shared past experience of the participants. It is part of the 'long conversation' of their relationship as mother and daughter. The speakers know what each other knows that is relevant, such as who Nicola or Dad is, or why a problem will be sorted out when Jess has 'spoken to Dad'. In that sense, they have no problem establishing a shared frame of reference for discussing the issue in question (the use and control of family funds). But this is not 'cumulative talk' as illustrated by Sequences 2.6 and 2.7 in Chapter 2. There, the speakers worked together in a non-competitive way to build a shared perspective on events. Here we see two people using language to pursue their individual interests and oppose those of the other person. Despite there being such strong contextual foundations for the talk,

Jess feels that her message is not getting through ('God you don't listen at all').

Amy and Jess are both using language as a tool to make things happen – or prevent things happening – but in accord with their own, separate vested interests or agendas. Jess tries to get her money, Amy tries to avoid giving it. The mother asserts her moral authority as a parent, the daughter asserts her independence as someone nearing adulthood. The structure of the talk, as well as its content, reflects this conflict of aims. Yet this is not a 'disputation' of the 'yes it is – no it's not' kind where each person simply asserts a point of view with no account taken of what anyone else says. Both Jess and Amy use language to define the positions they wish to uphold ('I can't afford for you to go to the pub, and I'm not going to'), to assault each other's positions ('I haven't spent fifteen pounds Mum'), offer compromises ('OK just give me a pound then') and generally struggle to pursue their interests in a way which is genuinely interactive.

To some observers, it might seem that Amy and Jess are merely voicing views that they have already formed quite firmly and unequivocally. But that does not do justice to the way in which language and thinking are integrated or to the role of dialogue in forming points of view, as I explained earlier in the chapter. In order to make some impact on the people around us – to make our views count – we need to be convincing and persuasive, not just clear and informative, because we are dealing with people who have views of their own and who aim to pursue their own interests. So quite what views we express – and perhaps even what views we are aware of having – will to some extent depend on whom we are in dialogue with at any particular time. Given a different protagonist, or the involvement of a third party ('Dad', for example), both the participants in Sequence 4.9 might well have put rather different cases, taken more or less flexible positions, or sought different levels of compromise. The reason is, of course, that during such an argument they are not only 'thinking on their feet', but doing so together. Their talk has some 'disputational' features, but the speakers also include some reasons in their responses to each other's remarks, giving it some 'exploratory' qualities.

Ways of orientating to the minds of others

Most of the examples of dialogue I have included in the book will not fit neatly into the three categories of 'cumulative', 'disputational' and 'exploratory' talk. These are idealizations, models of ways of using language which may rarely be found in any pure form. No system of categories could ever really do justice to the natural variety of language, and even short stretches of dialogue may have characteristics of more than one of each of these types of talk.[35] But this categorization is nevertheless useful for making sense of the messy, category-defying reality of conversation. We can hold the three models of talk up against examples of actual conversation and see whether they show the characteristics of one or more of the types. We can use 'cumulative', 'disputational' and 'exploratory' as concepts for discussing 'discussion'.

The notion of the three types of talk is also relevant for understanding the relationship between the ways in which we use language to solve problems and create knowledge and the kinds of intellectual orientation we adopt to each other as we do so. Each is a way of using language to create a particular kind of intersubjectivity. We can use language to join our intellects in an uncritical, non-competitive and constructive way, as typified by cumulative talk; or we may treat the intellectual activities of partners as a threat to our individual interests, as in disputational talk. In cumulative talk, language is used to build a joint identity, a shared, intersubjective perspective on the topic of conversation in which individual differences of perception or judgement are minimized (consider Sequences 2.6 and 2.7 in Chapter 2 again in light of this idea). Talk with disputational features, on the other hand, occurs when the participants work to keep their identities separate, and to protect their individuality (as Sequences 4.6 and 4.9 again both illustrate).

So what kind of mutual orientation is embodied in talk of an 'exploratory' kind? As my fellow-researcher Rupert Wegerif has elegantly expressed it: in exploratory talk, the instant, uncritical 'yes' of cumulative talk and the instant, self-defensive 'no' of disputational talk are both suspended.[36] Instead, a dialogue happens in which differences are treated explicitly, as matters for mutual exploration, reasoned evaluation and resolution. To engage in exploratory talk, with its explicit reasons, criticisms and evaluations, participants must not be primarily concerned with protecting their individual or joint identities and interests, but instead with discovering new and better ways of jointly making sense. In exploratory talk, speakers may usefully take the role of 'devil's advocate', questioning their own assumptions, testing the validity of their own points of view as well as those of their partners. Participants may be pursuing their joint interests, but they do so from a relatively detached perspective that is aimed at the joint but impersonal construction of explanations, answers or solutions.

The systemic linguist Michael Halliday talks of language having both *ideational* and *interpersonal* functions, which basically mean that it is used both for the sharing of information and for the creation and maintenance of social relationships.[37] The concept of the three types of talk helps us see how, in some kinds of conversation, these two functions are intertwined. The quality of our collective thinking together is crucially dependent on the ways in which we use language to orientate to each other's intellects.

Summary

The process of thinking collectively can be considered a rhetorical activity, in which shared knowledge and understanding is achieved through conflict and debate as well as through co-operation. We all use language to pursue particular interests, whether these be individual or shared, competitive or co-operative. I began the chapter by focusing on rhetorical uses of language, and suggested that even techniques used by public speakers can be considered as features of dialogue rather than monologue. I illustrated some ways that public speakers use to make their 'cases' for particular points of view more dramatic, memorable and persuasive; and then went on to consider how engagement in more personal and interactive kinds of dialogue involves ways of using language which are, in their own terms, no less rhetorical.

The analysis of rhetoric is very important for understanding how language is used as a tool for collective thinking. If we accept that the very nature of human dialogue requires us to say things in ways which take account of whom we are talking to, what we are trying to achieve, and also what we think are the aims and views of the people with whom we are dealing, we come closer to understanding one aspect of the power of language as a means for minds to work together. There is nothing intellectually or morally dubious about our persistent engagement in argument and persuasion: they are part of the essence of effective human collaborative action. Someone whose opinions were so fixed that they always stated them in the same way, no matter who they were addressing and despite the reactions they got to what they said, would be suffering from a kind of autistic disability. Taking this rhetorical, dialogic perspective, I suggested that our use of metaphors may be one of the linguistic means by which we provide a frame of reference for sharing our thoughts with others, so that the memorability and credibility of our accounts of events may be influenced by the manner in which we present them to others and so may affect the extent those accounts become collectively accepted. Our choice of metaphor is therefore something that will be shaped by context.

Next, I discussed the issues of power and control, and the relative status and influence of partners in dialogue. This was followed by a comparison of three models of discussion: 'cumulative talk', 'disputational talk' and 'exploratory talk'. I explained the value of these for distinguishing how partners in dialogue orientate to each other's perspectives. This conception of three types of talk, while far from adequate as a way of describing the natural variety of discussion, is nevertheless helpful for shedding some light on the nature of language as a tool for carrying out joint intellectual activity. It also has some practical applications, particularly for education, as I will explain in Chapter 6.

I mentioned in the chapter that the word 'argument' has more than one meaning: as a persuasive monologue, as a competitive dispute and as a reasonable dialogue. We can perhaps now see why these three meanings co-exist. All are concerned in some way with the competition of ideas, and all (even dispute) may have the ultimate aim of creating a broader consensus, a situation in which more people think similarly about some topic or issue than was the case before the dialogue commenced.

5 Communities

As I explained in Chapter 1, the emergence of language in our evolutionary pre-history was important not simply because it allowed individuals to co-ordinate their work activities, but because people became able to combine their mental capacities. Unlike other animals, who lacked such a sophisticated means of communication, people became able to create a collective consciousness, a mega-brain, a 'mental matrix'. The development of print, and subsequently of telecommunications, then made it possible for people to link their thoughts together in this way even when far apart. Today's computer-based communications offer new kinds of opportunities for collective thinking, as we will see later in this chapter.

In this chapter, I want to consider how our language use and joint intellectual activity is affected by the existence of communities. The Latin origins of the word 'community' relate it closely to 'communicate' and 'common', which make it an appropriate term for groups of people who share experience and interests and who communicate amongst themselves to pursue these interests. In pre-industrial times, communities were necessarily groups of people who lived close together, working together to survive and sharing the experience of everyday life. But as transport and communication systems developed, social relationships became more complex and scattered. It became increasingly possible for people to be members of communities without living in the same locality – and also to become members of more than one community. Today, community membership can be distributed, multiple and complex, and based as much on common interests as on common locality. For example, a woman living on a farm deep in the Welsh countryside may be an active member of her local village community, yet also be involved in the activities of a wider community of dairy farmers and of an international community of evangelical Christians. She may maintain her membership of the first community through visiting friends, shopping locally and attending neighbourhood council meetings; the second mainly through reading a farming journal and attending regional cattle auctions and agricultural shows; and the third through the Internet.

How communities enable collective thinking

The kind of groups I call 'communities' offer their members the following resources for joint intellectual activity:

• *A history*. Groups which persist over time accumulate a body of shared experience. Members will be likely to recall that experience together and reflect on it, and so gain a history. Shared experience will generate information and expertise, on which members can draw and which can be passed to new members.

• *A collective identity*. By sharing a history, knowledge, aims and the experience of doing things together, members can find meaning, purpose and direction for their own endeavours and relate these to the special contributions that others in the community make. Joining the community may involve some initiation or admission process.

• *Reciprocal obligations*. Members will have responsibilities towards each other, and so can expect to have access to each other's intellectual resources. There will be roles and ground rules for specifying appropriate behaviour.

• *A discourse*. Communities use language to operate, but they do not simply take language 'off the peg' and use it as given. One of the marvellous and distinctive design features of language is what is usually called its 'openness'. That is, language can be reshaped to suit new communicative demands as they emerge. New words and new ways of putting words together can be generated if people consider it necessary. If a group of people are striving to communicate about their special interests, they can adapt and extend language as a tool for doing so. The specialized language of a community can be called its *discourse*.

Fluency in the discourse is likely to be one of the obvious signs of membership.

An example will illustrate how language use is adapted to serve the needs of groups with special, shared interests. Sequence 5.1 is part of a recorded conversation between three people working together. I will tell you more about it after you have read it and – taking into account what you have read earlier in the book – after you have considered these questions:

- What do you think is going on in this conversation?
- What special features of this talk help you guess what it is being used for?
- In what ways does the sequence depend on 'common knowledge'?

Sequence 5.1: Not sure about the E

Norm: We put the E in, it makes it [slightly odd.
Peter: [we've got to think in terms of words are concerned we only use, do that once at a time.
Norm: That's true.
Kieran: Yeh.
Peter: And then the, the long, the long A minors afterwards will simply [be
Norm: [Yeh.
Kieran: Yeh, we can actually keep those cycling round as many times as we need to.
Norm: I'm not sure about the E.
Kieran: Right, OK.
Peter: I like it.
Norm: Yeh but except its, because then you've [got (*demonstrates*)
Peter: [yeh but hang on, I'm using G instead of E minor.
Norm: Yeh yeh, all right. Perhaps it works.
Kieran: Let's try it like that, it goes straight to the F. (*They try it*)
Kieran: Yeh I think it actually works out the same number of bars because we're holding the F and the G twice as long.
Norm: Yeh.
Peter: That's right.

This conversation came from a session in which three musicians were working out the arrangements for the score of a musical play. They were sitting together in a room with various musical instruments which they sometimes played, and they each had charts of parts of the score in front of them. You may have guessed its topic and function from the specialized vocabulary used – 'E minor', 'G', 'bars' and so on. At the point at which the sequence begins, one of the musicians (Norm) has disagreed with the others about one of the proposed arrangements – whether or not a sequence based on the E minor chord should be included. By using the technical code of chord names in conjunction with a demonstration of what he means, Norm is able to explain his concern to his partners. All three then use the same resources to think through the apparent problem to reach an agreement. This talk has, then, some 'exploratory' characteristics.

If you know very little about music, much of the talk in the sequence may seem incomprehensible 'musicspeak', an alien jargon. In that sense, it may not seem to fit the criterion for exploratory talk to be *explicit*. But 'explicitness' is a relative concept, a matter of context (as I explained in relation to Sequence 2.1 in Chapter 2, which is a similarly technical bit of dialogue). In analysing this kind of discussion, the relevant consideration is whether matters are made sufficiently explicit by the participants to each other. However incomprehensible to outsiders, technical language of this kind is of immense value to people who share the relevant knowledge. Amongst the initiated, it makes possible a very fast and efficient form of communication in which a great deal of shared knowledge can safely be taken for granted. Much of that knowledge is never made explicit in the talk; yet it is part of the hidden context, the foundations of the visible communication. One important source of such knowledge is membership of a relevant community.

In Sequence 5.1 the three participants draw on knowledge of what they have done earlier that day, and in previous rehearsals. Context is also provided by the joint physical activity of playing music, as they play notes and phrases to elaborate what they have said, to demonstrate points and explore possibilities together. But Norm and the others have resources of common knowledge which were not created only by their past joint activity. They use musical knowledge which they have gained from musical training and experience elsewhere, knowledge which is shared with many people with whom they have had no direct contact. Imagine a musician newly arrived from California who joined Norm and his colleagues in their rehearsals in Britain. If familiar with the styles of music involved, he or she would probably have little trouble joining in the activity, because of experience back home in doing the same kind of activity and using the same technical language for carrying it out. On that basis, Norm, the Californian and the others might be considered members of one international, widely distributed community of musical discourse. I will return to this idea in the next section.

Sequence 5.2 is another example of language being used amongst people who share specialized knowledge, as they work to get something done. The sequence comes from the research of Julian Orr, who recorded photocopier repair technicians at work. In the sequence, two men (a senior technical specialist and another technician) are working together to try to fix a machine which had repeatedly proved unreliable. Although it is unlikely that you will understand many of the technical terms they use, try to notice how they talk together about the problem. It may help to know that E053 and F066 are codes for types of observable fault for which diagnostic procedures can be found in a manual. *(The symbol (. . .) indicates a substantial, noticeable pause by a speaker.)*

Sequence 5.2: The false E053 error

Technical specialist:	See, this runs along with the problems we've run into when you have a dead shorted dicorotron. It blows the circuit breaker and you get a 24-volt interlock problem. And you can chase that thing forever, and you will NEVER, NEVER find out what that is.
Technician:	Yes, I know, E053, try four new dicors . . .
Technical specialist:	But, if you went in . . . OK, you won't . . . You lose your 24, that's what it is: you're losing your 24-volt out of the power supply, but that's not what it's caused by. Now the key there, though, is when you pull up your dC20 log, you get hits in the XER board.
Technician:	Yeah. The other thing is as you're going on and on and getting E053s, you get, yeah, . . . F066 . . . in the sequence . . .
Technical specialist:	If you're lucky enough for it to run long enough, you'll get an F066 problem which leads you back into the dicorotrons – you check them – yeah, I've got one that's a dead short. You change it and everything's fine, but if you don't . . . if you're not lucky enough

	to get that F066 or don't look at the dC20 log; it's really a grey area . . .
Technician:	Well, dC20 logs . . . when I ran into that I had hits in the XER a few times previously, so I was tending to ignore it until I was cascading through after an E053 which is primary, I'm cascading to see what else I've got – F066 – what the hell's this? Noise?
Technical specialist:	E053, which one's that?
Technician:	Well, that's a . . . that's a 24 . . . lock. . . .
Technical specialist:	24 Interlock failure? Yeah. We did . . . I did that not knowing when they changed the circuitry in the XER board, normally if you had a shorted dicorotron, it'd fry the XER board – just cook it. Now they've changed the circuitry to prevent frying of that, but now it creates a different problem.[1]

The two speakers in Sequence 5.2 are using language to share some past experience which is relevant to their joint task. But they do not do this simply by formulating proposals for dealing with the current fault. Instead, they spend most of the time telling each other 'stories' – reports on what happened on other occasions when they faced similar problems. So when (in his third turn in the conversation) the specialist says 'yeah, I've got one that's a dead short', he is here making a dramatized recreation of an occasion when he was less experientially wise than he is now, and so was drawn down a false track in pursuit of the cause of a fault. The technician uses the same technique again soon after, ending a report of an earlier experience with a quote (in italics) from his earlier, less knowledgeable self:

> . . . when I ran into that I had hits in the XER a few times previously, so I was tending to ignore it until I was cascading through after an E053 which is primary, I'm cascading to see what else I've got – *F066 – what the hell's this? Noise?*

The gist of this story told by the technician is 'don't always trust the obvious signs – error codes can be red herrings'. As Orr's careful analysis of the talk between the two men reveals, this is one of several attempts by the technician to signal, obliquely, to the specialist that he thinks they are wrong to place too much faith in the standard diagnostic procedures. It appears that one of the ground rules of this working community is that general technicians do not overtly contradict specialists.

In some ways, then, this technical talk is similar to that in Sequence 5.1, and serves a similar function: it enables two colleagues to share relevant experience and think out the solution to a problem together. But there is also an interesting difference in the way language is related to the joint activity, to 'getting on with the job'. In Sequence 5.1, the work is being done *through* the talk, while in Sequence 5.2, the talk is a *parallel activity* to the actual testing of the circuits in the machine – the talk and the joint physical task of repair complement each other. In the community of photocopier technicians, telling relevant stories about dealing with past problems is a way of thinking together. These 'war stories' (as Orr calls them) are told before, during and after repair activity, and are an intrinsic part of doing the job. They are a means for displaying experience and expertise, provide 'models' for doing the shared action in which the partners are engaged, and communicate technical knowledge in a memorable form. 'Storytelling' is therefore an important tool in the language tool-kit of these technicians.

Genres and communities of discourse

The concept of 'genre' is useful for understanding specialized uses of language. In linguistics, 'genre' means a conventionalized way of using language for a particular purpose, following ground rules which reflect the cultural traditions of a particular group or society.[2] Examples of genres would be scientific reports, recipes, letters, the question-and-answer episodes which are typical of classroom life – and narratives. The discourse of any community will include a repertoire of specialized genres. So we might say that in the work community of photocopier engineers, the narrative genre has an important function for sharing relevant experience. Particular genres will have fairly consistent functions within established communities (which linguists sometimes refer to as 'communities of discourse').[3]

In some genres – for example, in the discourses of science, civil engineering or accountancy – the language has a 'dry', unemotional quality. This not only reflects its function, it also embodies the kind of thinking that it is meant to represent. The processes of reporting scientific experiments, surveying buildings and conducting financial transactions are meant to be guided by rationality, rather than emotion, and this is reflected in the absence in such language of references to the personal feelings of those doing the work. Whatever they may have felt at the time, you will find few scientific journal articles reporting the delight and relief of researchers when their predictions were found to be supported by the results of an experiment. The ground rules of the genre of 'scientific reports' simply do not permit it (as science students soon discover if they submit reports which do so). In such writing, the 'agency' of the writer is often rendered completely invisible by the use of passive forms of verbs ('a survey was carried out' rather than 'I spent hours interviewing people'), so emphasizing the supposedly detached and impersonal nature of the process being described.

However, the impersonal style of such language should not obscure the fact that specialized discourse can be important for creating and maintaining professional and personal identities of members of an occupational community. One way of expressing your membership of the community of physicists, and being recognized as a member, is by talking and writing in an appropriate way. And not all discourses of working communities are formal and dry; emotions and attitudes may be expressed through the language of work. Talking informally together, scientists and accountants may express strong feelings about their work. In an active community, language may not only be used to think collectively through shared problems. It may also be used to develop a shared emotional or moral perspective on the everyday experience of working life. An interesting example, studied by the linguist Kathleen Odean,[4] is the slang used by stockbrokers on New York's Wall Street. It seems that members of that community of stockbrokers (almost all male) wish to redefine their work metaphorically as a matter of warfare and misogynistic sex. Stocks are commonly given female nicknames, and the acts of trading them are transformed into sexual acts: traders *ride Pamela*, or *pull out of Becky*. They *touch but don't penetrate* some parts of the market. When things go wrong, then speculators get *burned* or *blown out*. Traders *pound stocks* and *slaughter* them, or sell *cemetery spreads* leaving behind unfortunate investors as *widows and orphans*. It would be interesting to research how the increasing membership of women in this particular community affects the use of this kind of language.

A particularly chilling example of occupational discourse which came to public attention in the 1970s was the slang used by American soldiers in action in the Far East, in which Indo-Chinese people were described as 'geeks' and 'slants', and soldiers spoke about 'wasting' or 'losing' Vietnamese people rather than killing them. This kind of slang – common in all war-active military communities – enables soldiers to represent their victims as essentially different from 'real people'. Under the military dictatorship in Greece (1967–74) soldiers in special units responsible for torturing 'opponents of the regime' went through initiation procedures which included the learning of a special in-group jargon. Particular methods of torture were given euphemistic nicknames, such as 'tea party with toast'.[5] By using language in this way, members of military communities are thus able to use language to *jointly redefine* the moral significance of their actions and emphasize their joint identity.

At the beginning of the chapter, I suggested that being able to 'speak the discourse' is one sign that someone is a member of a community. I have explained that the knowledge and use of specialized discourses is valuable for collective thinking amongst members of communities, but we should be aware that saying something in the right way may too easily be taken by listeners as evidence that a speaker is sincere and truthful. In Spring 1996, the cultural studies journal, *Social Text*, published an essay suggesting a link between quantum mechanics and postmodernist philosophy (of the kind popular in cultural studies) by Alan Sokal, professor of physics at New York University. On the day of publication Sokal announced in another journal, *Lingua Franca*, that the article, 'Transgressing the Boundaries: Towards a Transformative Hermeneutics of Quantum Gravity', had in fact been a hoax. He also explained that the article contained several inaccurate, and even nonsensical, passages about physics, which anyone who had reasonable scientific knowledge should have been able to check. His aim was apparently to undermine the academic credibility of the postmodern critics of science whose work regularly appeared in *Social Text*. (Essentially, such critics argue that scientific ways of experimenting and reasoning are only one set of culturally based procedures for determining 'the truth', and that other cultural perspectives should be acknowledged as being potentially equally valid when the social and political implications of science are being considered.) The revelation of the hoax caused heated debates about science, postmodernism and the morality of Sokal's actions, which I will not get involved with here. More relevant is the fact that one of the main reasons for the success of Sokal's hoax was that he wrote his article in the discourse of two intellectual communities. Here are two short extracts from his article:

> It has thus become increasingly apparent that physical 'reality', no less than social 'reality', is at bottom a social and linguistic construct; that scientific 'knowledge', far from being objective, reflects and encodes the dominant ideologies and power relations of the culture that produced it; that the truth claims of science are inherently theory-laden and self-referential; and consequently, that the discourse of the scientific community, for all its undeniable value, cannot assert a privileged epistemological status with respect to counter-hegemonic narratives emanating from dissident or marginalized discourses.[6]

> More recently, a small group of physicists has returned to the full nonlinearities of Einstein's general relativity, and – using a new mathematical symbolism invented by Abhay Ashketar – they have attempted to visualize the structure of the corresponding quantum theory (Ashketar et al. 1992; Smolin 1992). The picture they obtain is intriguing: As in string theory, the space–time manifold is only an approximation valid at distances, not an objective reality. At small (Planck-scale) distances, the geometry of space-time is a *weave*: a complex interconnection of threads.[7]

The first of these extracts is written in the discourse of cultural studies: the academic community which writes and reads *Social Text*. By using it, Sokal encouraged the trust of the journal's editors and readers. He used appropriate technical terms (such as the 'transformative' and 'hermeneutics' of the title); made frequent, apparently positive references to important and well-respected scholars in the field; and appeared to offer support and agreement with the dominant postmodernist perspective of the cultural studies community.

The second extract is written more in the discourse of Sokal's own physics research community – a community with high academic status, with a discourse which is difficult for non-members to read critically. Using these two discourses as rhetorical tools, Sokal succeeded in his main aim. The editors of *Social Text* were made to look rather silly, not only because it was revealed that they had a poor understanding of the science that they were so willing to criticize, but also because they appeared to be so ready to accept even a flawed and badly constructed argument so long as it fitted their world-view and was presented in the right kind of language. The critics of science were shown to be very uncritical when it came to turning the lens on their own academic practices. Since the Sokal hoax, many people have asked whether a similar attempt would be as likely to be successful in other subjects. Some communities of discourse would almost certainly be harder to hoax in this way, such as that of research physicists like Sokal, because they are more closed to outsiders and the research they report in their journals usually involves experimental and mathematical data which would be difficult to fabricate convincingly. But there have been examples of fabricated results in all physical sciences, some of which have not come to light for some time. It is also worth noting that there are many recorded examples of unqualified charlatans and confidence tricksters carrying on quite successful careers for years in medicine, the law and accountancy by being able to speak convincingly in the professional discourse of the relevant occupational communities.

There is also another related problem that can arise from the dependency of communities on their discourses – one which is a kind of 'mirror image' of the situation in the Sokal hoax. People offering new and interesting ideas to members of a community, but doing so in ways that do not correspond with the communicative ground rules of the communities, may find that their ideas are ignored or rejected simply because they are not presented in the right kind of language. Members may find it difficult to communicate – and hence to engage intellectually – with people who lack the history of using the specialized thinking tool which is the discourse of a community of practice. What is more, trapped within their technical vocabularies, ways of organizing texts and contextual frames of reference, members of particular communities of discourse may find it hard to represent and share unconventional ideas about their shared area of interest – and so find it hard to conceive of radical alternatives to conventional views, or to develop new, fresh perspectives on the problems and issues with which they are dealing. Ironically, physicists and other scientists often seem resistant to the insights that this kind of perspective on their activities can offer.[8]

Communities of practice

In their book *Situated Learning*, the educational researchers Jean Lave and Etienne Wenger introduce the concept of 'community of practice'.[9] They apply this to groups which are united by common purposes and who engage in joint activity. Examples they give are midwives in rural Mexico, tailors in west Africa, quartermasters in the US Navy and the reformed drinkers of Alcoholics Anonymous. While members of some of these communities do happen to live in the same geographical area, their membership is not defined by that feature of their lives, but by their shared knowledge and activities. Communities of practice represent a way in which groups of people use their ability to share past experience to create joint understanding and co-ordinate ways of dealing with new experience. Lave and Wenger suggest that 'communities of practice' are social mechanisms for sharing and developing knowledge and expertise. In these communities, new members (apprentices) are trained by experienced members (experts). This is well illustrated by their Alcoholics Anonymous (AA) example.[10] It appears that, on joining AA, an 'apprentice' will be explicitly informed of the community's aims and practices – such as its 'Twelve Steps' to sobriety. These then form the context for discussions between apprentices and experts, as the experts try to help the newcomers use language to build a new, robust identity using the resources of their drinking experiences. Like the photocopier engineers studied by Orr, it seems that AA members also have their distinctive 'ways with words'; and they also make great use of storytelling. The narrative genre in this case is represented by a kind of biographical résumé, offered by old-timers as salutary tales to meetings:

> An apprentice alcoholic attends several meetings a week . . . At these meetings old-timers give testimony about their drinking past and the course of the process of becoming sober. In addition to 'general meetings,' where old-timers may tell polished, hour-long stories – months and years in the making – of their lives as alcoholics, there are also smaller 'discussion meetings,' which tend to focus on a single aspect of what in the end will be a part of the reconstructed life story [of the apprentice].[11]

So we can see that achieving full 'expert' membership of the AA community of practice does not just depend on the obvious behaviours of not drinking, attending AA meetings regularly and learning the formal rules and aims of the community. It also involves learning to 'speak the discourse' – acquiring the particular, conventionalized and specialized language repertoire of the community. The way AA apprentices learn is through exposure to the 'model' narratives of the experts, through speaking themselves and through getting feedback on their efforts. There is also a good deal of joint working with what a new member says:

> One speaker follows another by picking out certain pieces of what has previously been said, saying why it was relevant to him, and elaborating on it with some episode of his own. . . . other speakers will take the appropriate parts of the newcomer's comments, and build on this in their own comments, giving parallel accounts with different interpretations, for example, or expanding on parts of their own stories which are similar to parts of the newcomer's story, while ignoring the inappropriate parts . . . [12]

Within the AA community, new entrants are offered what Lave and Wenger call 'legitimate peripheral participation' in its activities. This participation enables the newcomers to use language in the two ways I described in Chapter 1 – as a *cultural tool* for gaining the benefit of the experience of others, for gaining social support and attempting to solve their problems with others who have similar interests; and as a *psychological tool* for reviewing their own past experience, organizing it into a special, AA kind of narrative, and so reconstructing their self-identities as 'non-drinking alcoholics'.

I suggested earlier that communities are typified by roles and ground rules that govern members' behaviour. Some members may have particular responsibility for guiding collective thinking activities. Obvious examples might be found in the ways in which chairs of business meetings, court judges and teachers direct and control talk. A more unusual example comes from research by Nathalie Muller and Anne-Nelly Perret-Clermont on a community-based programme for agricultural development in Madagascar, resourced by a Swiss foundation.[13] They describe the vital role that a local co-ordinator (a member of a village community) can play in ensuring that the community recognizes and prioritizes its needs and goals within the programme. This often happens in communal meetings. Observing one very effective co-ordinator, well respected in his community (whom they call 'Alex'), they noticed that he often used particular strategies in these meetings, such as:

- summarizing and recording ideas suggested (such as 'So one of the causes of the disappearance of the forests is bush fires?');
- 'jump-starting' discussions when they falter by reminding people of what has already been said ('Someone mentioned that young plants are rare');
- asking participants if they have anything else to add before closing a topic;
- interrupting discussions that are not progressing;
- reminding participants of the ground rules of the meetings if they transgress them.

Using these strategies, he was able to mobilize relevant individual experience and common knowledge, create shared frames of reference, and help the community work together to make original and useful analyses of their situation and needs. However, Muller and Perret-Clermont also observed that this equitable process of collective thinking and joint decision-making in these meetings was often threatened by roles and statuses of individuals in the community which predated the development programme, with authoritative individuals speaking out to protect their existing interests. On some occasions an existing landowner ('Tom') tried to take over the collective discussion in this way (for example, telling those present ' . . . you don't know how to talk, you don't know how to express yourselves'). However, Alex did little to police Tom's disregard for the ground rules – an inconsistency which could perhaps be explained by the fact that Tom was Alex's brother-in-law and Alex had gained in social status by joining Tom's family. The structures of communities exert their influence on the processes of collective thinking in many different ways.

Virtual communities

In the 1980s, a new concept of community began to be used by social scientists: the 'virtual community' of people linked by e-mail and other similar systems on the Internet. The communications researcher Howard Rheingold defined a virtual community as follows:

> Virtual communities are social aggregations that emerge from the Internet when enough people carry on . . . public discussions long enough, with sufficient human feeling, to form webs of personal relationships in cyberspace.[14]

He suggested that a group of Internet subscribers with shared interests could access a collective store of information and work on it together as an 'on-line brains trust' or a 'computer-assisted group mind'. For Rheingold, virtual communities emerged in response to a widespread 'hunger for community', a hunger which is increasingly unsated as more traditional types of communities disintegrate. However – bearing in mind the characteristics of a 'community' I listed at the beginning of this chapter – there are good reasons for being cautious about applying this term too widely. Not every group of interconnected Internet users deserves the title 'virtual community'. Most use of the Internet is made up of searches for information by individuals who have nothing in common but a short-term interest in a particular topic, and interactive web sites may only attract casual users and generate little shared, cumulative knowledge amongst a group. Compared with 'community of discourse' and 'community of practice', the term 'virtual community' has been used rather loosely, and some communications researchers like Neil Postman and Nessim Watson have therefore suggested that, unless it is more precisely defined, it will be of little value.[15] It is also worth noting that the idea of certain groups of people who are linked only through the Internet being called members of a 'community' has met with some resistance in popular debate. For example, in 1998 I read several letters to British newspapers which objected to journalists describing members of Internet-based pornography rings as members of an 'international virtual community of paedophiles'. The letters usually seemed to be fuelled by concerns that honouring a group of such people with the title of 'community' was inappropriate. But while we should not use the term too loosely, it must be accepted that communities of practice can pursue the 'common evil' as well as the 'common good', as so many earlier and more conventional criminal organizations (Chicago gangsters and Cornish shipwreckers, for instance) have demonstrated.

From what information is available, it seems that members of some on-line interest groups do organize themselves in ways which would match most, if not all, of the features I listed for a 'community'. They have special communication networks to which they control admission, a specialized discourse which is only comprehensible to initiated members, a shared, cumulative body of specialized knowledge and the active, collaborative pursuit of a set of common goals. They may even have ways of evaluating and policing members' mutual responsibilities and obligations to each other. An interesting example can be found in Nessim Watson's account of the activities of a fan club for an obscure North American rock band called Phish. I still have never heard Phish's music, and so have to take it on trust that they actually exist; but it seems that they attract a dedicated following, with many fans using 'Phish.net' to share information, critical responses to concerts and interpretations of songs. Apparently the band, who are themselves participants in Phish.net, have even altered the lyrics of some songs to reflect the fans' interpretations that they have read. The web site opens with a claim that it provides all the information anyone needs about 'the band, its <u>community</u>, and its culture' and addresses the reader as 'a new member of the <u>Phish Community</u>' (with words underlined as shown). What is more, Phish.net is used to express, and gain support for, judgements about how Phish fans should behave responsibly as community members. So when one fan accompanied a review of three New York concerts at the Beacon Theatre with the boast that they had gained entry by using forged tickets and congratulated other fans who had 'crashed' entry, many responses of the following kind were posted by contributors to the web site:

> do you really think that this sort of activity deserves a 'congrats'. I think not!!! . . . Pushing open doors to get into a show for free is childish, selfish, and risking the entire scene for everyone who paid to enjoy the show.

> This doesn't help Phish, the Beacon, or us . . . I am quite unimpressed, & more than a little disappointed. I posted this, 'cause I want everyone to think before they act. What you do, affects everyone!![16]

Synchronous and asynchronous forms of computer mediated communication

There are essentially two types of computer mediated communication (CMC): 'synchronous', in which people are simultaneously connected, and interact in real time (as they also do in face-to-face or telephone conversations); and 'asynchronous', in which messages are sent and read whenever any particular user is connected. CMC is a new medium for communication, and like the more established modes of spoken and written language it can carry a range of language styles and genres. Communications can be formal or informal, involve two or more participants, and so on. But some linguistic characteristics of CMC use are now becoming clear. Synchronous on-line talk is often a messy affair, in which the language looks much less prepared and monitored – more like talk, in many ways – than most conventional forms of writing.[17]

Here is a short example of a casual, synchronous on-line chat between friends (Marie and Alan) who are trying to work out how to improve a recipe for carrot cake.

Sequence 5.3: Recipes on-line

Marie: That was an ace carrot cake.
Alan: :-)
Marie: Can I have the recipe?
Marie: Only we have to work out why . . .
Marie: The filling goes runny. It shouldn't.
Alan: You made it too soon I think.
Alan: What was it? Yog . . .
Marie: What on earth do you mean?
Alan: Icing sugar?
Marie: Cream cheese and icing sugar. How can age be importa
Marie: nt.
Marie: ?

Synchronous on-line chat commonly consists of this kind of series of very short comments by users, who are thus able to keep up a fairly rapid exchange of ideas. However, 'turn-taking' is much harder to achieve smoothly in this medium than in face-to-face or telephone conversations, mainly because (without cues like intonation or gesture) it is more difficult to tell when someone has completed their 'turn'. As can be seen from the example, the software design of the particular interactive system ('First Class') being used in Sequence 5.3 is such that, if anyone pauses for more than a couple of seconds, their turn is treated as closed and any further words they write are represented as a new turn. (So Marie takes two turns to spell 'important'.) The coherence of the conversation is sometimes then disrupted, because one partner is not sure when the other has finished. Of course, that can sometimes also happen in spoken conversation, but is less likely (even on the telephone) because listeners can gather clues from intonation that speakers are closing their turn. Alan's use of the smiling face 'emoticon' [:-)] in the sequence also illustrates a way in which on-line communicators try to compensate for the absence of gesture and intonation in this medium by an imaginative adaptation of punctuation symbols. As any regular CMC user will know, emoticons are now fairly often used to communicate feelings.

In one particular form of synchronous CMC known as 'MUDs' (Multi User Domains), users take on the role of 'characters' whom they act out in a game scenario (say, an adventure based on J.R.R. Tolkien's *Lord of the Rings*) in which they move through a virtual landscape as they make the story unfold. In her book *Life on the Screen*[18] the cyberpsychologist Sherry Turkle explains how the nature of Internet encounters has made it possible for people to create shared fantasy environments, inhabited by virtual selves who together make events happen on the screen which can carry a considerable emotional charge. Under the protection of the anonymity which cyberspace offers, the real people involved may do things which they never have had the opportunity, courage, or even intention (in the sensible and more accountable contexts of their everyday lives) to do. One of the topics many people seem to like thinking together about on the Internet is sex. As in real life, some virtual sexual encounters (known as 'Tinysex' amongst the initiated) can be fleeting affairs, in which participants emerge with little history and disperse afterwards into the ether; but on some occasions participants build love lives in cyberspace which have continuity through time. For example, Turkle describes how two MUD characters eventually felt that their relationship justified first an engagement, and then a wedding ceremony on the MUD. The following dialogue is an extract from that wedding, as recorded by the person taking the role of the character Achilles. The other participants are his bride Winterlight and the 'priest' Tarniwoof (a third MUD user):

Tarniwoof says, 'At the engagement ceremony you gave one another an item which represents your love, respect and friendship for each other.'
Tarniwoof turns to you.
Tarniwoof says, 'Achilles, do you have any reason to give your item back to Winterlight?'
Winterlight attends your answer nervously.
Tarniwoof waits for the groom to answer.
You would not give up her gift for anything.
Tarniwoof smiles happily.
Winterlight smiles at you.[19]

We can see that even that brief piece of dialogue invokes information of past life on the MUD shared amongst the participants. In this way, people in cyberspace can use language to develop contextual foundations of shared past experience for current activity and make plans for a joint future.

MUDs have mainly been used for recreational purposes, but virtual scenarios have also been devised to help people to learn a language, and to act out simulations for occupational training. The use of other kinds of CMC (especially asynchronous e-mail) is now extensive in many educational communities. In my own institution (The Open University), by far the greater part of office correspondence, internally and externally, is now carried by e-mail rather than paper. This enables people to work together in new ways. I have now written a journal article with a co-author I have never met (achieved partly by working collaboratively on the same electronic text) and I supervise doctoral students in distant locations, using the 'First Class' e-mail and conferencing network. It is becoming increasingly common for students and tutors to communicate almost exclusively through e-mail and computer conferencing. Some idea of how this works can be gained from Sequence 5.4, which is part of an e-mail dialogue between one of my colleagues, Robin Goodfellow, and Helen Chappell who was a student tutored by Robin on an Open University educational technology course. They are talking about the nature of their on-line relationship as tutor and student.

Sequence 5.4: E-mail talk

From: Helen (student)@globalsite
To: Robin (tutor)@milton keynes
It's been a productive year, I've learnt a lot, thoroughly enjoyed it all (nodding approvingly). But I really wonder about your role in it. We never met, and most of my online interaction was with other students. I word-counted all the comments you made on my essays and incidental mail – total words 1,600. Translating this to spoken word at a generally accepted rate of 160–180 words per minute (BBC estimates) then you spoke directly and personally to me for about ten minutes in the entire course.

From: Robin (tutor)@milton keynes
To: Helen (student)@globalsite
Ah . . . but the online tutor's role is different from face-to-face teaching. In the hi-tech virtual classroom (pompously) the tutor's job is to facilitate online collaboration amongst the students. I did some counting and see that in every one of the computer conferences that were our 'classroom' interaction, you 'spoke' most out of all the students – not only that, but you are referred to by name in other people's messages more often than anyone else in the group. That puts you pretty much at the centre of our virtual community. I think as facilitator I did my job rather well.

From: Helen (student)@globalsite
To: Robin (tutor)@milton keynes
Our conferences were certainly fun, informative and witty places (smiling brightly but not too brightly). Not unlike an actual classroom except that it's all done through text, and classmates are dispersed around the world. But writing style needs to be much more informal, more personal, if the online environment is to come alive.

I now count as friends those of my fellow students who, like me, decided to take the plunge and start posting messages, sharing thoughts and feelings, instead of just doing collaborative tasks.

From: Robin (tutor)@milton keynes
To: Helen (student)@globalsite
But (furrowed brow, haggard look) being online adds hugely to the distance teacher's workload. Just imagine if every time one of your face-to-face students came to see you, and you were out, they could leave their words hanging in the air in your office for when you

returned. That is what it is like trying to 'moderate' a computer conference full of enthusiastic, knowledgeable adults, all poised to give back 100 words for every ten you give them. What with reading and summarising all that, plus sorting out individual students' problems, not to mention all those assignments (involuntary shudder). There didn't seem much time for socialising.[20]

We can see here two people thinking through the history of their on-line relationship, though not seeming to come to much agreement about it. Both make claims that seem to imply that they have rather different conceptions about what it should be like, or at least began with different expectations of what it should have been like. Helen seems to have expected Robin to have a more active and regular presence on screen, and probably also expected her tutor to take a direct teaching or guiding role in her learning. Robin, on the other hand, justifies his style of involvement by describing his role as a 'facilitator' rather than a teacher, and someone who has also done a lot of 'moderating' activity unseen by the students. It seems, then, as if Helen and Robin have implicitly been following rather different sets of ground rules for on-line distance education – and that this difference has not come to the surface as a topic for discussion until this rather late stage towards the end of the course. This is not an unusual situation in more conventional educational settings. Teachers and students often have different implicit understandings about how language should be used, and only very rarely is this brought into the open and resolved.

In another study of asynchronous CMC use in distance education,[21] Rupert Wegerif suggests that CMCs do offer good opportunities for creating communities of practice, into which students are inducted by the 'scaffolding' interactions with their tutors (and other students). But just as with more conventional communities, it is easy for newcomers to feel excluded and ignorant, and so to feel that entry to community membership is almost impossible. In fact, most of the problems he describes as affecting the CMC students' sense of being members of a community are similar to those which would apply in face-to-face higher education settings. For example, students who join the course late feel the lack of the common knowledge which, through shared experience, has developed in the group and which underpins the on-line discourse. Wegerif suggests that some self-conscious community building needs to be done by those running such courses, using on-line equivalents of the 'ice-breaking' activities which are often used to begin conventional training workshops.

The nature of CMC as a medium for collective thinking

CMC is a new communication medium, but nevertheless one whose use requires language skills. This means that the ways in which it is used, and the effectiveness of it for getting things done, will be influenced by many of the same factors as operate in more established forms of interaction. For example, the effective use of CMC for joint problem-solving will depend on the extent to which people develop secure foundations of shared understanding by sharing their individual knowledge resources, and the success of their joint activity is likely to depend on how well they establish shared ground rules for working together, and so on. In Sequence 5.4 Robin (the tutor) suggests that 'the online tutor's role is different from face-to-face teaching', but I am not very convinced by this claim that the medium is the message. It seems to me that an on-line tutor could choose to be authoritarian, didactic and interventional, just as a conventional tutor could act out his or her role in face-to-face teaching as a non-authoritarian facilitator. How we use CMC for doing education, business, or whatever will depend on our implicit conceptions of how such activities should be done, and not on the qualities of the medium itself.

So what distinctive qualities, if any, does CMC have as a medium for joint intellectual activity? The most significant, I believe, is that, compared with face-to-face conversation, telephone talk or correspondence by letter, CMC is a medium whose use is not defined by the constraints of real time. The two types of CMC use – synchronous and asynchronous – are not necessarily distinct, since some systems allow communication to be carried out either way. E-mail is usually asynchronous, with users sending messages which lie in their correspondent's electronic mailboxes, rather like conventional mail, until the addressee logs on and opens it; but it can be used for rapid interaction. MUDs, on the other hand, are usually carried out 'live' on-line, though some MUD scenarios carry on, in an episodic way, for weeks. Messages take only an instant to travel between correspondents, but need not necessarily be read immediately when they arrive. Recipients may have the choice of responding to them instantly when they do read them, or waiting until they have more time or they have had a chance to reflect on the contents and construct a suitable reply. This is how a student on an Open University course put it:

> Whereas in a face to face conference if someone raised an issue that was not really important to what you were doing you'd say look we can't discuss that – we've booked the room for two hours we have to get on. In CMC it might niggle and you go away and think about it and maybe get a book down from the shelf and come back the next day with some ideas on it . . . [22]

For doing joint problem-solving, or arguing about a particular complex issue, CMC therefore offers some of the advantages of speech (rapid interaction, informal register) together with some of those of written correspondence (the messages do not fade rapidly, and so can be considered in depth; pieces of text can be exchanged with precision; replies can be drafted, reviewed and redrafted before sending).

A second important quality may be its potential for allowing users to operate with a certain detachment from their real selves. A user can interact intellectually with other people without necessarily having to worry about the impact of their physical appearance, age, accent, and so on. People seem to find CMC particularly suitable for role play, often of a very absorbing and serious kind. But some researchers believe that what is available is more than this (if by role play we mean the self-evident taking on of another identity, as an actor does). Turkle, for example, argues that the nature of CMC offers a user something more akin to the creation of a 'flexible self', who in a range of character forms can gain experience which may be valuable as well as entertaining in the virtual communities of the Internet.[23] Different virtual characters and scenarios may create different contexts for engaging in collective thinking, and so have considerable creative potential. And, freed from the conformity pressures of personal contact which operate at 'real' meetings, participants may feel more able to be critical and to challenge existing consensuses.[24] From this perspective the potential of CMC as a medium for using language as a psychological and cultural tool is undoubtedly considerable.

On the other hand, any user knows that in all its current forms CMC is still a clumsy medium, one in which people try to do talk-like things but without the auxiliary systems of gesture and tone of voice for conveying emotions and subtle meanings. Although it has many spoken language characteristics, CMC is still essentially a literate activity, and so users have to rely on the self-conscious representation of emotions through language in a way that speakers do not. The extracts from CMC use I included earlier illustrate these limitations, as well as the strengths of the medium. For example, 'Winterlight attends your answer nervously' are the words of an author and not the involuntary gestural signals of a nervous bride. And in synchronous exchanges, at least, the expectation that the exchange will be rapid means that the reflective, considered quality of much written communication is lost. People may commit themselves to 'saying' something in the potentially permanent print of CMC which they would not normally write and send without much more cautious consideration. And even in asynchronous use, its 'timelessness' may be a relative matter. Used as the medium of communication for a developing community of practice, the rolling snowball of on-line talk gathers the contextual weight of accumulated common knowledge in the same way that more conventional talk does – as one Open University student involved in an on-line course on academic writing explained:

> The medium is not as asynchronous as it seems. If a bit of time is missed it is hard to catch up. You feel an observer of someone else's conversation. Before making a point you wonder if it has already been made and so have to read back – by the time you are ready the debate has moved on. It is therefore necessary to log on regularly – perhaps every day. This is especially true of collaborative work where your time and the other participants' time have to mesh together.[25]

Other evaluation studies have shown that certain kinds of students – those in older age groups, and more women than men – find the medium of CMC uncongenial, and will avoid distance education courses if this is the only kind of tutorial contact which is offered. Inevitably, those people who promote the use of CMC in education tend to be 'adept users' of the medium, and so easily underestimate the significance of psychological barriers and limited computer expertise on students' participation.[26]

To sum up, then, there is no doubt that CMC can be used to generate and maintain dispersed communities. It can be used conveniently and effectively for collective thinking. It combines in a useful way characteristics of speech and writing in ways which make it a welcome, valuable addition to our language toolbox. Some of the attitudinal problems people have with using it may be easily overcome once it becomes a more widely used, familiar, everyday medium. But CMC has some limitations which must be recognized; and, in many ways, its effective use for joint activity and the creation of new knowledge will depend on the same basic considerations that apply in any kind of language use. So, as in spoken conversation, e-mail correspondents working together will need firm contextual foundations for their communications, to establish ground rules for carrying out particular kinds of communication. Although physical appearance may be irrelevant, social and cultural factors can still affect interactions amongst virtual conversationalists. But whether or not a network of Internet users amounts to a virtual community will depend on how users relate to each other, rather than on the special properties of the medium. Like any other communicative medium, CMC will only be as good for collective thinking as its users make it.

Summary

In this chapter I drew on several conceptions of 'community' to consider how language for collective thinking depends on the shared, continuing activities of established groups with common interests and goals. The concepts of 'community of discourse' and 'community of practice' are useful for describing how groups of people with shared interests use and adapt language to think collectively in pursuing common interests. Within communities, knowledge resources are normally shared and developed through language; knowledge commonly exists in the form of discourse. Members of communities can develop special meanings for words, or even new words to pursue joint purposes if it seems necessary. They can also organize language into particular, specialized tools – the 'genres' that make up the repertoires of the discourses of communities. In this way, the language of the community gives members access to the history of experience of their group – the ways in which earlier members have found it appropriate and useful to use language for collective thinking – and so they learn from the efforts of the more experienced. Language also enables members to construct an identity for their group, and roles and identities for themselves within it. By their nature, because they are built out of the common knowledge of a community, discourses are relatively inaccessible to outsiders. Newcomers to communities may need to be 'apprenticed' to experienced 'experts' to become able to speak the discourse. The negative side of communities' dependence on their discourses is that members may become more concerned with the linguistic form in which ideas are presented, rather than with the content. This may make them uncritical of ideas so long as they are expressed in the appropriate discourse, and resistant to relevant ideas which are not presented in it.

6 Development through dialogue

This chapter is about how children learn to use language for collective thinking, and how other people help them do so. It is also about how the process of communicating with language contributes to children's intellectual development. To begin, here is some talk which I recorded while three children were playing together at home. Kay was 5 at the time, while her brother Alec and his friend Robert were both 9. She was listening to them telling each other jokes of the question-and-answer type.

Sequence 6.1: What a joke!

Robert: What's the difference between

Alec: (*interrupting*) Between a pelican and another pelican? Well, there's not much difference! (*laughs*)

Robert: No, between a banana and an elephant? Try lifting it. If you can't lift it, it's likely to (*loud noises from Kay*) to be a banana – to be an elephant.

Kay: What did the hippopotamus do when he's, uh, in the park?

Alec: I don't know.

Kay: Plays football (*giggles*).

Robert: Ho, ho, ho (*false laughter; Alec sighs*).

We can see that Alec and Robert have learned a common genre structure for joke telling, based on a question-and-answer sequence. This involves the joke teller leading their listener along an apparently predictable line of thought to a surprising, unexpected conclusion. It seems that Kay has also learned the structure of this genre; but she does not share their conception of how to use it to make a funny joke.

Joke telling relies on learning the genre, because audiences usually need to know this is the type of dialogue in which they are involved. (As illustrated by the occasional need for repair remarks like 'It was a joke' when this shared frame is not established.) To be successful the joke teller must do more than use a structure; they must build up the right kind of cohesive content. This is a rhetorical skill based on cultural ground rules. The boys share past experience of hearing these kinds of jokes and through this they have formed implicit criteria for what 'counts' as an appropriate, funny answer. It seems that Kay has not yet been drawn into this communal way of thinking.

However, children do seem to grasp the basic rhetorical and dialogical quality of joking quite early in life. Sequence 6.2 is an extract from a recording the researcher Dianne Horgan made of a conversation with her daughter Kelly (who was nearly 3 years old at the time).

Sequence 6.2: Do you love me?

Kelly: Mommy, do you love me?
Mother: Yes.
Kelly: Do you love me to HIT you? Ha, ha![1]

This example not only illustrates Kelly's developing understanding of humour, but also the awareness she has already developed of different meanings of the word 'love'. Verbal humour is not an incidental, peripheral part of human thinking; it is one manifestation of how language is involved with making collective sense of experience. Becoming able to tell jokes involves an appreciation of some important aspects of the relationship between minds: that you can usually take as 'common knowledge' the familiarity of your audience with appropriate genres; that if you know something that other people do not, surprises can be engineered; and that your listener's understanding of a word can be shaped by the contexts in which you offer it. As children communicate with people around them, they are learning to perceive and understand the world from the perspective of being a member of a community. This means their thinking is becoming more collective. But they are also becoming aware of the significance of the distinction between their knowledge and understanding and that of other people. So, as they communicate, they are also learning how to take account of people's individuality when thinking collectively.

You may recall Sequences 2.3 and 2.4 in Chapter 2 in which 15-year-old children, working in pairs but out of each other's sight, carried out an activity in which they were each given a slightly different version of a route map. Using only spoken language, the partners had to resolve these discrepancies and so help one of them find a route to their intended destination. Anne Anderson and her fellow researchers in Glasgow gave a similar activity to children aged between 7 and 13.[2] They found that the most striking age-related variation was that the younger children hardly ever used questions to find out what their partner knew, or to check that they understood the information they had been given. Yet – as the sequences in Chapter 2 also illustrate – asking questions is one of the best strategies for getting this kind of task done successfully. There is also an apparent paradox in that young children often bombard adult companions with questions. But this is not so paradoxical if we remember that the effective use of language depends not just on knowing communicative techniques or strategies, but realizing when to use them in particular situations. The younger children still had to learn how to link minds together effectively in this particular kind of task.

A socio-cultural perspective on development

Recent psychological and anthropological studies of adult–child relations, observed in many cultures, support the view that growing up is an 'apprenticeship in thinking', an induction into ways with words and ways of thinking.[3] The extent to which language is used to make matters explicit to young cultural apprentices seems to vary considerably between societies (and even between communities within them). Amongst some social groups, adults seem to rely quite heavily on the ability of children to make sense for themselves of what they are learning, while in others explanations are provided regularly. In some societies, demonstration rather than verbal explanation is preferred as a method of teaching – for example, amongst the Navajo, who consider language a sacred gift which should be used sparingly.[4] Nevertheless, throughout the world, conversation is one of the most important means by which children seek and receive guidance. One of the principal researchers in this field, Barbara Rogoff, calls the process of children's induction into the intellectual life of their community 'guided participation':

Guided participation involves collaboration and shared understanding in routine problem-solving activities. Interaction with
other people assists children in their development by guiding their
participation in relevant activities, helping them adapt their
understanding to new situations, structuring their problem-solving
attempts, and assisting them in assuming responsibility for
managing problem solving.[5]

This 'socio-cultural' explanation of cognitive development depicts
children's emergent understanding as the product of the collective
thinking of generations, made available to children through observation, joint activity and communication. This contrasts with more
biological and individualistic psychological accounts of cognitive
development, in which abilities and understanding are seen as emerging
through natural growth and individual discovery.[6] Socio-cultural
explanations recognize the role that parents and other people play in
helping children learn.

Guidance through dialogue

Of course, adults do not only allow children to participate in activities,
they also deliberately provide them with information and explanations
and instruct them in ways to behave. But this need not be thought of as
a one-way transmission process. Children may take an active role in
soliciting help or obtaining information and transforming what they
are given into their own new understanding. They can also contest what
they are given, and gain understanding from engaging in argument.
I can illustrate these points through the next sequence of dialogue.
Have you ever felt, during a conversation with a child, that a shift
in their understanding has taken place as a result of gaining some
new information? I remember feeling this during a conversation with
my daughter Anna, which happened when she was 2 years old. At that
time, I was regularly recording our talk in joint activities. On this
occasion, the topic of our conversation had continued from a little
earlier the same evening, when for the first time she had seen bats flying
round the house. I had pointed to the eaves, where I had said the bats
slept.

Sequence 6.3: Bats in the roof

Me: What did you think of the bats?
Anna: What?
Me: Did you like the bats?
Anna: Yeh.
Me: Think of those bats now, they're out flying around now. Aren't they?
Anna: They not going – are they lying on the roof?
Me: What about them?
Anna: Lie on the roof.
Me: Oh yeh.
Anna: They not, but not inside.
Me: Yeh, I think they do go inside the roof.
Anna: But not in.
Me: You don't think so?
Anna: Not in!
Me: Not in the roof? I think they go inside the roof. That's where they go to sleep in the day.
Anna: (*sounding confused*) But they, they not going *inside* it.
Me: Why? (*laughing*) Why do you think that?
Anna: (*also laughing*) But they are not going inside it.
Me: They can get inside it. There are little kind of holes round the edge of the roof, at the top of the walls and they creep in there.
Anna: They go there to bye-byes now?
Me: Yeh – no, they go to bye-byes in the day. They're just coming out now.
Anna: Are they not going to bye-byes now?
Me: No, they go to bye-byes in the day, in the morning, and they fly around all night. They get up at night and go out.

It seems that our earlier conversation, while watching the bats, had left Anna with some intellectual dissatisfaction with what she had heard me explain about the creatures' lifestyle. This motivated her to raise the issue of whether the bats' habit was to sleep lying on the roof, when I had offered the (apparently less believable) story that they slept inside it. When I would not confirm her existing belief, it can be seen from the transcript that she reiterated it five times, continuing to do so until I offered a more elaborated explanation of how the bats might enter the roof. She seemed to accept this explanation as reasonable, because in her next statement she asked if the bats were now going 'there' to sleep. As we continued on this topic, it became apparent to me that she did not understand that the bats were nocturnal, and so I tried also to explain this feature of their lifestyle.

An interesting point to note about Sequence 6.3 is that both the topics for which I provided Anna with explanations were raised by her, not by me. The developmental psychologist Jean Piaget suggested that one of the motivations for intellectual development was the 'cognitive conflict' that periodically arises between children's experience of the world and their understanding of it.[7] He saw this as happening mainly through children's direct involvement with the physical world, but also through communication with other children exposing them to alternative conflicting perspectives. However, Piaget may have underestimated the importance of the role that adult–child conversation plays in development. Young children's direct experience of the world usually takes place in social settings, and is often accompanied by talk about it. That is, new experiences are likely to be mediated by language. What is more, conversation is one of the most important kinds of experience that children have; there is no reason to think that the information they gain through it is any less significant than that obtained by other means (such as by seeing, touching, and so on).

Nevertheless, Piaget's notion of 'cognitive conflict' is still very useful. The information children gain through language may well be, or at least appear to be, incompatible with experience gained in other ways, or with their existing understandings formed through past experience. Language provides both a means for generating a motivating kind of cognitive conflict – and also a means for resolving it, by engaging in some joint thinking with an adult, as Anna did with me. Using language, children can actively test their understanding against that of others, and may use argument to elicit relevant information and explanations from adults about what they perceive – and what they want to know. There is little doubt that children who are unable to ask more knowledgeable people about the world they are discovering, either because adults are unco-operative or because the children themselves lack the communicative ability or confidence to do so, are being denied valuable learning experience as developing thinkers.[8]

Interactions with parents and other older people also provide young children with ways of using language that they can appropriate and adapt for later use. A good example of this comes from Mariëtte Hoogsteder's observations of adults and children engaged in the play task of assembling blocks of increasing sizes on to a spindle. When one

2-year-old made a mistake in choosing a block, his father pointed out his error and remarked 'that's a joke, I think', at which the boy took the block away and tried again. Later, the boy decided to rebuild the tower himself. As he was doing so, the following interaction took place.

Sequence 6.4: Building blocks

Child: Shall we continue with this one?   *Child selects too small a block and places it on the spindle.*

Father: Well yes, do you think so?

Child: (*laughs*) <u>Joke</u>!

Father: Oh.[9]   *Child takes off the wrong block and selects the right one.*

Hoogsteder suggests that the boy had taken the wrong block on purpose, so that he could turn the tables and tease his father as he had been teased himself. The father's earlier guidance led to learning of a kind he may not have envisaged. The boy appropriated his father's ironic comment on his earlier effort ('that's a joke, I think') and used it in conjunction with his 'wrong' choice to make an original, creative contribution to the dialogue. In this way, the child not only created his own 'joke' but also demonstrated to his father that he had some understanding of how the blocks should be put together.

You may recall from Chapter 3 that the Russian literary scholar Bakhtin said that we take the words we use from other people's mouths.[10] The meanings of words are generated in context, through dialogue, and when we speak we almost always do so in partial response to what others have said. We 'appropriate' ways of using language from the people with whom we interact. The relevance of Bakhtin's ideas for analysing Sequence 6.4 is fairly clear. Consider what relevance you think they have for the next example, Sequence 6.5. This is an extract from a conversation with two young girls which was recorded by my colleague Janet Maybin in her research on children's informal talk. They are telling her about the sister of one of them, who had got pregnant.

Sequence 6.5: She did the best thing

Janet: So does your sister live quite near you?
Nicole: She lives with us

Karlie: Cause [she's only quite young
Nicole: [she's young, she's sixteen
Janet: Ah right
Karlie: She did the best thing about it though, didn't she, Nicole?
Nicole: She didn't tell a soul, no-one, that she was pregnant
Karlie: Until she was due, when she got into hospital, then she told them
Nicole: On Saturday night she had pains in her stomach and come the
         following Sunday my mum was at work and my sister come to the
         pub and my aunt Ella was in it and my sister went in there and said
         'I've got pains in my stomach' so my auntie Ella went and got my
         mum, and took her to hospital, and my mum asked her if she was
         due on and she said 'No, I've just come off' and when they got her
         to hospital they said 'Take her to maternity'. My mum was crying!
Janet: Your mum didn't realise she was pregnant?
Nicole: No, and my mum slept with her when she was ill!
Karlie: My dad said she did – Terri did the best thing about it – her sister's
         Terri
Nicole: Or if she did tell, as she's so young, she weren't allowed to have
         him[11]

We can see that Nicole quotes her sister and the hospital staff in her
account of this unusual childbirth. Karlie also recycles language from
an earlier event, but in a less obvious way. We first hear her expressing
her opinion that Nicole's sister 'did the best thing about it'. Later,
though, these same words emerge as an apparent quotation from her
father. It seems that she was so impressed by her father's comment that
she appropriated it for her own use. Although her father may not have
made his comment in a self-conscious attempt to guide Karlie's moral
development, by recycling his remark she implicitly supports the moral
sentiments that it expresses – or at least she shows that she felt they were
appropriate sentiments to voice in this later conversation with another
adult (the researcher). For children, 'recycling' the language they hear
may be an important way of assimilating the collective ways of thinking
of the community in which they are growing up.

Providing a 'scaffolding' for learning

In Chapter 3, I described how teachers commonly use techniques
like 'elicitations', 'recaps' and 'reformulations' when interacting with
students. These techniques are deliberate guidance strategies for
generating a common frame of reference during an episode of teaching-

and-learning. James Wertsch observed parents of young children using two other rather similar techniques.[12] The first, which he calls 'establishing a referential perspective', is when an adult responds to a child's apparent lack of comprehension by referring to other shared knowledge. Imagine, for instance, that while on a country walk a parent says to a child: 'look, there's a tractor'. If this reference fails (that is, the child does not seem to realize which object is being referred to), the adult may then say something like 'can you see, that big green thing with enormous wheels in the field?' In doing this, the adult is drawing on resources of common knowledge to build a shared contextual frame of reference, based on the reasonable assumption that the child's understanding of basic features like colour and appearance will help them identify the strange object in question. Coupled with this technique, adults use a kind of reverse process which Wertsch calls 'abbreviation'. This is when, over the course of time, an adult begins to assume that new common knowledge has been successfully established, and so, when talking to the child, makes progressively more abbreviated or cryptic references to what is being discussed. For example, the next time the same parent and child are out in the countryside, the parent may first point out 'another big green tractor', but then later just refer to 'the tractor'. In these ways, by gradually and systematically creating and assuming more common knowledge, adults support and encourage children's developing understanding of language and the world it describes.

To use any of these teaching techniques effectively, an adult has to make careful judgements about what a child understands at any one point in time, to base their communications with the child upon these judgements, and adapt the kind of intellectual support they give the child to take account of their developing knowledge and understanding. If they do so systematically while engaged in a joint activity with a child, the adult can enable the child to make progress which they would not have been able to do alone. The adult's intellect provides a temporary support for the child's own, until a new level of understanding has been achieved. To provide this 'scaffolding', as Jerome Bruner and others have called it,[13] an adult may not only offer useful information and guiding suggestions, they may even intervene to simplify slightly the task in hand. (As, for example, when an adult helps a young child get started on a jigsaw puzzle by assembling all the edge pieces.) Effective 'scaffolding' reduces the learner's scope for failure in the task, while encouraging their efforts to advance. 'Scaffolding' helps a learner to accomplish a task which they would not have been able to do on their own. But it is a special, sensitive kind of help which is intended to bring the learner closer to a state of competence which will enable them eventually to complete such a task on their own.

Creating an intermental development zone

The notion of 'scaffolding' is closely related to one of the ideas of the Russian psychologist Vygotsky, whose work I discussed in Chapter 1. Vygotsky suggested that the usual measures of children's intellectual ability, such as IQ tests, are too static and decontextualized to be of real educational value. He pointed out that children differ in their responsiveness to guidance, instruction and opportunities for learning. So two children who currently have reached a similar level of, say, mathematical understanding, could be expected to achieve similar results in a standardized maths test. But, given (as he put it) 'good instruction' by a teacher, one of those children might very quickly grasp new mathematical concepts and computational skills, while the other – even if similarly motivated – might only be able to make a little progress. By measuring the difference between the original independent capability of each child and what they were able to achieve when given some intellectual guidance and support, educators could make a more useful, dynamic assessment of these children's educational potential and needs. The difference between their original and eventual achievement was what Vygotsky called each child's *zone of proximal development* (often today referred to by the acronym ZPD). In his last major work, he returned to this concept and used it to argue that 'Instruction is only useful when it moves ahead of development'.[14] That is, good teaching should draw children just beyond their existing capabilities to 'stretch' their intellect and so help them to develop. He seems to have wanted the concept to be used to ensure that individual children received teaching appropriate to their potential, rather than their actual, achievements. Vygotsky's conception of the ZPD embodied his view that intellectual development is something sensitive to dialogue and situational factors, a process by which *intra*mental (individual) processes can be facilitated and accelerated by *inter*mental (social) activity.

I went back to Vygotsky's original account of the ZPD while writing this book, and also read again what several other sociocultural researchers had written about it.[15] This made me realize that I have developed a rather different conception of a 'zone' of intellectual development. This is probably because I am less interested than Vygotsky in assessing individuals and more in understanding the quality of teaching-and-learning as an 'intermental' or 'interthinking' process. For a teacher to teach and a learner to learn, they must use talk and joint activity to create a shared communicative space, an 'intermental development zone' (IDZ) on the contextual foundations of their common knowledge and aims. In this intermental zone, which is reconstituted constantly as the dialogue continues, the teacher and learner negotiate their way through the activity in which they are involved. If the quality of the zone is successfully maintained, the teacher can enable a learner to become able to operate just beyond their established capabilities, and to consolidate this experience as new ability and understanding. If the dialogue fails to keep minds mutually attuned, the IDZ collapses and the scaffolded learning grinds to a halt.

Like Vygotsky's original idea of the ZPD, the concept of an 'intermental development zone' still focuses attention on how a learner progresses under guidance in an activity, but in a way which is more clearly related to the variable contributions of both teacher and learner. The IDZ is a continuing event of contextualized joint activity, whose quality is dependent on the existing knowledge, capabilities and motivations of both the learner and the teacher. Vygotsky suggested that 'good', appropriate instruction could influence development. But if we say that the contribution of a teacher is significant in determining what a learner achieves on any particular occasion, we must accept that this achievement is a joint one, the product of a process of interthinking. The progress of the two hypothetical mathematics students I mentioned above might well be greatly affected by who taught them, because teachers do not offer the same quality of continuing intermental support, and individual students respond differently to the same teacher. This has obvious implications for researching cognitive development and evaluating the process of teaching-and-learning. As well as observing the progress a learner, or a class of learners, makes with the support of a particular teacher through a particular activity, we should also observe how the teachers and learners use language and other means of communicating to create an IDZ during the activity. I will return to these ideas a little later, in relation to teaching-and-learning in school.

Learning together

As well as learning from the guidance and example of experts, children (and novices of all ages) also learn the skills of thinking collectively by acting and talking with each other. Any account of intellectual development based only on the guidance of young people by older members of their community would of course be inadequate. As members of a younger generation, we often rebel against the learning that our elders prescribe, and often question the values inherent in the given knowledge of our community. We use language to generate some of our own common understandings and to pursue our own interests. Each generation is active in creating the new knowledge they want, and in doing so the communal resources of the language tool-kit may be transformed. Yet even the rebellious creativity of a new generation is inevitably, in part, the product of a dialogue between generations.

I now want to look at some examples of children involved in activities without an adult present. The nature of the collective thinking involved is usually very different in such circumstances. Language offers children a means for simulating events together in play, in ways which may enable the participants to make better sense of the actual experiences on which the play is based. The Dutch psychologist Ed Elbers has provided some excellent examples of children engaged in this kind of play activity. Like many children, when they were aged 6 and 7 his two daughters enjoyed setting up play 'schools' together with toy animals. They would act out scenarios in which, with one of them as the teacher, the assembled creatures would act out the routines of a school day. But Elbers noticed that one typical feature of their play school was that incidents which disrupted classroom life took place with surprising frequency. Sequence 6.6 is one such example (translated by Elbers from the Dutch). Margareet is the elder girl, being nearly 8 years old, and here takes the role of the teacher. Elisabeth, her younger (6-year-old) sister, acts out the role of a rather naughty student.

Sequence 6.6: Play school

Margareet: Children, sit down.
Elisabeth: I have to go to the toilet, Miss.
Margareet: Now, children, be quiet.
Elisabeth: I have to go to the toilet.
Margareet: I want to tell you something.
Elisabeth: (*loud*) I have to go to the toilet!
Margareet: (*chuckles*) Wait a second.
Elisabeth: (*with emphasis*) Miss, I have to go to the toilet!!
Margareet: OK, you can go.
Elisabeth: (*cheekily*) Where is it? (*laughs*)
Margareet: Over there, under that box, the one with the animals on, where the dangerous animals . . . (*chuckles*) under there.
Elisabeth: Really?
Margareet: Yes.[16]

In this sequence we can again see, as in Sequences 6.4 and 6.5, a child appropriating an adult's way with words. 'Now, children, be quiet' is exactly the kind of teacher-talk that Margareet will have heard every day in 'real' school. But Elbers suggests we can also interpret this sequence as an example of children reflecting together on the rules which govern their behaviour in school, and how the robustness of these rules can be tested. They can play with ideas of power and control, without risking the community sanctions which 'real life' behaviour would incur. Teachers normally have to be obeyed, and children are not meant to leave the class during lessons – but given the legitimate excuse of having to go to the toilet, how can a child not get her way? Sometimes, in setting up this kind of activity, the girls (out of role) would discuss how best to ensure that such disruptive incidents occurred. For example:

Sequence 6.7: Setting up the play school

Margareet: You should choose four children who always talk the most; those children must sit at the front near the teacher. It'll be fun if they talk.
Elisabeth: (*to one of the toy pupils*) You, you sit here and talk, right?
Margareet: The desks are behind each other, then they can only . . . then I have to turn round all the time, if the children talk.[17]

These kinds of examples illustrate something important about how language use in play activities may contribute to children's development. Language can be used by them to simulate social life, to create virtual contexts in which they can use dramatized activity to think together about the ways in which life is carried out in the communities in which they are cultural apprentices.

The next example comes from the research by Janet Maybin which also provided Sequence 6.5. She asked children in her project to wear radio microphones so that she could record their conversations throughout the school day. Sequence 6.8 is part of such a recording for a girl of 11 called Julie, which begins while she is doing a mathematics problem in class with a partner. She then goes out to the girls' toilets and eventually returns to the classroom.

Sequence 6.8: In and out of class

Julie: Three pounds twelve I make Tom Ato. Back in a second. Miss can I go to the toilet please?

Teacher: Yes all right.

(*Sound of Julie's heels as she goes down the corridor. When she enters the toilets the acoustics on the tape change abruptly, with the tiled walls making the voices echo. Carol and Nicole are already there*)

Julie: Oh, hi. Where did you get your hair permed?

Nicole: (*indistinct*)

Julie: You're not going out with Sasha, are you?

Nicole: Yea.

Julie: Are you?

Nicole: Yes, I hope so (*laughs*)

Julie: You've got darker skin than me, I've got a sun tan. (*pause*) (*to Carol*) I should think so too, it's disgusting, that skirt is! Aii . . . don't! (*Nicole starts tapping her feet on the tiled floor*) Do you do tap dancing? (*both girls start tapping their feet and singing*)

Julie and Nicole: 'I just called to say I love you / And I mean it from the bottom of my heart.'

Julie: Caught you that time, Carol – ooh! What's the matter, Carol, don't show your tits! (*laughs*) (*to Nicole*) I went like this to Carol, I says, I pull down her top, I went phtt 'don't show your tits!' (*Nicole laughs*)

(*Julie leaves the toilets, walks down the corridor, re-enters the classroom and sits down*)

Julie: Turn over – six plates of chips – oh I've nearly finished my book. I've got one page to do.[18]

Janet Maybin points out that the conversation in the toilets seems to belong to a different world from that of the maths classroom. The frame of reference changes completely. In the toilets, the girls are no longer students but young adolescents jointly interpreting their femininity. Yet in doing so they are still recycling earlier language experience, transforming the 'given' into the 'new', using *risqué* words and song lyrics that they have appropriated from older children or adults.

Sequence 6.8 shows that, in the informal setting of the girls' toilet, Julie and her friends have no problems in sharing ideas and developing shared understandings about their experiences of life. But this does not necessarily mean that they know how to use language effectively for thinking together in other kinds of situations, or that they will inevitably learn all the communication strategies they will need from each other or from the informal guidance adults provide outside school. For example, Maybin's research of children's informal conversations captured little talk of the kind which in Chapter 4 I called 'exploratory', in which reasons are made explicit and ideas are critically considered. Of course, play activities may not generate any obvious need for such talk. But observational research in classrooms on children's activities in pairs and groups generally shows that much of it is unproductive, with more 'disputational' than 'exploratory' talk happening. Sequence 6.9, for example, is a fairly typical episode of interaction amongst a group of four 11-year-olds writing together at the computer, recorded by the teacher and researcher Madeline Watson. The three girls (Jenny, Katy, Annie) have sat down at the screen in such a way that the fourth member, Colin, has had to get a stool and sit behind, sometimes leaning on the girls' shoulders. He has made it clear that he thinks the girls lack computer expertise, and that he should tell them what to do.

Sequence 6.9: At the computer

Jenny: No   *Katy goes to press DELETE.*
Annie: Now delete. Yeh. That's it.   *Jenny pushes her hand out of the*
        And then nuh *(sounds*   *way. Colin pushes over and goes to*
        out the letter n)*   *press the key.*

Colin:	For God's sake.	*Jenny pushes Colin's hand out of the way.*
Katy:	Stop it Colin.	*Colin gets off stool.*
Colin:	You're not doing any of mine (*speaks in aggressive high voice to Katy*).	
Annie:	Now space.	*Raises hand towards keyboard.*
Katy:	(*high pitched – arguing with Colin*) I know. She's just doing the title.	
Annie:	No a bit – delete one of those spaces. There you have to	*Annie leans across Jenny at keyboard to press DELETE.*
Katy:	(*still arguing with Colin*) We're meant to be doing the title. It's the title.	
Annie:	Hang on.	*Jenny pushes Annie's arm up off the keyboard.*[19]

This is the kind of talk which gives group work a bad name. Classroom research has shown that the educational potential value of collaborative activity is often squandered because students do not communicate effectively. Anna Sfard and Carolyn Kieran provide a particularly clear illustration of this in their research on mathematics education in Montreal. A class of 13-year-olds had been asked to answer questions about a worksheet containing a graph showing hours of daylight throughout the year in an Arctic settlement called Alert, which is reproduced as Figure 1. Sequence 6.10 is part of a long and ultimately unproductive conversation between two boys in the class, Ari and Gur. They are addressing the question 'During which period of time did the number of hours of daylight increase most rapidly?' As you read it, see if you can tell what interpretation each boy seems to be making of the graph.

Sequence 6.10: Daylight

Gur: One hundred.
Ari: 60 to 100. From day 60 to 100.
Gur: Cause, oh no, no, no no no no. Look, look. Up here. It's day 100 to day – to day
Ari: What are you talking about?

READING CONTINUOUS GRAPHS

The number of hours of daylight on any given day is a function of what day it is in the year, and of the latitude of the location. The number of hours of daylight in Alert, NWT (near the North Pole) was recorded every day in 1993. The graph below shows the information.

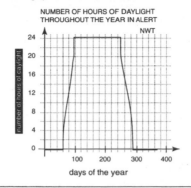

Describe what happened to the number of hours of daylight over the year by answering the following questions.
(1) How many hours of daylight were there on January 1, 1993?
(2) For how many days did this occur before there was a change in the number of hours?
(3) During which period of time did the number of hours of daylight increase most rapidly?
        From day _____ to day _____
(4) What was the maximum number of hours of sunlight in Alert?
        For how long did this last?
        _____ days

(5) Describe what happened when the number of hours started to decrease.

Figure 1: The activity sheet being studied by Ari and Gur in Sequence 6.10

Gur: 55.
Ari: Where?
Gur: Look, it changed most rapidly in between here and here. You see?
Ari: Oh? It's exactly the same.
Gur: No, because see, it moves up (*mumble*)
Ari: It goes up most rapidly
Gur: So it's from day 100.
Ari: To day 100.
Gur: No, from day 100 to day . . .
Ari: No, No, No.
Gur: 2 hundred and sixty.
Ari: That's not how you're supposed to do it.[20]

From the transcript and video, it was clear to Sfard and Kieran that, while Ari clearly understood that the question needed them to attend to the first sloping climb on the graph, it seemed that Gur either mistakenly read the high middle plateau of the graph as a representation of rapid change, or completely misunderstood the question they had been asked to address. The boys had ample opportunity to resolve and reconcile their different understandings, but they never managed to do so. They engage in talk which is mainly 'disputational', in which neither actively seeks information nor offers explicit explanations. They use the word 'it' to make unclear references to various possible things – the question they have been set, the line of the graph, hours of daylight, and so on. They never use their common access to the worksheet to build contextual foundations for their talk, and so never establish a clear, shared focus or frame of reference. Their talk is, as Sfard and Kieran put it, 'discursively incoherent'.[21] Ari obviously began the activity knowing how to read the graph, while if Gur learned anything at all it is in spite of, rather than because of, his communications with Ari.

Even though neither Ari nor Gur may have been behaving in a deliberately awkward or difficult way, they may nevertheless have been acting out this activity as an episode of the 'long conversation' of their relationship in which they habitually orientated to each other in this inexplicit, mildly unco-operative way. That is, the nature of their communication might have been shaped more by what the linguist Michael Halliday calls the 'interpersonal' function of language than by its 'ideational' function as a tool for getting their task done.[22] The same is probably true of Jenny and the others in Sequence 6.9. There is no avoiding the interpersonal function of language, of course. As I suggested in Chapter 4, all interactions, however much focused on a joint intellectual task, must involve participants in an intersubjectivity, a way of orientating to each other's minds. We cannot, and should not, try to ignore the interpersonal function of language, but we can try to help participants ensure that interpersonal orientations are compatible with what they are trying jointly to achieve.

Educating children in collective thinking

The communication problems we have been considering are not only found in school. In all situations, in work and at home, people – often despite their good intentions – find it difficult to communicate effectively. This is not surprising. The ground rules of everyday communication are usually taken for granted, and there may be little encouragement from other people to reflect and improve on how things are normally done. Some ways of using language to get things done may not be used much in the informal activities of everyday childhood life, and so children can hardly be expected to learn them. This offers a clear and useful role for schools, which are special institutional settings created for guiding intellectual development. Education should help children to gain a greater awareness and appreciation of the discourse repertoire of wider society and how it is used to create knowledge and carry out particular activities. It should give them access to ways of using language which their out-of-school experience may not have revealed, help them extend their repertoire of language genres and so enable them to use language more effectively as a means for learning, pursuing interests, developing shared understanding and generally getting things done.

Throughout the 1990s my colleagues and I began to produce classroom-based activities for developing children's use of language as a tool for thinking collectively. The background and first stages of this research were described in my earlier book, *The Guided Construction of Knowledge*.[23] In the most recent five-year phase of this research, Lyn Dawes, Rupert Wegerif, Karen Littleton and I have been working closely with primary teachers in Milton Keynes to develop a practical programme of 'Talk Lessons' for children aged 8–11. These lessons have a careful balance of teacher-led and group-based activities. We have designed teacher-led activities to raise children's awareness of how they talk together and how language can be used in joint activity for reasoning and problem-solving. These teacher-led activities are coupled with group-based tasks in which children have the opportunity to practise ways of talking and collaborating, and these in turn feed into other whole-class sessions in which teachers and children reflect together on what has been learned. The group tasks include topics directly relevant to the National Curriculum for English, science and citizenship.[24] We have also created computer-based activities using specially designed software. (As other researchers have also found, computer-based activities can be excellent for stimulating and focusing children's discussion.[25])

A good example of our computer-based group activities is one designed by Rupert Wegerif which is related directly to the citizenship

curriculum. In an interactive narrative called *Kate's Choice* children
meet a girl called Kate who faces a moral dilemma. One of her friends
tells her he has stolen from the local shop, for reasons which are not
entirely selfish, and she promises not to reveal his crime. But as the
story unfolds, various pressures make Kate doubt whether she should
keep this promise. The children have to talk together and decide what
Kate should do. One of the story frames from *Kate's Choice* is shown
as Figure 2.

In order to evaluate the Talk Lessons, we have made comparisons
between children in 'target' classes who have done them, with 'control'
classes of similar children who have not been involved in the
programme. One specific kind of comparison we have made is
to video-record groups of both 'target' and 'control' children doing
Kate's Choice and other computer-based activities. This comparison
reveals striking differences between children who have done the Talk
Lessons and those who have not. Compared with children of similar
age, experience and background in the same city who have not done the
lessons – and compared with their own prior selves before doing them

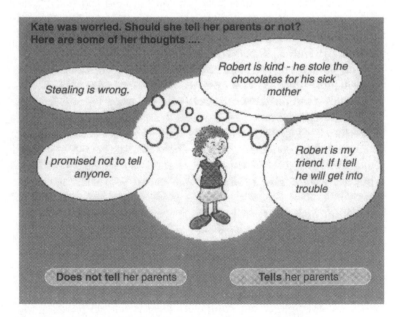

Figure 2: A frame from the computer program *Kate's Choice*

– children who have done the programme discuss issues in more depth and for longer, participate more equally and fully, and provide more reasons to support their views.[26]

Our analysis of recordings of the group activities shows that the improved ability of the 'target' children to think together critically and constructively can be related directly to the structure and content of their talk. Here, to illustrate this, are two examples of groups working on *Kate's Choice*. The first group is from a 'control' class who have not done the Talk Lessons, while the second is one of the 'target' classes who have.

The children in each of the following sequences (6.11 and 6.12) have reached the same point in *Kate's Choice*, where they are looking at the picture shown as Figure 2 above. Kate has discovered that her friend Robert stole the chocolates from a shop, and has already promised him that she will not tell anyone. The children have been asked to talk about the best action that Kate could take in these particular circumstances before moving on.

Sequence 6.11: *Kate's Choice* – Kirsty, Jessica and Jacob

Kirsty: Wait (*reading from screen*). 'Kate was worried. Should she tell her parents or not?' Does . . . no.
'Talk together and decide what Kate should do. Then click on one of those.' Tells her parents I think.
Jessica: Do you think that? (*looking across to Jacob*)
Jacob: Yes.
Kirsty: I think that. 'Tells her parents'.
(*Jessica clicks the mouse to indicate their choice*)

Sequence 6.12: *Kate's Choice* – Gavin, Sara and Tammy

Gavin: (*reading from screen*) 'Kate was worried. Should she tell her parents or not. Here are some of her thoughts. Stealing is wrong. I promised not to tell anyone. Robert is my friend, if I tell he will get into trouble. Robert is kind. He stole the chocolates for his sick mother. Talk together and decide what Kate should do. Then click on one of these buttons.'
'Does not tell her parents' or 'Tells her parents.'
Right we've got to talk about it.
(*Tammy looks at Sara, who unfolds her arms and puts her finger to her mouth*)

Tammy: What do you think? (*Tammy points at Gavin*)
Sara: What do you think?
Gavin: I think even though he is her friend then um she shouldn't tell of
         him because em well she should tell of him em because was, was,
         if he's stealing it it's not worth having a friend that steals is it?
Tammy: No.
Sara: Why? I don't agree.
Tammy: He said why. I think that one as well do you?
(*Tammy points to the screen and looks at Sara*)
Gavin: I think she should tell her parents. Do you?
(*Gavin looks at Sara*)
Tammy: I think I'm I think even though he is her friend because he's
         stealing she should still tell her parents and her parents might give
         her the money and she she might be able to go to the shop and
         give them the money.
Sara: I think um.
Gavin: But then she's paying for the thing he stole so I think he should
         get the money anyway. He should have his [own money
Sara: [I think that he
         should go and tell his [mother (. . .)
Tammy: [Even though she has promised
Sara: Because he's, well you shouldn't break a promise really should
         you?
Gavin: What's it worth having a friend if he's going to steal?
Tammy: If he steals (. . .) If you know he's stolen if she don't tell her
         parents then he will be getting away with it.
(*Tammy looks at Sara*)
Gavin: It's not worth having a friend that steals is it?
(*Gavin looks at Sara. 3 second pause*)
Sara: OK then.
(*Sara clicks the mouse to indicate their choice*)

You may have noticed that the group in Sequence 6.11 spend little time considering their joint decision, and this is typical of children who have not done the Talk Lessons. This is in obvious contrast with the group in Sequence 6.12, where all the children offer opinions and give reasons to support them. They ask for each other's views and check agreement. They make relevant information explicit. They build common knowledge effectively, and their reasoning is visible – to us as well as to members of the group – in their talk. They engage critically and constructively with each other's ideas, by challenging suggestions and offering their own reasons and alternatives. So we see Gavin, in his second contribution, reasoning that Kate 'should tell' because a friend who steals is not worthy of trust. Sara later offers her own counter to this ('you shouldn't break a promise . . .'). They actively seek each other's ideas. They may not always reason well, or allow each other the conversational space that they perhaps ought, but they *are* using language as a tool for joint, rational thinking.

Encouraging exploratory talk

The quality of the discussion in Sequence 6.12 can be related to the idea of 'exploratory talk', which I defined in Chapter 4 as follows:

> *Exploratory talk* is that in which partners engage critically but constructively with each other's ideas. Relevant information is offered for joint consideration. Proposals may be challenged and counter-challenged, but if so reasons are given and alternatives are offered. Agreement is sought as a basis for joint progress. Knowledge is made publicly accountable and reasoning is visible in the talk.

This is the kind of talk which we can see Sara, Tammy and Gavin beginning to use. There is good reason for wanting children to use this kind of talk in group activities, because, as I explained in Chapter 4, it embodies a valuable kind of 'co-reasoning', with speakers following ground rules which help them to share knowledge, evaluate evidence and consider options in a reasonable and equitable way. It is an effective way of using language to think collectively, and the process of education should ensure that every child is aware of its value and able to use it effectively.[27] However, observational research evidence suggests that very little of it naturally occurs in classrooms when children work together in groups. Most of the talk observed tends to be 'disputational' or 'cumulative' and – as in Sequence 6.9 – only involving some of the children and amounting to no more than a brief and superficial consideration of the relevant topics.

When a teacher asks students to 'discuss' a topic, the teacher is usually expecting a certain quality of interaction to take place. A competitive disputation, or the passive acceptance by most members of a group of one assertive person's viewpoint, would almost certainly not be what any teacher had in mind. But one other clear finding of classroom research, including my own, is that teachers rarely make such expectations clear and explicit.[28] That is, the ground rules which are used for generating particular functional ways of using language – spoken or written – are rarely taught. In all levels of education, from primary school to university, students usually seem to be expected to work out the ground rules for themselves.

Identifying exploratory talk

Although talk which has exploratory features can be identified by a careful, detailed and fairly laborious analysis of recorded discussion, my colleague Rupert Wegerif and I have designed a convenient computer-based method which helps us locate this kind of co-reasoning activity. The origins of this lie in the fact that we noticed that children who had done the Talk Lessons seemed to use some words – 'because', 'if' and 'why' – much more often than those who had not. These are words which speakers commonly use to *account for* their opinions. This made us wonder whether the frequent occurrence of these words was associated with exploratory talk. In Chapter 3, I described the use of a computer concordancer for examining the incidence of key words in the context of continuous talk or written text. We used the same computerized method for tracking the occurrence of 'because', 'if', 'why' and 'I think' in the whole of the talk we had recorded of 'target' and 'control' groups doing problem-solving activities. A small part of the results of a concordance search for 'because' in our data is shown below, targeting the group in Sequence 6.12 doing *Kate's Choice*.

Part of the concordance search for 'because': Gavin, Sara and Tammy doing *Kate's Choice*

Kate's Choice   Full search for <because>

1 . . . he is her friend then um she shouldn't tell of him **because** em well she should tell of him.
2 . . . she should tell of him em **because** was, was, if he's stealing it it's not worth having a friend
. . .
3 . . . I think I'm I think even though he is her friend **because** he's stealing she should still tell her parents and . . .
4 . . . **Because** he's, well you shouldn't break a promise really should you . . .
5 . . . I think that he should go to the policeman first **because** he is the most important person there and um like he . . .
6 . . . No, **because** his Mum's in prison, isn't she? I mean in hospital . . .

With this computer-based text analysis we did two things. First, we looked back at the transcripts and videos to check whether the frequent occurrence of these key words was a reliable indication of the occurrence of talk of an exploratory, co-reasoning kind. We were able to confirm that this was so. Where we located a high incidence of 'because', 'if', and so on, we regularly found evidence that children were engaged in critical, constructive discussion. Next, we made a quantitative, statistical comparison of the incidence of the key words in the talk of the 'target' and 'control' groups, to see if children who had done the Talk Lessons used them more frequently. This showed us that the children who had done the Talk Lessons used these words significantly more than the children who had not. In other words, the Talk Lessons had fulfilled our aim of guiding children into an 'exploratory' way of using language to think together.[29]

Another interesting finding from our research relates to Vygotsky's theory of cognitive development, which I discussed in Chapter 1. You may recall that Vygotsky proposed that there is a close relationship between the use of language as a cultural tool (in social interaction) and the use of language as a psychological tool (for organizing our own, individual thinking). He also suggested that our involvement in joint activities may generate understanding which we then 'internalize' as individual knowledge and capabilities. Although this claim has been treated with great interest by development psychologists, surprisingly little evidence has been offered to support or refute it. We decided to try to test this hypothesis, using our 'target' and 'control' classes. We gave children in both sets of classes a psychological test called the *Raven's Progressive Matrices*, which has been commonly used as a general measure of non-verbal reasoning. The test consists of a series of analogical shape puzzles. The owners of the Raven's test would not allow me to reproduce a suitable example here, but a very similar kind of puzzle is shown in Figure 3.[30]

As an additional way of assessing any effects of the Talk Lessons on children's problem-solving skills, we gave both sets of children the Raven's test before the target children did the Talk Lessons, and then again after the series of lessons had been completed. Using two matched versions of the test, we were able to assess the children's thinking both collectively (as they did the test in groups) and individually (when they did the other version of the test alone). From doing so, we discovered two interesting things. First, by examining the recorded talk of the

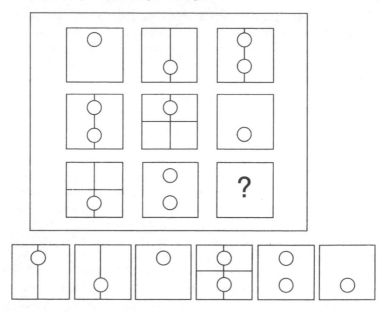

Which of these six completes the set?

Figure 3: An analogical puzzle similar to that being attempted by the
children in Sequences 6.13 and 6.14

groups, we found that groups who used more exploratory talk tended
to solve the Raven's puzzles more successfully. When we compared
the failures of groups in 'target' classes on specific problems in
the pre-lessons test with their successes on the same problems
in the post-lessons test, we could see how the 'visible reasoning' of
exploratory talk in the transcripts had enabled them to do so. Here, for
illustration, are two sequences from the talk of children in the same
group. They are doing one of the Raven's test items (D9) which poses
them basically the same problem as the puzzle in Figure 3. Sequence
6.13 was recorded before they did the series of Talk Lessons, while
Sequence 6.14 was recorded after they had done so.

Sequence 6.13: Graham, Suzie and Tess doing Raven's test item D9 (before the Talk Lessons)

Tess: It's that.
Graham: It's that, 2.
Tess: 2 is there.
Graham: It's 2.
Tess: 2 is there Graham.
Graham: It's 2.
Tess: 2 is there.
Graham: What number do you want then?
Tess: It's that because there ain't two of them.
Graham: It's number 2, look one, two.
Tess: I can count, are we all in agree on it?
(*Suzie rings number 2 – an incorrect choice – on the answer sheet*)
Suzie: No.
Graham: Oh, after she's circled it!

Sequence 6.14: Graham, Suzie and Tess doing Raven's test item D9 (after the Talk Lessons)

Suzie: D9 now, that's a bit complicated it's got to be.
Graham: A line like that, a line like that and it ain't got a line with that.
Tess: It's got to be that one.
Graham: It's going to be that don't you think? Because look all the rest have got a line like that and like that, I think it's going to be that because . . .
Tess: I think it's number 6.
Suzie: No I think it's number 1.
Graham: Wait no, we've got number 6, wait stop, do you agree that it's number 1? Because look that one there is blank, that one there has got them, that one there has to be number 1, because that is the one like that. Yes. Do you agree?
            (*Tess nods in agreement*)
Suzie: D9 number 1.
(*Suzie writes '1', which is the correct answer*)

In Sequence 6.13, the talk is not 'exploratory' but rather the type of talk which (in Chapter 4) I called 'disputational', which is associated with competitive activity and individualized decision-making. Cycles of assertion and counter-assertion, forming sequences of short utterances which rarely include explicit reasoning, are typical of disputational talk. We can see that Tess does offer a reason – a good reason – for her view, but Graham ignores it and she seems to give up in the face of his stubbornness. Suzie has taken the role of writer and she says little. At the end, having ringed the answer Graham wanted, she disagrees with it. It is not the right answer, but they all move on to the next problem anyway.

Sequence 6.14 illustrates some ways in which the talk of the same children changed after doing the programme of Talk Lessons and how this helped them to solve the problem. The children's language clearly shows characteristics of exploratory talk. Graham responds to opposition from Tess by giving an elaborated explanation of why he thinks 'number 1' is the correct choice. This clear articulation of reasons leads the group to agree on the right answer. Such explanations involve a series of linked clauses and so lead to longer utterances. All three children are now more equally involved in the discussion. Compared with their earlier attempt, language is being used more effectively by the group as a tool for thinking together about the task in which they are engaged.

These 'before-and-after' comparisons of Raven's test performances therefore confirmed that the Talk Lessons were changing the quality of children's joint reasoning. But, as we hoped, the results also provided some evidence which is relevant to Vygotsky's hypothesis about the link between intermental (social) activity and intramental (individual) development. We found that the 'target' children became significantly better at doing the Raven's test *individually*, compared with the 'control' children who had not done the Talk Lessons. That is, the 'target' children appeared to have improved their individual reasoning capabilities by taking part in the group experience of explicit, rational, collaborative problem-solving. This is despite the fact that the 'target' children had no more experience or training in doing the Raven's puzzles, together or alone, than the 'control' children. These results therefore support Vygotsky's claim.

Of course, we cannot be sure exactly what the 'target' children learned from their experience that made the difference. It may be that some gained from having new, successful problem-solving strategies explained to them by their partners, while others may have benefited from having to justify and make explicit their own reasons. But a more radical and intriguing possibility is that children may have improved their reasoning skills by 'internalizing' the ground rules of exploratory talk, so that they became able to carry on a kind of silent rational dialogue with themselves. That is, the Talk Lessons may have helped them become more able to generate the kind of rational thinking which depends on the explicit, dispassionate consideration of evidence and competing options.

The role of the teacher

The role of the teacher in the Talk Lessons is crucial for their success. To explain, I must first refer to some other research I have also been involved in for several years, in Mexican schools, with Sylvia Rojas-Drummond and her colleagues at the University of Mexico. One of the aims of this research was to help improve the quality of teaching in primary schools, and so we decided to compare teachers whose students had been found to achieve particularly good results in reading comprehension and independent problem-solving in mathematics, with teachers in similar state schools whose classes had not made such significant achievements. In Chapter 3 I described some techniques which teachers use to build shared contextual foundations with their students, such as recapping past activity, eliciting relevant knowledge from students, elaborating the replies they receive, and in various ways helping students perceive key issues and continuity in their educational experience. I suggested that teachers can use these techniques to build shared contextual foundations for their classroom activities with students, and so help the students make better sense of their educational experience. Using video recordings of classroom life, and focusing on the teachers' use of these techniques, the Mexican researchers and I tried to discover whether the better teachers and those who were less successful differed in the ways they interacted with their students. Essentially, we were trying to see whether the better teachers were providing a more effective 'scaffolding' for their students' learning, and what kinds of learning they appeared to be encouraging.[31]

Our analysis of the recordings in the Mexican schools covered several features of classroom interaction, including teachers' uses of questions. We looked at the content of tasks, activities and discussions, at the extent to which teachers encouraged students to talk together, and the kinds of explanations teachers provide to students for the tasks they set them. The results of this time-consuming and complex analysis can be summarized as follows. We found that the more effective teachers could be distinguished by the following characteristics:

1 *They used question-and-answer sequences not just to test knowledge, but also to guide the development of understanding.* These teachers often used questions to discover the initial levels of students' understanding and adjust their teaching accordingly, and used 'why' questions to encourage students to reason and reflect on what they were doing.

2 *They taught not just 'subject content', but also procedures for solving problems and making sense of experience.* This included teachers demonstrating to children the use of problem-solving strategies, explaining to children the meaning and purpose of classroom activities, and using their interactions with children as opportunities for encouraging children to make explicit their own thought processes.

3 *They treated learning as a social, communicative process.* This was represented by teachers doing such things as organizing interchanges of ideas and mutual support amongst students, encouraging students to take a more active, vocal role in classroom events, explicitly relating current activity to past experience and using students' contributions as a resource for building the 'common knowledge' of the class.

There is, of course, much more to effective teaching than the use of particular talk techniques. The better Mexican teachers and those who were less effective were all using elicitations, recaps, reformulations, and so on. The crucial difference between the two sets of teachers was how and when they used them, and what they used them to teach. They differed significantly in the extent to which they helped children to see the relevance of past experience and common knowledge, and in the opportunities they provided for children to explain their own understanding or misunderstanding.

The findings of our research are in accord with those of other researchers in various parts of the world.[32] This has encouraged my colleagues and me – and the teachers with whom we have been working closely in both the UK and Mexico – to believe that it is useful for teachers to become aware of the techniques they use in dialogue and what they are trying to achieve by using them. Teachers have found this approach useful for examining their own practice. Even very good teachers, who probably do these things without being aware that they do, seem nevertheless to appreciate gaining this meta-awareness.

This brings me back to the concept of an 'intermental development zone' (IDZ) that I discussed earlier in this chapter. If we combine it with ideas about community-based ways of using language that I discussed in Chapter 5, we can redefine the role of teacher. Think of a teacher not simply as the instructor or facilitator of the learning of a large and disparate set of individuals, but rather as the potential creator of a 'community of enquiry' in a classroom, in which individual students can take a shared, active and reflective role in the development of their own understanding.[33] The students are apprentices in collective thinking, under the expert guidance of their teacher. The quality of their educational experience, and to some extent at least their commitment to their own education, will be affected by the extent to which what they are doing in class has continuity, a comprehensible purpose and scope for their own active participation. The teacher has to use classroom activities to develop IDZs with students, and among students, to fulfil these conditions.

The success of the Talk Lessons programme depends on teachers creating communities of enquiry in their classrooms and using class-room activities to create IDZs. Group activities like *Kate's Choice* offer children good opportunities to practise and evaluate ways of thinking together away from the teacher's authoritative presence. But as the comparisons of 'control' and 'target' classes show, children need first to be guided in how to talk and work together. In the Talk Lessons, teachers organize and lead activities, provide children with information and guidance and help them to recognize and reflect on what they have learned. They talk explicitly with children about the goals of classroom activities. In the early stages of the Talk Lessons, teachers also talk with children about what counts as good, productive discussion and agree on some very clear ground rules for making it happen. These rules are then put up on the classroom wall, as a constant source of reference. The rules generated by two of our project classes looked like these:

OUR GROUND RULES FOR TALK
We have agreed to:
Share ideas

Give reasons
Question ideas
Consider
Agree
Involve everybody
Everybody accepts responsibility

OUR TALKING RULES
*We share our ideas and listen to each other
*We talk one at a time
*We respect each other's opinions
*We give reasons to explain our ideas
*If we disagree we ask 'why'?
*We try to agree in the end

During the programme of Talk Lessons, each teacher is expected to demonstrate 'exploratory' ways of talking for the children in whole-class sessions – for example, asking 'Why?' at appropriate times, giving examples of reasons for opinions, and checking that a range of views is heard. Each Talk Lesson consists of a careful balance of teacher-led, whole-class sessions and 'talk groups' in which children work and talk together, without constant supervision, on problem-solving activities which can only be completed successfully through talk and co-operation. Also, in 'debriefing' discussions at the ends of lessons, teachers review with the whole class what has been done, and what they might have learned from it. The organized continuity of this IDZ experience helps children to consolidate learning, gain educational benefit from their activity – and hopefully see that following the ground rules for exploratory talk does get good results.

Once the ground rules for exploratory talk have been established in a class, they are there as common knowledge which can be invoked by the teacher or children. Sequence 6.15 is an example of a teacher reviewing the ground rules for exploratory talk with a group of children (aged 10–11 years) just before they go off to do an activity together (without the teacher). The activity is one from the Talk Lessons, called *Dogs' Home*, in which children have to talk and decide together how best to match each of a motley set of stray dogs with an appropriate family of owners.

Sequence 6.15: Revisiting the ground rules

Teacher: OK. Right, now – the idea of this lesson isn't just to match the dogs with the owners – that's one of the main things. But the other main thing is to think really carefully about how you do it, and how you talk to each other while you are doing it. If you think back to the talking lessons you've had so far, you've got to try and remember what were the good ways of talking to each other, and the useful ways that helped you find out what other people were thinking. Right, now, can you think of any useful ways of finding out what somebody else is thinking?

Thomas: Ask questions?

Teacher: Ask questions. Well, that's what I've just done to you now. I've asked questions, to find out what you think about it. So you could ask each other questions, couldn't you? I'm going to ask you to ask a very definite question – I'm going to give you cards to remind you every single time to ask this question. What do <u>you</u> think? Not a difficult question, it's just that you might forget to ask it. And when somebody's answered the question, you say to them: <u>Why</u> do you think that? So what have they got to give to you then?

Anna: An answer.

Teacher: An answer. And what will the answer tell you then? Tell you the reason they think it. So – what do you think, and why do you think that? So, say there's three of you in this talking group, right? And one of you will ask the other two people that question, OK? What do you think and why do you think it. There's lots of other questions you can ask as well, aren't there? Now if somebody's telling you what they think, what will you have to do, what will you have to do, to make sure you understand what they are thinking?

Thomas: What do you mean by that?

Teacher: Yes, ask them another question. If you are not sure, get them to talk about it a little, and then they can probably tell you, can't they? You'll have to listen carefully, won't you? Were there any other rules that we thought were useful? I can't remember any? Give reasons, discuss it, make sure everybody in the group gets a go – not just you because you've got the loudest voice and think your opinion is the most important! Everybody gets a go.

Darien: Don't leave anybody out!

Teacher: Don't leave anybody out. Right, so – if you want to, if you find it easier you could cut these up once you've read them. Read it through first, then you can cut it into strips – cut out the dogs and match each one with a family. If you find it easier you could do that. You've got to read it through together first, so that you've all understood what the families are like. OK? Before we start then, why are you doing this lesson, what's the reason for it, what are you trying to end up with doing? Somebody else – Gary? What do you think? You're half asleep as usual – in your dozy morning state.

Gary: To try to find out what other people's opinions are.

Teacher: Exactly! I wish I'd said that! To find out what other people's opinions are. And how will you do it?

Gary: By asking questions?

Teacher: By asking questions, talking to them. So that's all we need to know, isn't it – it's the talk that's important.

In the first part of this sequence we can see the teacher attempting to give continuity to her students' educational experience by *exhorting* them to recall their past shared activities as a preliminary to beginning new ones:

> If you think back to the talking lessons you've had so far, you've got to try and remember what were the good ways of talking to each other, and the useful ways that helped you find out what other people were thinking.

By drawing their attention back to this past shared experience, the teacher tries to ensure that the children will enter the talk activity with an appropriate frame of reference – the ground rules. She also *elicits* bits of educationally relevant past experience or knowledge from individual students. She then *elaborates* and *reformulates* what the child has said for the benefit of the rest of the class. She is not an unusual teacher in using these techniques. As I explained in Chapter 3, they are the common linguistic tools of a teacher's trade. This teacher is unusual, however, because she is using these techniques to guide children, expressly and explicitly, into effective ways of using language to think together.

At the time I am writing, the Talk Lessons project is continuing. Interest in our findings has been shown by those involved in the policy and practice of the teaching of science, mathematics and citizenship. Teachers involved have said that they can see the influence of children's learning of the ground rules on their work across the curriculum, and even in their playtime activity. From the data we have gathered so far, it seems that the Talk Lessons have most effect in schools which serve populations of low average income, in which levels of educational attainment are low. At the turn of the millennium, the lead school in our project was specially congratulated by the Secretary of State for Education on its improved educational standards (as measured by the performance of our 'target' children on national tests). The project has grown into a full-scale programme in primary schools of one education authority in England, aimed at raising standards of achievement across the curriculum, with other pilot schemes beginning elsewhere in the UK and in Mexico. Of all the areas of everyday life in which the implementations of the study of language and collective thinking might have a practical impact, education is, I believe, the one which offers the most tangible and long-term benefits.

Summary

I have concentrated in this chapter on the ways in which language use is involved in the development of children's understanding, and their induction into ways of using language for collective thinking. In the early part, I explained how an influential group of psychologists have redefined cognitive development as a dialogue, rather than a process of individual discovery and growth. From this 'socio-cultural' perpective, the guidance of children into ways of thinking collectively is a vital aspect of human development, and one in which language is necessarily closely involved. I illustrated how this kind of guidance happens in casual, incidental ways, as adults and children go about their joint activities, and in more structured kinds of teaching-and-learning. I suggested that the concept of an 'intermental development zone' (IDZ) is useful for explaining how dialogue supports the process of teaching-and-learning.

Young people learn a great deal about how to think collectively from interacting with each other. As the younger generation, there are lessons that they can only learn amongst themselves, away from the guiding or constraining influence of their elders. They may be more or less receptive to the guidance adults offer on any particular occasion, but nevertheless they will actively participate in many informal dialogues with adults which contribute to the development of their own understanding and skills in communication. In such dialogues, knowledge of generations is shared and children acquire some valuable tools for creating knowledge together.

I also suggested, however, that out-of-school everyday life does not provide many children with adequate experience or guidance in the use of language as a tool for collective thinking. It is not to their benefit, or to that of society in general, that they should be expected to discover or infer this kind of important cultural knowledge for themselves, or to live their social lives without it. Such experience and guidance can, and should, be provided by schools. The Talk Lessons programme illustrates how these ideas can be put into practice.[34]

7 Conclusions

One of my main aims in this book has been to encourage readers to see the relationship between language and thought from a new perspective. In this chapter, I will begin by summarizing the implications of adopting this 'intermental' perspective for our understanding of language, thinking and the relationships between individuals and communities. I will then briefly discuss the methods needed for future research into interthinking. Finally, I will describe some of the practical implications of this kind of research for our everyday lives.

For anyone with a serious interest in interthinking, the good news is that the work of psychologists, linguists, sociologists and others has provided some valuable concepts, interesting findings and useful research methods. The bad news is that because this research is spread across several different disciplines, it lacks coherence. Different groups of researchers have their own discourses and research agendas, with not much dialogue taking place between them. Members of each discipline speak mainly to each other, in ways that draw heavily on the common knowledge of their disciplines (as a reader of this book might expect), so even the same words ('language', 'discourse' and 'context', for example) can mean different things in different research communities. My guess is that most of the researchers whose work I have drawn on throughout the book would not even recognize the study of collective thinking as one of their concerns.

The experience of trying to draw these disparate ideas and world-views together has confirmed my view that we need a fresh perspective on language and thought, one that is not commonly employed in psychology, linguistics or any other apparently relevant field of research. From this 'intermental' perspective, we can recognize language as a system designed to support the essentially collective nature of human thinking.

Our interthinking ancestors

I began this book with some ideas about the role of language in human prehistory. I would like you to consider this topic again now, having read the earlier chapters, because it is very relevant to understanding some of the implications of adopting this new perspective. I suggested that, with the emergence of language, members of our species did not simply become able to share information and co-ordinate individual activity. Rather, they gained a completely new way of using their minds in combination for solving problems, transforming individual experience into shared knowledge and making shared knowledge available to individuals. Language enabled our ancestors to become able to do something which, so far as we are aware, no other life-form has ever been capable: to represent experience in a shared communicative space, where they could jointly consider it, take it apart, reconstruct it as a simplified model, and plan ways of dealing with it. One of language's design features that suits it well for this purpose is that it is a flexible, 'open' system – its symbols, words and structures have no fixed associations of meaning and can be recombined infinitely – so new meanings can be negotiated and new elements introduced as emerging circumstances demand. The design of language embodies one of our species' greatest natural assets for survival: an improvisational adaptability to changing environmental circumstances.

The Darwinian slogan 'the survival of the fittest' is often mistakenly associated with the image of two creatures battling for food or territory, with one winning out in the end. Evolution is not about individual survival, but the continuation of families and communities of related individuals over generations. Language enables individuals with diverse talents, dispositions and experiences to collaborate in sophisticated ways when solving problems. It transforms a group of diverse individuals into complementary contributors to a collective mind. If we recognize ourselves as a species designed for collaborative, language-based thinking, this helps explain some of our psychological characteristics which, from the more usual individualistic perspective of cognitive psychology, are enigmatic. For example, it is puzzling that we seem to be very effective at storing information in memory, but notoriously unreliable at accessing it. The tip-of-the-tongue problem – where you are sure you know a word, or a fact, but cannot immediately recall it – is a common experience and one that has intrigued psychologists for years.[1] People who suffer the trauma of brain injury through illness, accident or medical intervention sometimes find that 'lost' memories of long-gone events may be recovered in some detail, running like radio programmes, unbidden and in great detail through their minds.[2] Such memories may include, for example, snatches of conversation, tunes and the words for songs, which on being set down are found to be based in real experience much earlier in their lives, but which the person involved did not ever remember learning. Why should humans waste cognitive space storing information that they have not self-consciously learned, or that cannot readily be accessed? One possible explanation is that, given our normal, collective and communicative lifestyle as a species, we do not have to rely on individual attempts to recall information: we can do it together.[3] We can stimulate each other's recall through offering ideas of our own and commenting on suggestions that are made. 'Tip-of-the-tongue' frustrations can often be resolved with conversational assistance. Under evolutionary conditions, creatures who were good at storing information in memory and could use joint communicative effort to recall it and make sense of it might well have had the advantage over individuals with similar storage capacity but who had to rely on individual recall.

Thinking communities

The term 'community' is suitable for describing a social unit – larger and looser than a family, smaller and more cohesive than a society – whose activities are based on foundations of past shared experience, common interests and language-based ways of thinking together (as in 'communities of practice' and 'communities of discourse'). The continued life of communities depends on each new generation benefiting from the experience of previous ones, and on people with special knowledge and expertise teaching it to others. Language is the prime tool of teaching-and-learning. Education happens in conversations where the combined mental resources of teacher and learner are focused on developing the learner's understanding. The socio-cultural concept of 'scaffolding' is a useful metaphor for the intellectual involvement of a teacher with a learner's efforts during joint activity.[4] But while socio-cultural psychologists have described the 'shared thinking' of adults and children as they engage in dialogue and joint activity, they usually have done so in order to determine its influence on individual children's development.[5] That is, they have studied 'intermental' activity in order to understand the 'intramental', while I am suggesting that we should also try to explain children's development as *interthinkers*. To do so, we need to understand how experienced members of communities act as *discourse guides*, guiding children (or other novices) into ways of using language for thinking collectively. The socio-cultural concepts of 'guided participation' and 'legitimate peripheral participation' are useful too for describing this process.

Communally, we forge language into specialized tools for getting particular jobs done. The linguists' concept of 'genre' is valuable for understanding how communal activities produce and require particular varieties of language.[6] Job interviews, church services, chat shows, sales encounters, cookery recipes and pub conversations have characteristic language forms and structures because they are different kinds of social activities. This is well accepted in linguistics. But from an intermental perspective, we can see that language genres are also related to conventional, collective ways of thinking in particular communities and societies. People unfamiliar with a community's ways with words are likely to be excluded from its activities. Those familiar with its genres know how to use language to participate, how to work with others to get things done. Expert members of communities can use language features to recognize when a particular kind of activity is taking place, and this enables them easily to draw on past experience relevant to the joint intellectual activity they become engaged in. Genres are templates for interthinking, which, like all social conventions, both facilitate and constrain what we do.[7]

We all rely on habitual ways of making sense of life. Language genres enable us to cope with the experiential data that life throws at us, to put it in some kind of order and to gain the help of others in dealing with it. Even apparently 'recreational' genres may have an important interthinking function. As the linguist Guy Cook has suggested, fictional literature enables a reader to participate vicariously in the continuous thought processes of the writer.[8] Authors of novels do not usually offer practical information, or make specific proposals for dealing with life's problems. Instead, they offer readers a persuasive, historically contextualized, cohesive account of human life unfolding. In stories, the natural complexity and inscrutability of life is reduced: events can be linked in causal chains, characters can be seen to reap the consequences of their choices. Through reading fiction (or experiencing it through stage or screen productions) we can not only experience life vicariously, we can also play with new ways of making sense of it. We may, with varying degrees of seriousness, treat fictional narratives as analogies for explaining our own lives. It is also worth noting that a common consequence of the popularity of a work of fiction is that people who have read it, talk about it. In Latin American countries *telenovellas* (television 'soaps') have been successfully used to stimulate popular debate about political matters. The popular BBC radio series 'The Archers' was apparently introduced to promote the consideration of agricultural issues amongst the British farming community; its aficionados, now found as much in towns as in the British countryside, often discuss its plots together today. When fiction becomes canonical literature, as have the works of Shakespeare in the English-speaking world, whole sections of libraries and university courses are set up to give its collective consideration a legitimate community base.

Interthinking in context

As I explained in Chapter 2, linguists commonly use the concept of 'context' to describe the physical and social features of a situation in which language is used. This rather static notion of context does not capture the dynamic, interactive way in which people create frameworks for joint understanding in conversation, yet 'context' still seems to me the most appropriate term for describing what they create. As listeners, we continually try to relate what we hear to what else is going on and to any relevant past experience. For joint understanding to be achieved, speakers have to help listeners with this difficult task. That is, contextualizing has to be done co-operatively. In successful communication, 'context' is not located in the mind of either speaker or listener, and neither does it exist in the world around them; it is negotiated and maintained by mutual effort. In Chapter 6 I introduced the idea of an 'intermental development zone' (IDZ) to explain the way a teacher and learner can both contribute to the learning process by setting up and maintaining a shared, contextual frame of reference.

Intermental development zones are vehicles of contextual knowledge which teachers use to steer learners through joint activity towards new understanding.

An intermental perspective can explain some other interesting design features of language. Words carry with them the history of their use, but they also gather new meanings in new contexts. This means that the same collection of words can never be guaranteed the same interpretation by different listeners. If we think of language as a system for accurately transmitting ideas and information between speakers, this may seem to be a problem. But if we consider language as a medium designed for collective thinking, this feature, the 'necessary indeterminacy' of language as the linguist David Bloome calls it, is a strength rather than a weakness.[9] Human communication partners need not just take what the other gives and then go and carry out individual activities, as do the honey-bees; they can use information which has been shared as an intellectual resource, working on it to make better sense than they might alone. By bringing different contextualizing resources to the task of making sense of experience, individuals can add to the richness of the collective intellect. Common knowledge and understanding is the product of their interaction.

A persuasive argument

I have suggested that communication is necessarily co-operative, yet much of our communication is concerned with argument, persuasion and the exercise of control. An intermental perspective helps to reconcile these aspects of communicative life. We talk and write to influence what other people think and do, to pursue our interests and to make the things happen that we wish to happen. But to be persuasive, we must lead our listeners down discourse paths which lead to the conclusions we want them to draw. It will not help if they lack contextual information which supports our case, or if our ideas are expressed in an inappropriate incomprehensible discourse, and so we try to choose our words accordingly and 'scaffold' our listeners' interpretation of them. We recycle the words of authoritative voices and use other rhetorical techniques on the assumption that they will activate listeners' own relevant past experience.

To be persuasive, we must offer listeners ways of interpreting experience to 'change their minds'. As I mentioned in Chapter 4, cognitive scientists have argued that metaphor is a vital feature of human thinking.[10] I see no reason to disagree with this claim. But for those researchers, metaphor-making is treated only as an *intra-mental* activity – a creative way in which individuals make sense of experience. From an intermental perspective, however, metaphors can be recognized as rhetorical techniques in the communal language tool-kit, which can be selected to suit particular occasions and aims, and which refer to relevant shared experience amongst speakers.[11] They may be culture-specific: what would be the use of employing the metaphorical image of 'scaffolding' amongst a people who did not construct buildings? Attractive new metaphors are those which persuade us to see new likenesses in the complex data of experience. They can be used to give common knowledge a culturally robust, memorable form. Participants in conversations may take them up and develop them further as ways of modelling reality. Metaphors persist or fade, depending on their perceived value, as resources in the collective thinking of communities.

Using language, we can link our intellects together in a variety of ways. We may build the uncritical, non-competitive and constructive relationship of 'cumulative talk', in which individual differences of perception or judgement are minimized. We may treat our talk partners as a threat to the pursuit of our individual interests, in 'disputational talk', in which the participants work to keep their identities separate, and to protect their individuality. Or we may engage in a dialogue in which differences are treated explicitly, as matters for mutual exploration, reasoned evaluation and resolution, which I called 'exploratory talk'. Exploratory talk, with its explicit reasons, criticisms and evaluations, is a model of dialogue in which participants are not primarily concerned with protecting their separate identities and interests, but instead with ways of jointly and rationally making sense. The notion of exploratory talk captures an ideal – of a discussion in which all participants are striving, in a committed but unselfish manner, to establish the best solution. Each participant can make a creative contribution to the sense-making and the most useful interpretation may be arrived at eventually through a discussion of the various individual interpretations offered.[12] Of course, these models of talk are simplifications of complex reality which will need to be refined, or even replaced, as we learn more about the nature of interthinking.

Ways of researching interthinking

When studying interthinking, we are in the odd, but interesting, position of having to use the process we are trying to understand in order to understand it. That is, as in the scientific study of any complex phenomenon, researchers have to gather observations of it, find ways of describing it in words (using metaphors, narratives and other modelling tools) and then, by a process of rational debate, agree upon the best explanation of what they have found. What is more, researchers have to use their own knowledge as language users and interthinkers to interpret the data they gather. So what methods do we have at our disposal? Earlier chapters have shown how several well-established types of research – conversation analysis, ethnography, computer-based text analysis, experimental action research and so on – have already provided valuable insights into how we use language to think together. Different methods can make their own distinctive contribution to understanding, and in cross-disciplinary research there is no reason why researchers should not combine them.[13] But we do need to use methods which do justice to conversation as an interactive, continuing process of making meaning. Thinking together with language is a problematic process, and the constructing of common knowledge involves regular monitoring and repair by those involved. Through recording and analysing language as it is used in the accomplishment of everyday activities, we can begin to understand how people give continuity to their shared understanding, and to explain how and why they succeed or fail. My favourite metaphorical image for this kind of analysis is watching a school of dolphins from a moving ship (not least because this has the advantage of associating a very laborious, desk-bound process with a much more relaxed and leisurely one). If we notice that a particular dolphin has a white mark or other distinctive feature, each time an animal with that feature appears we assume it is the same one, travelling between sightings under the surface of the sea. In this way, the occasional sightings of individual animals can tell us about the continuous, co-ordinated activities of the school as a whole. For discourse analysts, key words, language patterns and topics appear and reappear in continuous stretches of language like surfacing dolphins. Some conversational dolphins may regularly appear together, suggesting that their relationship is significant. Others, even some apparently prominent members of the school, seem to get lost along the way. Analysts can use these observations to build models of the process of interthinking, and so begin to explain how people develop shared, coherent lines of thought and follow them through to achieve practical outcomes – or, just as importantly, how they fail to do so.

It is, of course, difficult to show how people develop common knowledge using short samples of talk, because the 'long conversations' between people in a community, carried on over hours, days or even longer, illustrate it best. But these are difficult to record and analyse. One profound problem for analysts is that, as communicative relationships develop, participants take progressively more common knowledge for granted amongst themselves. Though their talk becomes no less clear to them, it becomes less explicit to an analyst who, arriving at some point in their 'long conversation', lacks the contextualizing knowledge of their shared history. There has been no research tracking the conversations of particular sets of people over fairly long periods of time. Perhaps this is what is most needed now.[14]

Processes and outcomes

Another goal for future research should be to relate the processes of communication to the outcomes of joint activity. That is, it would be useful to know if certain ways of communicating are particularly effective for the successful solving of problems or completion of tasks. A little has been done on this, as I described in Chapter 6, and its results are very encouraging; but most researchers of spoken language, such as sociolinguists, discursive psychologists and conversation analysts, do not seem to share my interest in evaluating communication or assessing its outcomes. On the other hand, people with a practical interest in the effectiveness of communication in business, counselling, law and other important areas of everyday activity have shown surprisingly little interest in the careful analysis of talk. Yet by combining practical concerns with careful analysis, applied research on collective thinking might transform the quality of education and working life.

'Talking' is often unfavourably compared with 'doing', but language enables people to combine their intellects to get things done. Our survival today depends no less on the effective combination of minds than was the case for our prehistoric ancestors. Yet most people are relatively unaware of how the process of thinking collectively is achieved. They have no idea whether they do it well or badly, and even less how they might improve on the ways they build knowledge and understanding with others. They may be unaware of how other people exercise control over collective endeavours, and may feel powerless in making their own ideas carry influence. Crucial conversations happen every day, in which people strive to find solutions, argue cases, build relationships and teach-and-learn, but they frequently do not succeed in their efforts. As a result, misunderstandings persist, good reasons go unheard, and useful lessons are not learned. A better understanding of interthinking could help us to overcome some of these enduring human problems. As individuals as well as community members, it is in our enlightened self-interest to do so.

Notes

1 Language as a Tool for Thinking

1 S. Pinker, *The Language Instinct*, London, Penguin, 1994, p. 15. See also S. Pinker, 'Facts about human language relevant to its evolution', in J-P. Changeux and S. Chavailon (eds) *Origins of the Human Brain*, Oxford, Clarendon Press, 1995, pp. 263–83. Some other recent, rather different, but also nevertheless individualistic approaches to language and thinking are presented in A. Gopnik and A.N. Meltzoff, *Words, Thoughts and Theories*, London, MIT Press, 1997; and P. Carruthers and J. Boucher (eds) *Language and Thought: Interdisciplinary Themes*, Cambridge, Cambridge University Press, 1998. The latter book begins with the editors setting out a 'clean dichotomy' between a 'communicative conception of language' and a 'cognitive conception', which are treated as if they are difficult to reconcile.

2 Guy Browning, in the regular column 'Office Politics', *The Guardian*, 6 March 1999.

3 See, for example, J. Fodor, *The Modularity of Mind*, London, MIT Press, 1983. Pinker (see n. 1) also takes this point of view.

4 From an interview with Studs Terkel by Huw Richards in *The Times Higher Educational Supplement*, 26 June 1998, p. 18.

5 L.S. Vygotsky, *Thought and Language*, Cambridge, MA, MIT Press, 1962. [The title of the original 1934 Russian publication, *Myshlenie i rech'*, translates more accurately as 'Thinking and Speech'.]

6 Vygotsky's contribution to psychology is discussed in detail in J.V. Wertsch (ed.) *Culture, Communication and Cognition: Vygotskian Perspectives*, Cambridge, Cambridge University Press, 1985.

7 L.S. Vygotsky, *Mind in Society*, Cambridge, MA, Harvard University Press, 1978, p. 26. This book was constructed from a collection of Vygotsky's essays by the American psychologist Michael Cole and his colleagues.

8 See, for example, J. Bruner, *Acts of Meaning*, Cambridge, MA, Harvard University Press, 1990; and B. Rogoff, *Apprenticeship in Thinking: Cognitive Development in Social Context*, New York, Oxford University Press, 1990.

9 M.A.K. Halliday, 'Towards a language-based theory of learning', *Linguistics and Education*, 1993, vol. 5, no. 2, pp. 93–116.

10 J. Austin, *How to do Things with Words*, Oxford, Oxford University Press, 1962.

11 *The Oxford Dictionary of Quotations*, 1979 edition, London, Book Club Associates, p. 269. This often-quoted version is based on the report of a listener in the audience at the Oxford debate, as no official transcription of Huxley's speech was made.

12 G. Wells, 'Using the tool-kit of discourse in the activity of learning and teaching', *Mind, Culture and Activity*, 1996, vol. 3, no. 2, pp. 74–101.

13 This approach to learning about tools was pioneered by Vygotsky's student A.N. Leont'ev (for example, A.N. Leont'ev, *Problems of the Development of Mind*, Moscow, Progress Publishers, 1981). For interesting and more recent discussions of the cognitive implications of the use of tools and other artefacts, see G. Salomon (ed.) *Distributed Cognitions: Psychological and Educational Considerations*, Cambridge, Cambridge University Press, 1993.

2   Laying the Foundations

1 David Crystal's *Dictionary of Linguistics and Phonetics* (Oxford, Blackwell, 1985, p. 71) explains that 'context' is sometimes used by linguists to refer to nothing more than the parts of a spoken utterance or written text which are near to a word on which they are focusing. But the term 'context of situation' is also used by linguists to refer to 'the whole set of external features *considered relevant* to the linguistic analysis of an utterance' (Crystal, 1985, p. 72). The way psychologists use the notion of 'context' also varies considerably. For example, it is interesting to compare the range of uses and definitions within two books with very similar titles: P. Light and G. Butterworth (eds) *Context and Cognition*, Hemel Hempstead, Harvester-Wheatsheaf, 1992; and A.C. Qhelhas and F. Pereira, *Cognition and Context*, special issue of *Análise Psicológica*, Lisbon, ISPA, 1998.

2 M.A.K. Halliday and R. Hasan, *Language, Context, and Text: Aspects of Language in a Social-Semiotic Perspective*, London, Oxford University Press, 1989. Within the Hallidayan tradition of systemic functional linguistics, 'context' is tied to situations in which language texts are generated. For a short, clear explanation of this approach, see J. Martin, 'Genre and literacy – modeling context in educational linguistics', *Annual Review of Applied Linguistics*, 1993, vol. 13, pp. 141–72.

3 Adapted from P. Medway, 'Constructing the virtual building: language on a building site', in J. Maybin and N. Mercer (eds) *Using English: From Conversation to Canon*, London, Routledge with the Open University, 1996, p. 109.

4 Cited in S. Romaine, 'Pidgin English advertising', in C. Ricks and L. Michaels (eds) *The State of the Language*, London, Faber and Faber, 1990, p. 197.

5 Most *Tok Pisin* words are derived from English words. For example, 'eplikeson' is really a variant of 'application', 'skul' of 'school', 'ekseptim' is derived from 'accept him' and 'long' from 'belong'. Using this knowledge, you may guess that 'skul long fama' can be roughly translated as 'school belong(ing to) farmers' – that is, an agricultural training institution. Suzanne Romaine offers the following complete translation into standard English of what the student says: 'I sent my application to the school board and then they considered and accepted me and I'm going to agricultural school.'

6 The educational researchers Edwards and Furlong were perhaps the first to express clearly this important idea of the reciprocal relationship between language and context: 'It is not a matter of the context determining what is said, because the process is reciprocal. [Speakers] create through talk the very context on which they rely to support that talk'. (A.D. Edwards and V.F. Furlong, *The Language of Teaching*, London, Heinemann, 1978, p. 57.) In recent years, conversation analysts seem to be the researchers most aware of this. See, for example, P. Drew and J. Heritage (eds) *Talk at Work: Interaction in Institutional Settings*, Cambridge, Cambridge University Press, 1992.

7 'Map' is one of several activities devised in the early 1980s by the National Foundation for Educational Research for the purpose of assessing the oral communication skills of British children. The sequences transcribed here were recorded by The Open University and can be heard on the audiocassette for *Talk and Learning 5–16: An Inservice Pack on Oracy for Teachers*, Milton Keynes, The Open University, 1991.

8 For other examples of the use of ground rules in analysing language use, see D. Edwards and N. Mercer, *Common Knowledge*, London, Methuen/Routledge, 1987; Y. Sheeran and D. Barnes, *School Writing: Discovering the Ground Rules*, Milton Keynes, Open University Press, 1991; and N. Mercer, *The Guided Construction of Knowledge: Talk Amongst Teachers and Learners*, Clevedon, Multilingual Matters, 1995.

9 This research is reported in N. Mercer and J. Longman, 'Accounts and the development of shared understanding in Employment Training Interviews', *Text*, 1992, vol. 12, no. 1, pp. 103–25; and in J. Longman, 'Professionals and clients: form filling and the control of talk', in Maybin and Mercer (eds) *Using English*, pp. 116–21.

10 J. Coates, 'No gap, lots of overlap', in D. Graddol, J. Maybin and B. Stierer (eds) *Researching Language and Literacy in Social Context*, Clevedon, Multilingual Matters, 1994, p. 181.

11 This sequence was recorded during the *Spoken Language and New Technology (SLANT)* project, which was a joint venture of the University of East Anglia and The Open University, funded by the Economic and Social Research Council. It involved schools in Buckinghamshire, Cambridgeshire, Northamptonshire and Norfolk, and is reported in R. Wegerif and P. Scrimshaw (eds) *Computers and Talk in the Primary Classroom*, Clevedon, Multilingual Matters, 1997.

12 R. Shuy, *Language Crimes: The Use and Abuse of Language Evidence in the Courtroom*, London, Blackwell, 1993, p. 24.

13 Shuy, *Language Crimes*, p. 24.

14 Shuy, *Language Crimes*, p. 32.

15 H. Marriott, 'Deviations in an intercultural business negotiation', in A. Firth (ed.) *The Discourse of Negotiation: Studies of Language in the Workplace*, London, Pergamon, 1995, pp. 260–1.

16 Marriott, p. 263.

17 Marriott, p. 262.

18 D. Tannen, *Conversational Style: Analysing Talk Amongst Friends*, Norwood, NJ, Ablex, 1984. For a general discussion of conversational styles, see also J. Maybin, 'Everyday talk', in Maybin and Mercer (eds) *Using English*.

19 H. Garfinkel, 'A conception of, and experiments with, "trust" as a condition of stable concerted actions', in O.J. Harvey (ed.) *Motivation and Social Interaction*, New York, Ronald Press, 1963.

20 This research is reported in M. Cole, J. Gay, J. Glick and D. Sharpe, *The Cultural Context of Learning and Thinking*, New York, Basic Books, 1971. This sequence is given as cited by Ulric Neisser in L.B. Resnick (ed.) *The Nature of Intelligence*, New York, Lawrence Erlbaum, 1976, pp. 135–6.

21 The talk of job-counselling interviews, and the problems of understanding that arise in them, are described in Mercer and Longman, 'Accounts'. Problems which arise in interrogations of suspects by police are discussed in G. Gudjonsson, *The Psychology of Interrogations, Confessions and Testimony*, Chichester, John Wiley and Sons, 1992. Research on medical consultations and other kinds of client–professional talk is described in Drew and Heritage, *Talk at Work*.

22 D. Eades, 'Communicative strategies in Aboriginal English', in Maybin and Mercer (eds) *Using English*.

23 I. Malcolm, 'Speech events in the Aboriginal classroom', *International Journal of the Sociology of Language*, 1982, no. 36, pp. 115–34. For more on these kinds of cross-cultural language issues in education, see N. Mercer and J. Swann (eds) *Learning English: Development and Diversity*, London, Routledge with The Open University, 1996.

3 The Given and the New

1 For this idea of the 'long conversation' I am grateful to Janet Maybin. See J. Maybin, 'Children's voices: talk, knowledge and identity', in D. Graddol, J. Maybin and B. Stierer (eds) *Researching Language and Literacy in Social Context*, Clevedon, Multilingual Matters, 1994.

2 The conversational 'maxims' stated by Grice include the maxim of relevance ('be relevant') and the maxim of quantity ('Make your contribution as informative as required', and 'do not make your contribution more informative than is required'). See, for example, H.P. Grice, 'Logic and conversation', in P. Cole and J. Morgan (eds) *Syntax and Semantics*, vol. 3: *Speech Acts*, New York, Academic Press, 1975.

3 E. Stokoe, *Exploring Gender and Discourse in Higher Education*, Doctoral Thesis, University of Leicester, 1996, pp. 253–4.
4 D. Middleton and D. Edwards, 'Conversational remembering: a social psychological approach', in D. Middleton and D. Edwards (eds) *Collective Remembering*, London, Sage, 1990, p. 25.
5 Most psychological research on memory, perception and learning has been done in laboratories – places in which experimenters strive to eliminate the influence of everyday experience – or in clinical settings, where inevitably the focus has been on abnormal, pathological thinking and behaviour. This means that normal thinking and communicating has been excluded from most research on human cognition, with much of the content of cognitive psychology being based on the study of people doing things outside the contexts of everyday social life. This 'decontextualized' tradition of research unfortunately continues, with researchers within the immensely influential field of 'cognitive science' (which uses computers as a basis for modelling the human mind) quite deliberately ignoring cultural, social and emotional influences on thinking because to include them would, as Howard Gardner has aptly put it, 'unnecessarily complicate the cognitive-scientific enterprise': H. Gardner, *The Mind's New Science*, New York, Basic Books, 1985, p. 6.
6 This sequence was video-recorded by the BBC for the Open University course *U210 The English Language: Past, Present and Future*, Milton Keynes, The Open University, 1996.
7 These functions of classroom language are dealt with in more detail in N. Mercer, *The Guided Construction of Knowledge: Talk Amongst Teachers and Learners*, Clevedon, Multilingual Matters, 1995.
8 The structuring of most classroom talk into three part units – Initiation, Response, and Feedback – was first clearly revealed by the classic research of the linguists Sinclair and Coulthard. (J. Sinclair and M. Coulthard, *Towards an Analysis of Discourse: The English Used by Teachers and Pupils*, London, Oxford University Press, 1975.)
9 For examples of conversation analysis research, see D. Boden and D. Zimmerman (eds) *Talk and Social Structure: Studies in Ethnomethodology and Conversation Analysis*, Cambridge, Polity Press, 1991; P. Drew and J. Heritage (eds) *Talk at Work: Interaction in Institutional Settings*, Cambridge, Cambridge University Press, 1992. The short list of transcription symbols I provide here is only a subset of those normally used by conversation analysts. See Drew and Heritage for a more complete list. (*Note also that a full set of the transcription symbols I have used in the book is included in the Preface.*)
10 This sequence, recorded in the UK, comes from a research project on occupational counselling interviews, described in N. Mercer and J. Longman, 'Accounts and the development of shared understanding in Employment Training Interviews', *Text*, 1992, vol. 12, no. 1, pp. 103–25.
11 This example comes from one of the most influential linguistic works on cohesion: M.A.K. Halliday and R. Hasan, *Cohesion in English*, London, Longman, 1976, p. 17.

12 F. Scott Fitzgerald, *The Great Gatsby*, Harmondsworth, Penguin Books, 1973, p. 103. (First published in 1926.)

13 Adapted from Stokoe, *Exploring Gender and Discourse*, p. 186.

14 P. Gibbons, *Discourse Contexts for Second Language Development in the Mainstream Classroom*, Doctoral Thesis, University of Technology, Sydney, Australia, 1995. I have slightly adapted her transcription of the talk and the analysis to relate it to the style and content of this book.

15 Bakhtin actually wrote: 'the word does not exist in a neutral or impersonal language (it is not, after all, out of a dictionary that the speaker gets their words!), but rather exists in other people's mouths' (M. Bakhtin, *The Dialogic Imagination*, Austin, TX, University of Texas Press, 1981). Many researchers now believe that Bakhtin was also the author of work published under the name of Volosinov – for example: V. Volosinov, *Marxism and the Philosophy of Language*, New York, Seminar Press, 1973.

16 B. Louw, 'Irony in the text or insincerity in the writer? The diagnostic potential of semantic prosodies', in M. Baker, G. Francis and E. Tognini-Bonelli (eds) *Text and Technology: In Honour of John Sinclair*, Philadelphia, PA, John Benjamins, 1993.

17 P. Larkin, *The Whitsun Weddings*, London, Faber and Faber, 1964, p. 27.

4 Persuasion, Control and Argument

1 M. Atkinson, *Our Master's Voices: The Language and Body Language of Politics*, London, Methuen, 1994.

2 Adapted from Atkinson, *Our Master's Voices*, p. 63.

3 See R. Wooffitt, 'Rhetoric in English', in J. Maybin and N. Mercer (eds) *Using English: From Conversation to Canon*, London, Routledge with the Open University, 1996, pp. 122–43. Also, J.O. Thompson, 'Televangelical language: a media speech genre', in Maybin and Mercer (eds) *Using English*, pp. 156–61.

4 Quoted in S. Clark (ed.) *Malcolm X Talks to Young People: Speeches in the US, Britain and Africa*, New York, Pathfinder, 1991, p. 23.

5 Wooffitt, 'Rhetoric in English', p. 130.

6 Cited in J. Heritage and D. Greatbatch, 'Generating applause: a study of rhetoric and response at party political conferences', *American Journal of Sociology*, 1986, vol. 92, part 1, p. 123 (my italics).

7 See J. Sen, R. Sharma and A. Chakravarty, '"The light has gone out": Indian traditions in English rhetoric', in Maybin and Mercer (eds) *Using English*, pp. 150–5.

8 See D. Sutcliffe and A. Wong (eds) *The Language of Black Experience*, Oxford, Blackwell, 1986. Also, G. Smitherman, *Talkin and Testifyin*, Detroit, MI, Wayne State University Press, 1986.

9 These examples come from N. Rees, *Graffiti 2*, London, Unwin, 1980; and N. Rees, *Graffiti 3*, London, Unwin, 1981 (as cited in G. Cook, 'Language play in English', in Maybin and Mercer (eds) *Using English*, p. 213).

10 J. Burchill, '99 and counting', *The Guardian*, Saturday 4 January 1999, p. 6.

11 This conception of attitudes as generated through interaction is explained in more detail in J. Potter and M. Wetherell, *Discourse Analysis and Social Psychology*, London, Sage, 1994.

12 See G. Lakoff and M. Johnson, *Metaphors We Live By*, Chicago, IL, University of Chicago Press, 1980; G. Lakoff, *Women, Fire and Dangerous Things: What Categories Reveal About the Mind*, Chicago, IL, University of Chicago Press, 1987.

13 For an interesting critique of Lakoff's treatment of metaphors, and from a rhetorical perspective, see D. Edwards, 'Categories are for talking: on the cognitive and discursive bases of categorization', *Theory and Psychology*, 1991, vol. 1, no. 4, pp. 515–42.

14 Lakoff's circulated article was subsequently published as G. Lakoff, 'Metaphor and war', in B. Hallet (ed.) *Engulfed in War: Just War and the Persian Gulf*, Honolulu, Matsunaga Institute for Peace, 1991.

15 Lakoff, 'Metaphor and war'.

16 M. Bakhtin, *The Dialogic Imagination*, Austin, TX, University of Texas Press, 1981.

17 M.A.K. Halliday, *An Introduction to Functional Grammar*, London, Edward Arnold, 1985. The concept of 'grammatical metaphor' is clearly exemplified in J. Martin, 'Genre and literacy – modeling context in educational linguistics', *Annual Review of Applied Linguistics*, 1993, vol. 13, pp. 141–72.

18 G. Kress and R. Hodge, *Language as Ideology*, London, Routledge and Kegan Paul, 1979; R. Fowler, R. Hodge, G. Kress and A. Trew (eds) *Language and Control*, London, Routledge and Kegan Paul, 1979.

19 N. Fairclough (ed.) *Critical Language Awareness*, London, Longman, 1992.

20 D. Edwards, *Discourse and Cognition*, London, Sage, 1997. The idea that our choice of words is shaped in ways both obvious and subtle by our motivations was one of Freud's insights on the 'psychopathology of everyday life'. For Freud, 'slips of the tongue' were never accidental. See S. Freud, 'The psychopathology of everyday life', in A.A. Brill (ed.) *The Basic Writings of Sigmund Freud*, New York, Modern Library, 1938. (Freud's article was first published in 1904.)

21 R. Davis, *Writing Dialogue for Scripts*, London, A. and C. Black, 1998, pp. 27–8.

22 H. Sacks, 'On doing "being ordinary"', in J. Atkinson and J. Heritage (eds) *Structures of Social Action: Studies in Conversation Analysis*, Cambridge, Cambridge University Press, 1984 (my italics).

23 R. Wooffitt, *Telling Tales of the Unexpected: The Organisation of Factual Discourse*, Hemel Hempstead, Harvester-Wheatsheaf, 1992, pp. 163–4. As is the case for many other examples of other researchers' speech data that I have cited, this is a simplified version of Wooffitt's original transcription.

24 R. Wooffitt, 'Rhetoric in English', p. 142.

25 See S. Goodman, 'Market forces speak English', in S. Goodman and D. Graddol (eds) *Redesigning English: New Texts, New Identities*, London, Routledge with the Open University, 1996.

26 Goodman, 'Market forces', p. 148.

27 From M. Lynch and D. Bogen, *The Spectacle of History: Speech, Text and Memory at the Iran–Contra Hearings*, Durham, NC, Duke University Press, 1996, p. 195.

28 Adapted from S. Levinson, 'Activity types and language', in P. Drew and J. Heritage (eds) *Talk At Work: Interaction in Institutional Settings*, Cambridge, Cambridge University Press, 1992, pp. 82–3.

29 Levinson, 'Activity types', p. 84.

30 See E. Loftus and K. Ketcham, *The Myth of Repressed Memory*, New York, St Martin's Press, 1994; B. Andrews, J. Morton, D. Bekerian, C. Brewin, G. Davies and P. Mollon, 'The recovery of memories in clinical practice: experiences of British Psychological Society practitioners', *The Psychologist: Bulletin of the British Psychological Society*, 1995, vol. 8, no. 3, pp. 209–14; and G. Gudjonsson, 'The members of BFMS, the accusers and their siblings', *The Psychologist: Bulletin of the British Psychological Society*, 1996, vol. 10, no. 3, pp. 111–15.

31 D. Tannen, *Talking from 9 to 5*, London, Virago Press, 1994, p. 234.

32 Adapted from B. Kleiner, 'The modern racist ideology and its reproduction in "pseudo-argument"', *Discourse and Society*, 1998, vol. 9, no. 2, pp. 187–215.

33 The term 'exploratory talk' was first used to describe this kind of discussion by the educational researchers Douglas Barnes and Frankie Todd. See D. Barnes and F. Todd, *Communication and Learning in Small Groups*, London, Routledge and Kegan Paul, 1977. Also D. Barnes and F. Todd, *Communication and Learning Revisited*, Portsmouth, NH, Heinemann, 1995. For more classroom-based examples of these types of talk, see N. Mercer, *The Guided Construction of Knowledge: Talk Amongst Teachers and Learners*, Clevedon, Multilingual Matters, 1995; N. Mercer, 'The quality of talk in children's collaborative activity in the classroom', *Learning and Instruction*, 1996, vol. 6, no. 4, pp. 359–79; and R. Wegerif and P. Scrimshaw (eds) *Computers and Talk in the Primary Classroom*, Clevedon, Multilingual Matters, 1997.

34 The *Tracks* software was designed by Rupert Wegerif. See R. Wegerif, 'Using computers to help coach exploratory talk across the curriculum', *Computers and Education*, 1996, vol. 26, no. 1–3, pp. 51–60.

35 For discussions of the capabilities and limitations of various methods for categorizing and analysing the talk of joint activities, see N. Mercer, 'Socio-cultural perspectives and the study of classroom discourse', in C. Coll and D. Edwards (eds) *Teaching, Learning and Classroom Discourse*, Madrid, Infancia y Aprendizaje, 1996; R. Wegerif and N. Mercer, 'A dialogical framework for researching peer talk', in Wegerif and Scrimshaw (eds) *Computers and Talk in the Primary Classroom*; and R. Wegerif and N. Mercer, 'Using computer-based text analysis to integrate quantitative and qualitative methods in the investigation of

collaborative learning', *Language and Education*, 1997, vol. 11, no. 3, pp. 271–86.

36 R. Wegerif, 'Two images of reason in educational theory', *The School Field*, 1999, vol. IX, no. 3/4, pp. 78–105. Wegerif draws on the ideas of Habermas in this account. See J. Habermas, *The Theory of Communicative Action*, vol. 1, Cambridge, Cambridge University Press, 1991.

37 Halliday, *Introduction to Functional Grammar*.

5 Communities

1 From J.E. Orr, 'Sharing knowledge, celebrating identity: community memory in a service culture', in D. Middleton and D. Edwards (eds) *Collective Remembering*, London, Sage, 1990, p. 177.

2 The linguist Jim Martin has suggested that genres should not simply be considered styles of language use but rule-governed, goal-orientated social processes – ways of jointly getting things done for which communities have their own sets of ground rules (J. Martin, 'Genre and literacy – modeling context in educational linguistics', *Annual Review of Applied Linguistics*, 1993, vol. 13, pp. 141–72).

3 The linguist John Swales, who has done much to develop this concept, has suggested that to count as a community of discourse a group of people must not only have special, shared interests; they should also have an agreed set of common, public goals, their own network of communication, and a specialized way of using language. For me, however, this definition is slightly too narrow to be useful. The requirement of having 'a set of common, public goals' is a particular problem, as it seems to exclude any group of people who are not either employees of the same (or same kind of) institution, or members of a professional association, even if they regularly communicate together for shared purposes and use a customized language or discourse to do so. Swales' definition would not recognize the musicians in Sequence 5.1 or the technicians in Sequence 5.2 as members of a community. See J. Swales, *Genre Analysis: English in Academic and Research Settings*, Cambridge, Cambridge University Press, 1990.

4 K. Odean, 'Bear hugs and Bo Dereks on Wall Street', in C. Ricks and L. Michaels (eds) *The State of the Language*, London, Faber and Faber, 1990.

5 M. Haritos-Fatouros, 'The official torturer: a learning model for obedience to the authority of violence', *Journal of Applied Social Psychology*, 1988, vol. 8, no. 13, pp. 1107–20.

6 A. Sokal, 'Transgressing the boundaries: towards a transformative hermeneutics of quantum gravity', *Social Text*, 1996, no. 46/47, pp. 217–18. Sokal's own analysis of this hoax can be found in A. Sokal and J. Bricmont, *Intellectual Impostures*, New York, Profile, 1998.

7 Sokal, 'Transgressing the boundaries', p. 223.

8 See G.N. Gilbert and M. Mulkay, *Opening Pandora's Box: A Sociological Analysis of Scientists' Discourse*, Cambridge, Cambridge

University Press, 1984; and H.M. Collins, *Changing Order: Replication and Induction in Scientific Discourse*, London, Sage, 1985.

9 J. Lave and E. Wenger, *Situated Learning: Legitimate Peripheral Participation*, Cambridge, Cambridge University Press, 1991.

10 Based on a study of one local AA group in the USA by Carol Cain, as reported in Lave and Wenger, *Situated Learning*.

11 Lave and Wenger, *Situated Learning*, pp. 79–80.

12 Lave and Wenger, *Situated Learning*, p. 83.

13 N. Muller and A.N. Perret-Clermont, 'Cultural, institutional and interpersonal aspects of "Thinking and Learning Contexts"', paper presented at the 8th Conference for Research in Learning and Instruction, Göteborg, Sweden, August 1999.

14 H. Rheingold, *The Virtual Community: Homesteading on the Electronic Frontier*, Reading, MA, MIT Press, 1993, p. 5.

15 N. Postman, *Technopoly: The Surrender of Culture to Technology*, New York, Vintage Books, 1993; N. Watson, 'Why we argue about virtual community: a case study of the Phish.net fan community', in S. Jones (ed.) *Virtual Culture: Identity and Communication in Cybersociety*, London, Sage, 1997.

16 Quoted in Watson, 'Why we argue', p. 111.

17 See S.J. Yates, 'English in cyberspace', in S. Goodman and D. Graddol (eds) *Redesigning English: New Texts, New Identities*, London, Routledge with The Open University, 1996; and J. Gains, 'Electronic mail – a new style of communication or just a new medium? An investigation into the text features of e-mail', *English for Special Purposes*, 1999, vol. 18, pp. 81–101.

18 S. Turkle, *Life on the Screen: Identity in the Age of Internet*, London, Weidenfeld and Nicolson, 1996.

19 Turkle, *Life on the Screen*, p. 195.

20 R. Goodfellow and H. Chappell, 'Chatline in virtual classrooms', *The Times Higher Education Supplement*, 24 January 1999, p. 32.

21 R. Wegerif, 'The social dimension of asynchronous learning networks', *Journal of Asynchronous Learning Networks*, 1998, vol. 2, issue 1, pp. 34–49.

22 Quoted in Wegerif, 'Social dimension', p. 43.

23 Turkle, *Life on the Screen*.

24 See M. Poster, *The Mode of Information: Poststructuralism and Social Context*, Cambridge, Polity Press, 1990.

25 Quoted in Wegerif, 'Social dimension', p. 38.

26 S. Hennessy, M. Flude and A. Tait, *An Investigation of Students' and Tutors' Views on Tutorial Provision: Overall Findings of the RTS Project (Phases I and II)*, Milton Keynes, The Open University, 1999. The notion of 'adept users' comes from a study of schoolteachers' induction into ICT by Lyn Dawes. See L. Dawes, 'First connections: teachers and the National Grid for Learning', *Computers and Education*, 1999, vol. 33, no. 4, pp. 235–52.

6 Development through Dialogue

1 From p. 236 of D. Horgan, 'Learning to make jokes: a study of metalinguistic abilities', in M.B. Franklin and S.S. Barten (eds) *Child Language: A Reader*, Oxford, Oxford University Press, 1988.

2 A.H. Anderson, A. Clark and J. Mullin, 'Introducing information in dialogues: forms of introducing chosen by young speakers and the responses elicited from young listeners', *Journal of Child Language*, 1991, no. 18, pp. 663–87.

3 See, for example, S.B. Heath, *Ways with Words: Language, Life and Work in Communities and Classrooms*, Cambridge, Cambridge University Press, 1983; and B. Rogoff, *Apprenticeship in Thinking*, New York, Oxford University Press, 1990.

4 B. Rogoff, J. Mistry, A. Göncü and C. Mosier, 'Guided participation in cultural activity by toddlers and caregivers', *Monographs of the Society for Research in Child Development*, 1993, vol. 58, no. 7.

5 From Rogoff, *Apprenticeship in Thinking*, p. 191. For further discussion of 'guided participation' and other related concepts, see B. Rogoff, 'Observing sociocultural activity on three planes: participatory appropriation, guided participation and apprenticeship', in J. Wertsch, P. del Rio and A. Alvarez (eds) *Sociocultural Studies of Mind*, Cambridge, Cambridge University Press, 1995, pp. 139–63.

6 The socio-cultural (Vygotskian) account of cognitive development is usually contrasted with the more individualistic theory of Jean Piaget. Piaget did not rule out the influence of social interaction or guidance, especially in moral development, but compared with Vygotsky he did not see adults as playing as important a part in shaping children's development. For a short and accessible comparison of Piaget's and Vygotsky's theoretical perspectives, see J.R. Tudge and P.A. Winterhof, 'Vygotsky, Piaget and Bandura: perspectives on the relations between the social world and cognitive development', *Human Development*, 1993, vol. 36, pp. 61–81.

7 See, for example, J. Piaget, *The Equilibriation of Cognitive Structures*, Chicago, IL, University of Chicago Press, 1985. See also W. Doise and G. Mugny, *The Social Development of the Internet*, Oxford, Pergamon Press, 1984.

8 See J. Collins, *The Quiet Child*, London, Cassell, 1996.

9 From M. Hoogsteder, *Learning Through Participation* (Doctoral Thesis published as Monograph), Utrecht, University of Utrecht, 1995, p. 110.

10 See n. 15, Ch. 3.

11 From J. Maybin, 'Children's voices: talk, knowledge and identity', in D. Graddol, J. Maybin and B. Stierer (eds) *Researching Language and Literacy in Social Context*, Clevedon, Multilingual Matters, 1994, pp. 142–3.

12 J. Wertsch, 'Adult–child interaction as a source of self-regulation in children', in S.R. Yussen (ed.) *The Growth of Reflection in Children*, Orlando, FL, Academic Press, 1985.

13 This conception of 'scaffolding' is attributed to D. Wood, J. Bruner and G. Ross, 'The role of tutoring in problem-solving', *Journal of Child Psychology and Child Psychiatry*, 1976, vol. 17, pp. 89–100. The educational relevance of the concept is discussed in J. Maybin, N. Mercer and B. Stierer, '"Scaffolding" learning in the classroom', in K. Norman (ed.) *Thinking Voices*, London, Hodder and Stoughton, 1992.

14 From L.S. Vygotsky, 'Thinking and speech', in R.W. Riber and A.S. Carton (eds) *The Collected Works of L.S. Vygotsky*, volume 1: *Problems of General Psychology*, New York, Plenum, 1987. (Vygotsky's article was first published in 1934.) See also Chapter 6 of L.S. Vygotsky, *Mind in Society: The Development of Higher Psychological Processes*, Cambridge, MA, Harvard University Press, 1978.

15 See, for example, D. Newman, P. Griffin and M. Cole, *The Construction Zone*, Cambridge, Cambridge University Press, 1989; G. Wells, 'Using the tool-kit of discourse in the activity of learning and teaching', *Mind, Culture and Activity*, 1996, vol. 3, no. 2, pp. 74–101; and Chapter 7, 'A cultural approach to ontogeny', in M. Cole, *Cultural Psychology: A Once and Future Discipline*, Cambridge, MA, Harvard University Press, 1996.

16 From E. Elbers, 'Sociogenesis and children's pretend play: a variation on Vygotskian themes', in W. de Graaf and R. Maier (eds) *Sociogenesis Re-examined*, New York, Springer, 1994, p. 230.

17 Adapted from Elbers, 'Sociogenesis', p. 231.

18 Maybin, 'Children's voices', p. 141.

19 From M. Watson, 'The gender issue: is what you see what you get?', in R. Wegerif and P. Scrimshaw (eds) *Computers and Talk in the Primary Classroom*, Clevedon, Multilingual Matters, 1997.

20 Figure 1 and Sequence 6.10 come from A. Sfard and C. Kieran, 'Cognition as communication: dissecting students' mathematical interaction to see what makes it effective', *Mind, Culture and Activity* (in press).

21 Sfard and Kieran, 'Cognition as communication'.

22 M.A.K. Halliday, *Language as a Social Semiotic: The Social Interpretation of Language and Meaning*, London, Edward Arnold, 1978.

23 N. Mercer, *The Guided Construction of Knowledge: Talk Amongst Teachers and Learners*, Clevedon, Multilingual Matters, 1995.

24 The 'Talk Lessons' are available as L. Dawes, N. Mercer and R. Wegerif, *Thinking Together*, Birmingham, Questions Publishing Co., 2000; also see L. Dawes, 'Developing exploratory talk', in L. Grugeon, L. Hubbard, C. Smith and L. Dawes, *Teaching Speaking and Listening in the Primary School*, London, David Fulton Press, 1998.

25 See R. Wegerif, N. Mercer and L. Dawes, 'Software design to support discussion in the primary classroom', *Journal of Computer Assisted Learning*, 1998, vol. 14, pp. 199–211. See also K. Littleton and P. Light (eds) *Learning with Computers: Analysing Productive Interaction*, London, Routledge, 1999, in which contributors analyse a range of activities involving learners of different ages.

26 This research is reported in detail in N. Mercer, R. Wegerif and L. Dawes, 'Children's talk and the development of reasoning in the classroom', *British Educational Research Journal*, 1999, vol. 25, no. 1, pp. 95–111; and R. Wegerif, N. Mercer and L. Dawes, 'From social interaction to individual reasoning: an empirical investigation of a possible socio-cultural model of cognitive development', *Learning and Instruction*, 1999, vol. 9, no. 6, pp. 493–516.

27 For other similar evidence about the value of 'exploratory' types of talk in problem-solving, see S. Teasley, 'Talking about reasoning: how important is the peer group in peer collaboration?', in L. Resnick, R. Saljo, C. Pontecorvo and B. Burge (eds) *Discourses, Tools and Reasoning: Essays on Situated Cognition*, Berlin, Springer Verlag, 1997, p. 369; S. Lyle, 'An investigation in which children talk themselves into meaning', *Language and Education*, 1993, vol. 7, no. 3, pp. 181–96; and also D. Barnes and F. Todd, *Communication and Learning Revisited*, Portsmouth, NH, Heinemann, 1995.

28 Mercer, *Guided Construction of Knowledge*.

29 Our methods of analysis are explained in R. Wegerif and N. Mercer, 'Using computer-based text analysis to integrate quantitative and qualitative methods in the investigation of collaborative learning', *Language and Education*, 1997, vol. 11, no. 3, pp. 271–86.

30 More information about the Raven's test can be found in J. Raven, J. Court and J.C. Raven, *Manual for Raven's Progressive Matrices and Vocabulary Scales*, Oxford, Oxford Psychologists Press, 1995.

31 This research is reported in R. Wegerif, S. Rojas-Drummond and N. Mercer, 'Language for the social construction of knowledge: comparing classroom talk in Mexican pre-schools', *Language and Education*, 1999, vol. 13, no. 2, pp. 133–50; also S. Rojas-Drummond, G. Hernandez, M. Velez and G. Villagran, 'Cooperative learning and the appropriation of procedural knowledge by primary school children', *Learning and Instruction*, 1998, vol. 8, no. 1, pp. 37–62; and N. Mercer, 'Development through dialogue: a socio-cultural perspective on the process of being educated', in A.C. Quelhas and F. Pereira (eds) *Cognition and Context*, Lisbon, Instituto Superior de Psicologia Aplicada, 1998.

32 In a substantial and extended programme of research Brown and Palincsar in California showed how strategic, 'contingent' interactions by teachers can provide effective 'scaffolding' for their students' development of understanding. A. Brown and A.S. Palincsar, 'Guided, co-operative learning and individual knowledge acquisition', in L. Resnick (ed.) *Knowing, Learning and Instruction*, New York, Lawrence Erlbaum, 1989.

33 The concept of 'community of enquiry' is usually attributed to the philosopher Matthew Lipman, who has played a leading role in promoting the teaching of 'thinking skills'. See M. Lipman, *Philosophy for Children*, Montclair, NJ, Institute for the Advancement of Philosophy for Children, 1970.

34 For availability of the Talk Lessons see Note 24.

7 Conclusions

1 This common phenomenon was first given serious attention by the psychologists Roger Brown and David McNeill. See R. Brown and D. McNeill, 'The "tip of the tongue" phenomenon', *Journal of Verbal Learning and Verbal Behavior*, 1996, no. 5, pp. 325–37.

2 See Chapter 15, 'Reminiscence', in O. Sacks, *The Man Who Mistook his Wife for a Hat*, London, Duckworth, 1985.

3 D. Middleton and D. Edwards, 'Conversational remembering: a social psychological approach', in D. Middleton and D. Edwards (eds) *Collective Remembering*, London, Sage, 1990.

4 See, for example, J. Wertsch, *Voices of the Mind: A Socio-cultural Approach to Mediated Action*, Cambridge, MA, Harvard University Press, 1991; N. Mercer and C. Coll (eds) *Proceedings of the First Conference for Socio-cultural Research*, vol. 3: *Teaching, Learning and Interaction*, Madrid, Infancia y Aprendizaje, 1994; J. Wertsch, P. del Rio and A. Alvarez (eds) *Sociocultural Studies of Mind*, Cambridge, Cambridge University Press, 1995, pp. 139–63; and G. Wells, *Dialogic Inquiry: Towards a Sociocultural Practice and Theory of Education*, Cambridge, Cambridge University Press, 1994.

5 See, for example, the discussion of 'shared thinking' in Chapter 7 in B. Rogoff, *Apprenticeship in Thinking*, New York, Oxford University Press, 1990.

6 See G. Kress and P. Knapp, 'Genre in a social theory of language', *English in Education*, 1992, vol. 26, pp. 4–15; J. Martin, 'Genre and literacy – modeling context in educational linguistics', *Annual Review of Applied Linguistics*, 1993, vol. 13, pp. 141–72; C. Berkenkotter and T. Huckin, *Genre Knowledge in Disciplinary Communications*, Hillsdale, NJ, Lawrence Erlbaum, 1995; and D. Russell, 'Rethinking genre in school and society: an activity theory analysis', *Written Communication*, 1997, vol. 14, no. 4, pp. 504–54.

7 Some psychologists have begun to use the term 'distributed cognition' to describe how human knowledge is embodied as a collective resource in the tools, machines and social routines we build and use together. See, for example, L. Resnick, J. Levine and S. Behrend (eds) *Socially Shared Cognitions*, Hillsdale, NJ, Lawrence Erlbaum, 1991; G. Salomon (ed.) *Distributed Cognitions: Psychological and Educational Considerations*, Cambridge, Cambridge University Press, 1993.

8 G. Cook, *Discourse and Literature*, Oxford, Oxford University Press, 1995.

9 D. Bloome, 'Necessary indeterminacy and the microethnographic study of reading as a social process', *Journal of Research in Reading*, 1993, vol. 16, no. 2, pp. 98–111.

10 G. Lakoff and M. Johnson, *Metaphors We Live By*, Chicago, IL, University of Chicago Press, 1980; G. Lakoff, *Women, Fire and Dangerous Things: What Categories Reveal About the Mind*, Chicago, IL, University of Chicago Press, 1987.

11 See D. Edwards, 'Categories are for talking: on the cognitive and discursive bases of categorization', *Theory and Psychology*, 1991, vol. 1, no. 4, pp. 515–42.

12 The term 'exploratory talk' was first used in this way by the educational researcher Douglas Barnes. See, D Barnes and F. Todd, *Communication and Learning in Small Groups*, London, Routledge and Kegan Paul, 1977; and D. Barnes and F. Todd, *Communication and Learning Revisited*, Portsmouth, NH, Heinemann, 1995.

13 For a comparative review of many methods of analysing talk, see D. Edwards and D. Westgate, *Investigating Classroom Talk* (2nd edn), London, Falmer Press, 1994.

14 For further discussions of methodological aspects of researching talk as collective thinking, see S. Draper and A. Anderson, 'The significance of dialogue in learning and observing learning', *Computers and Education*, 1991, vol. 17, no. 1, pp. 93–107; R. Wegerif and N. Mercer, 'Using computer-based text analysis to integrate quantitative and qualitative methods in the investigation of collaborative learning', *Language and Education*, 1997, vol. 11, no. 3, pp. 271–86; and C. Crook, 'Computers in the community of classrooms', in K. Littleton and P. Light (eds) *Learning with Computers: Analysing Productive Interaction*, London, Routledge, 1999.

Bibliography

Anderson, A.H., Clark, A. and Mullin, J., 'Introducing information in dialogues: forms of introducing chosen by young speakers and the responses elicited from young listeners', *Journal of Child Language*, 1991, no. 18, pp. 663–87.

Andrews, B., Morton, J., Bekerian, D., Brewin, C., Davies, G. and Mollon, P., 'The recovery of memories in clinical practice: experiences of British Psychological Society practitioners', *The Psychologist: Bulletin of the British Psychological Society*, 1995, vol. 8, no. 3, pp. 209–14.

Atkinson, M., *Our Master's Voices: The Language and Body Language of Politics*, London, Methuen, 1994.

Austin, J., *How to Do Things with Words*, Oxford, Oxford University Press, 1962.

Bakhtin, M., *The Dialogic Imagination*, Austin, TX, University of Texas Press, 1981.

Barnes, D. and Todd, F., *Communication and Learning in Small Groups*, London, Routledge and Kegan Paul, 1977.

Barnes, D. and Todd, F., *Communication and Learning Revisited*, Portsmouth, NH, Heinemann, 1995.

Berkenkotter, C. and Huckin, T., *Genre Knowledge in Disciplinary Communications*, Hillsdale, NJ, Lawrence Erlbaum, 1995.

Bloome, D., 'Necessary indeterminacy and the microethnographic study of reading as a social process', *Journal of Research in Reading*, 1993, vol. 16, no. 2, pp. 98–111.

Boden, D. and Zimmerman, D. (eds) *Talk and Social Structure: Studies in Ethnomethodology and Conversation Analysis*, Cambridge, Polity Press, 1991.

Brown, A. and Palincsar, A.S., 'Guided, co-operative learning and individual knowledge acquisition', in L. Resnick (ed.) *Knowing, Learning and Instruction*, New York, Lawrence Erlbaum, 1989.

Brown, R. and McNeill, D., 'The "tip of the tongue" phenomenon', *Journal of Verbal Learning and Verbal Behavior*, 1996, no. 5, pp. 325–37.

Browning, G. in the regular column 'Office Politics', *The Guardian*, 6 March 1999.

Bruner, J., *Acts of Meaning*, Cambridge, MA, Harvard University Press, 1990.

Burchill, J., '99 and counting', *The Guardian*, Saturday 4 January 1999, p. 6.

Carruthers, P. and Boucher, J. (eds) *Language and Thought: Interdisciplinary Themes*, Cambridge, Cambridge University Press, 1998.

Clark, S. (ed.) *Malcolm X Talks to Young People: Speeches in the US, Britain and Africa*, New York, Pathfinder, 1991.

Coates, J., 'No gap, lots of overlap', in D. Graddol, J. Maybin and B. Stierer (eds) *Researching Language and Literacy in Social Context*, Clevedon, Multilingual Matters, 1994.

Cole, M., *Cultural Psychology: A Once and Future Discipline*, Cambridge, MA, Harvard University Press, 1996.

Cole, M., Gay, J., Glick, J. and Sharpe, D., *The Cultural Context of Learning and Thinking*, New York, Basic Books, 1971.

Collins, H.M., *Changing Order: Replication and Induction in Scientific Discourse*, London, Sage, 1985.

Collins, J., *The Quiet Child*, London, Cassell, 1996.

Cook, G., *Discourse and Literature*, Oxford, Oxford University Press, 1995.

Cook, G., 'Language play in English', in J. Maybin and N. Mercer (eds) *Using English: From Conversation to Canon*, London, Routledge with the Open University, 1996.

Crook, C., 'Computers in the community of classrooms', in K. Littleton and P. Light (eds) *Learning with Computers: Analysing Productive Interaction*, London, Routledge, 1999.

Crossley, N., *Intersubjectivity: The Fabric of Social Becoming*, London, Sage, 1996.

Crystal, D., *Dictionary of Linguistics and Phonetics*, Oxford, Blackwell, 1985.

Davis, R., *Writing Dialogue for Scripts*, London, A. and C. Black, 1998.

Dawes, L., 'Teaching talking', in R. Wegerif and P. Scrimshaw (eds) *Computers and Talk in the Primary Classroom*, Clevedon, Multilingual Matters, 1997.

Dawes, L., 'Developing exploratory talk', in L. Grugeon, L. Hubbard, C. Smith and L. Dawes, *Teaching Speaking and Listening in the Primary School*, London, David Fulton Press, 1998.

Dawes, L., 'First connections: teachers and the National Grid for Learning', *Computers and Education*, 1999, vol. 33, no. 4, pp. 235–51.

Dawes, L., Mercer, N. and Wegerif, R. *Thinking Together*, Birmingham, Questions Publishing Co., 2000.

Doise, W. and Mugny, G., *The Social Development of the Intellect*, Oxford, Pergamon Press, 1984.

Draper, S. and Anderson, A., 'The significance of dialogue in learning and observing learning', *Computers and Education*, 1991, vol. 17, no. 1, pp. 93–107.

Drew, P. and Heritage, J. (eds) *Talk at Work: Interaction in Institutional Settings*, Cambridge, Cambridge University Press, 1992.

Eades, D., 'Communicative strategies in Aboriginal English', in J. Maybin and N. Mercer (eds) *Using English: From Conversation to Canon*, London, Routledge with the Open University, 1996.

Edwards, A.D. and Furlong, V.F., *The Language of Teaching*, London, Heinemann, 1978.

Edwards, D., 'Categories are for talking: on the cognitive and discursive bases of categorization', *Theory and Psychology*, 1991, vol. 1, no. 4, pp. 515–42.

Edwards, D., *Discourse and Cognition*, London, Sage, 1997.

Edwards, D. and Mercer, N., *Common Knowledge*, London, Methuen/Routledge, 1987.

Edwards, D. and Westgate, D., *Investigating Classroom Talk* (2nd edn), London, Falmer Press, 1994.

Elbers, E., 'Sociogenesis and children's pretend play: a variation on Vygotskian themes', in W. de Graaf and R. Maier (eds) *Sociogenesis Re-examined*, New York, Springer, 1994.

Fairclough, N. (ed.) *Critical Language Awareness*, London, Longman, 1992.

Fodor, J., *The Modularity of Mind*, London, MIT Press, 1983.

Fowler, R., Hodge, R., Kress, G. and Trew, A. (eds) *Language and Control*, London, Routledge and Kegan Paul, 1979.

Freud, S., 'The psychopathology of everyday life', in A.A. Brill (ed.) *The Basic Writings of Sigmund Freud*, New York, Modern Library, 1938. (Freud's article was first published in 1904.)

Gains, J., 'Electronic mail – a new style of communication or just a new medium? An investigation into the text features of e-mail', *English for Special Purposes*, 1999, vol. 18, pp. 81–101.

Gardner, H., *The Mind's New Science*, New York, Basic Books, 1985.

Garfinkel, H., 'A conception of, and experiments with, "trust" as a condition of stable concerted actions', in O.J. Harvey (ed.) *Motivation and Social Interaction*, New York, Ronald Press, 1963.

Gibbons, P., *Discourse Contexts for Second Language Development in the Mainstream Classroom*, Doctoral Thesis, University of Technology, Sydney, Australia, 1995.

Gilbert, G.N. and Mulkay, M., *Opening Pandora's Box: A Sociological Analysis of Scientists' Discourse*, Cambridge, Cambridge University Press, 1984.

Golay Schilter, D., Perret, J-F., Perret-Clermont, A-N. and Guglielmo, F., 'Sociocognitive interactions in a computerised industrial task', in K. Littleton and P. Light (eds) *Learning with Computers: Analysing Productive Interaction*, London, Routledge, 1999.

Goodfellow, R. and Chappell, H., 'Chatline in virtual classrooms', *The Times Higher Education Supplement*, 24 January 1999, p. 32.

Goodman, S., 'Market forces speak English', in S. Goodman and D. Graddol (eds) *Redesigning English: New Texts, New Identities*, London, Routledge with the Open University, 1996.

Gopnik, A. and Meltzoff, A.N., *Words, Thoughts and Theories*, London, MIT Press, 1997.

Graddol, D.J., Cheshire, J. and Swann, J., *Describing Language* (2nd edn), Buckingham, Open University Press, 1994.

Grice, H.P., 'Logic and conversation', in P. Cole and J. Morgan (eds) *Syntax and Semantics*, vol. 3: *Speech Acts*, New York, Academic Press, 1975.

Gudjonsson, G., *The Psychology of Interrogations, Confessions and Testimony*, Chichester, John Wiley and Sons, 1992.

Gudjonsson, G., 'The members of BFMS, the accusers and their siblings', *The Psychologist: Bulletin of the British Psychological Society*, 1996, vol. 10, no. 3, pp. 111–15.

Habermas, J., *The Theory of Communicative Action*, vol. 1, Cambridge, Cambridge University Press, 1991.

Halliday, M.A.K., *Language as a Social Semiotic: The Social Interpretation of Language and Meaning*, London, Edward Arnold, 1978.

Halliday, M.A.K., *An Introduction to Functional Grammar*, London, Edward Arnold, 1985.

Halliday, M.A.K., 'Towards a language-based theory of learning', *Linguistics and Education*, 1993, vol. 5, no. 2, pp. 93–116.

Halliday, M.A.K. and Hasan, R., *Cohesion in English*, London, Longman, 1976.

Halliday, M.A.K. and Hasan, R., *Language, Context, and Text: Aspects of Language in a Social-Semiotic Perspective*, London, Oxford University Press, 1989.

Haritos-Fatouros, M., 'The official torturer: a learning model for obedience to the authority of violence', *Journal of Applied Social Psychology*, 1988, vol. 8, no. 13, pp. 1107–20.

Harré, R. and Gillett, G., *The Discursive Mind*, London, Sage, 1994.

Heath, S.B., *Ways with Words: Language, Life and Work in Communities and Classrooms*, Cambridge, Cambridge University Press, 1983.

Hennessy, S., Flude, M. and Tait, A., *An Investigation of Students' and Tutors' Views on Tutorial Provision: Overall Findings of the RTS Project (Phases I and II)*, Milton Keynes, The Open University, 1999.

Heritage, J. and Greatbatch, D., 'Generating applause: a study of rhetoric and response at party political conferences', *American Journal of Sociology*, 1986, vol. 92, part 1, p. 123.

Hoogsteder, M., *Learning Through Participation* (Doctoral Thesis published as Monograph), Utrecht, University of Utrecht, 1995.

Horgan, D., 'Learning to make jokes: a study of metalinguistic abilities', in M.B. Franklin and S.S. Barten (eds) *Child Language: A Reader*, Oxford, Oxford University Press, 1988.

Kleiner, B., 'The modern racist ideology and its reproduction in "pseudo-argument"', *Discourse and Society*, 1998, vol. 9, no. 2, pp. 187–215.

Kress, G. and Hodge, R., *Language as Ideology*, London, Routledge and Kegan Paul, 1979.

Kress, G. and Knapp, P., 'Genre in a social theory of language', *English in Education*, 1992, vol. 26, pp. 4–15.

Lakoff, G., *Women, Fire and Dangerous Things: What Categories Reveal About the Mind*, Chicago, IL, University of Chicago Press, 1987.

Lakoff, G., 'Metaphor and war', in B. Hallet (ed.) *Engulfed in War: Just War and the Persian Gulf,* Honolulu, Matsunaga Institute for Peace, 1991.

Lakoff, G. and Johnson, M., *Metaphors We Live By*, Chicago, IL, University of Chicago Press, 1980.

Larkin, P., *The Whitsun Weddings*, London, Faber and Faber, 1964.

Lave, J. and Wenger, E., *Situated Learning: Legitimate Peripheral Participation*, Cambridge, Cambridge University Press, 1991.

Leont'ev, A.N., *Problems of the Development of Mind*, Moscow, Progress Publishers, 1981.

Levinson, S., 'Activity types and language', in P. Drew and J. Heritage (eds) *Talk At Work: Interaction in Institutional Settings*, Cambridge, Cambridge University Press, 1992.

Light, P. and Butterworth, G. (eds) *Context and Cognition*, Hemel Hempstead, Harvester-Wheatsheaf, 1992.

Lipman, M., *Philosophy for Children*, Montclair, NJ, Institute for the Advancement of Philosophy for Children, 1970.

Littleton, K. and Light, P. (eds) *Learning with Computers: Analysing Productive Interaction*, London, Routledge, 1999.

Loftus, E. and Ketcham, K., *The Myth of Repressed Memory*, New York, St Martin's Press, 1994.

Longman, J., 'Professionals and clients: form filling and the control of talk', in J. Maybin and N. Mercer (eds) *Using English: From Conversation to Canon*, London, Routledge with the Open University, 1996. pp. 116–21.

Louw, B., 'Irony in the text or insincerity in the writer? The diagnostic potential of semantic prosodies', in M. Baker, G. Francis and E. Tognini-

Bonelli (eds) *Text and Technology: In Honour of John Sinclair*, Philadelphia, John Benjamins, 1993.

Lyle, S., 'An investigation in which children talk themselves into meaning', *Language and Education*, 1993, vol. 7, no. 3, pp. 181–96.

Lynch, M. and Bogen, D., *The Spectacle of History: Speech, Text and Memory at the Iran–Contra Hearings*, Durham, NC, Duke University Press, 1996.

Malcolm, I., 'Speech events in the Aboriginal classroom', *International Journal of the Sociology of Language*, 1982, no. 36, pp. 115–34.

Marriott, H., 'Deviations in an intercultural business negotiation', in A. Firth (ed.) *The Discourse of Negotiation: Studies of Language in the Workplace*, London, Pergamon, 1995.

Martin, J., 'Genre and literacy – modeling context in educational linguistics', *Annual Review of Applied Linguistics*, 1993, vol. 13, pp. 141–72.

Maybin, J., 'Children's voices: talk, knowledge and identity', in D. Graddol, J. Maybin and B. Stierer (eds) *Researching Language and Literacy in Social Context*, Clevedon, Multilingual Matters, 1994.

Maybin, J., 'Everyday talk', in J. Maybin and N. Mercer (eds) *Using English: From Conversation to Canon*, London, Routledge with the Open University, 1996.

Maybin, J., Mercer, N. and Stierer, B., '"Scaffolding" learning in the classroom', in K. Norman (ed.) *Thinking Voices*, London, Hodder and Stoughton, 1992.

Medway, P. 'Constructing the virtual building: language on a building site', in J. Maybin and N. Mercer (eds) *Using English: From Conversation to Canon*, London, Routledge with the Open University, 1996.

Mercer, N., *The Guided Construction of Knowledge: Talk Amongst Teachers and Learners*, Clevedon, Multilingual Matters, 1995.

Mercer, N., 'Socio-cultural perspectives and the study of classroom discourse', in C. Coll and D. Edwards (eds) *Teaching, Learning and Classroom Discourse*, Madrid, Infancia y Aprendizaje, 1996.

Mercer, N., 'The quality of talk in children's collaborative activity in the classroom', *Learning and Instruction*, 1996, vol. 6, no. 4, pp. 359–79.

Mercer, N., 'Development through dialogue: a socio-cultural perspective on the process of being educated', in A.C. Quelhas and F. Pereira (eds) *Cognition and Context*, special issue of *Análise Psicológica*, Lisbon, Instituto Superior de Psicologia Aplicada, 1998.

Mercer, N. and Coll, C. (eds) *Proceedings of the First Conference for Socio-cultural Research*, vol. 3: *Teaching, Learning and Interaction*, Madrid, Infancia y Aprendizaje, 1994.

Mercer, N. and Longman, J., 'Accounts and the development of shared understanding in Employment Training Interviews', *Text*, 1992, vol. 12, no. 1, pp. 103–25.

Mercer, N. and Swann, J. (eds) *Learning English: Development and Diversity*, London, Routledge with The Open University, 1996.

Mercer, N., Wegerif, R. and Dawes, L., 'Children's talk and the development of reasoning in the classroom', *British Educational Research Journal*, 1999, vol. 25, no. 1, pp. 95–111.

Middleton, D. and Edwards, D., 'Conversational remembering: a social psychological approach', in D. Middleton and D. Edwards (eds) *Collective Remembering*, London, Sage, 1990.

Muller, N. and Perret-Clermont, A.N., 'Cultural, institutional and interpersonal aspects of "Thinking and Learning Contexts"', paper presented at the 8th Conference for Research in Learning and Instruction, Göteborg, Sweden, August 1999.

Newman, D., Griffin, P. and Cole, M., *The Construction Zone*, Cambridge, Cambridge University Press, 1989.

Norman, K. (ed.) *Thinking Voices: The Work of the National Oracy Project*, London, Hodder and Stoughton, 1992.

Odean, K., 'Bear hugs and Bo Dereks on Wall Street', in C. Ricks and L. Michaels (eds) *The State of the Language*, London, Faber and Faber, 1990.

Open University, *Talk and Learning 5–16: An Inservice Pack on Oracy for Teachers*, Milton Keynes, The Open University, 1991.

Open University, U210 *The English Language: Past, Present and Future*, Milton Keynes, The Open University, 1996.

Orr, J.E., 'Sharing knowledge, celebrating identity: community memory in a service culture', in D. Middleton and D. Edwards (eds) *Collective Remembering*, London, Sage, 1990.

Oxford Dictionary of Quotations, 1979 edition, London, Book Club Associates.

Piaget, J., *The Equilibriation of Cognitive Structures*, Chicago, IL, University of Chicago Press, 1985.

Pinker, S., *The Language Instinct*, London, Penguin, 1994.

Pinker, S., 'Facts about human language relevant to its evolution', in J-P. Changeux and S. Chavailon (eds) *Origins of the Human Brain*, Oxford, Clarendon Press, 1995.

Poster, M., *The Mode of Information: Poststructuralism and Social Context*, Cambridge, Polity Press, 1990.

Postman, N., *Technopoly: The Surrender of Culture to Technology*, New York, Vintage Books, 1993.

Potter, J. and Wetherell, M., *Discourse Analysis and Social Psychology*, London, Sage, 1994.

Qhelhas, A.C. and Pereira, F., *Cognition and Context*, special issue of *Análise Psicológica*, Lisbon, Instituto Superior de Psicologia Aplicada, 1998.

Raven, J., Court, J. and Raven, J.C., *Manual for Raven's Progressive Matrices and Vocabulary Scales*, Oxford, Oxford Psychologists Press, 1995.

Rees, N., *Graffiti 2*, London, Unwin, 1980.

Rees, N., *Graffiti 3*, London, Unwin, 1981.

Resnick, L.B. (ed.) *The Nature of Intelligence*, New York, Lawrence Erlbaum, 1976.

Resnick, L., Levine, J. and Behrend, S. (eds) *Socially Shared Cognitions*, Hillsdale, NJ, Lawrence Erlbaum, 1991.

Rheingold, H., *The Virtual Community: Homesteading on the Electronic Frontier*, Reading, MA, MIT Press, 1993.

Richards, H., interview with Studs Terkel, *The Times Higher Educational Supplement*, 26 June, 1998.

Rogoff, B., *Apprenticeship in Thinking: Cognitive Development in Social Context*, New York, Oxford University Press, 1990.

Rogoff, B., 'Observing sociocultural activity on three planes: participatory appropriation, guided participation and apprenticeship', in J. Wertsch, P. del Rio and A. Alvarez (eds) *Sociocultural Studies of Mind*, Cambridge, Cambridge University Press, 1995.

Rogoff, B., Mistry, J., Göncü, A. and Mosier, C., 'Guided participation in cultural activity by toddlers and caregivers', *Monographs of the Society for Research in Child Development*, 1993, vol. 58, no. 7.

Rojas-Drummond, S., Hernandez, G., Velez, M. and Villagran, G., 'Co-operative learning and the appropriation of procedural knowledge by primary school children', *Learning and Instruction*, 1998, vol. 8, no. 1, pp. 37–62.

Romaine, S., 'Pidgin English advertising', in C. Ricks and L. Michaels (eds) *The State of the Language*, London, Faber and Faber, 1990.

Rommetweit, R., 'Language acquisition as increasing linguistic structuring of experience and symbolic behavior control', in J.V. Wertsch (ed.) *Culture, Communication and Cognition: Vygotskian Perspectives*, Cambridge, Cambridge University Press, 1985.

Russell, D., 'Rethinking genre in school and society: an activity theory analysis', *Written Communication*, 1997, vol. 14, no. 4, pp. 504–54.

Sacks, H., 'On doing "being ordinary"', in J. Atkinson and J. Heritage (eds) *Structures of Social Action: Studies in Conversation Analysis*, Cambridge, Cambridge University Press, 1984.

Sacks, O., *The Man Who Mistook his Wife for a Hat*, London, Duckworth, 1985.

Salomon, G. (ed.) *Distributed Cognitions: Psychological and Educational Considerations*, Cambridge, Cambridge University Press, 1993.

Scott Fitzgerald, F., *The Great Gatsby*, Harmondsworth, Penguin Books, 1973 (first published in 1926).

Sen, J., Sharma, R. and Chakraverty, A., '"The light has gone out": Indian traditions in English rhetoric', in J. Maybin and N. Mercer (eds) *Using English: From Conversation to Canon*, London, Routledge with the Open University, 1996.

Sfard, A. and Kieran, C., 'Cognition as communication: dissecting students' mathematical interaction to see what makes it effective', *Mind, Culture and Activity* (in press).

Sheeran, Y. and Barnes, D., *School Writing: Discovering the Ground Rules*, Milton Keynes, Open University Press, 1991.

Shuy, R., *Language Crimes: The Use and Abuse of Language Evidence in the Courtroom*, London, Blackwell, 1993.

Sinclair, J. and Coulthard, M., *Towards an Analysis of Discourse: The English Used by Teachers and Pupils*, London, Oxford University Press, 1975.

Smitherman, G., *Talkin and Testifyin*, Detroit, MI, Wayne State University Press, 1986.

Sokal, A., 'Transgressing the boundaries: towards a transformative hermeneutics of quantum gravity', *Social Text*, 1996, no. 46/47, pp. 217–52.

Sokal, A. and Bricmont, J., *Intellectual Impostures*, New York, Profile, 1998.

Stokoe, E., *Exploring Gender and Discourse in Higher Education*, Doctoral Thesis, University of Leicester, 1996.

Sutcliffe, D. and Wong, A. (eds) *The Language of Black Experience*, Oxford, Blackwell, 1986.

Swales, J., *Genre Analysis: English in Academic and Research Settings*, Cambridge, Cambridge University Press, 1990.

Tannen, D., *Conversational Style: Analysing Talk Amongst Friends*, Norwood, NJ, Ablex, 1984.

Tannen, D., *Talking from 9 to 5*, London, Virago Press, 1994.

Teasley, S., 'Talking about reasoning: how important is the peer group in peer collaboration?', in L. Resnick, R. Saljo, C. Pontecorvo and B. Burge (eds) *Discourses, Tools and Reasoning: Essays on Situated Cognition*, Berlin, Springer Verlag, 1997.

Thompson, J.O., 'Televangelical language: a media speech genre', in J. Maybin and N. Mercer (eds) *Using English: From Conversation to Canon*, London, Routledge with The Open University, 1996.

Tudge, J.R. and Winterhof, P.A., 'Vygotsky, Piaget and Bandura: perspectives on the relations between the social world and cognitive development', *Human Development*, 1993, vol. 36, pp. 61–81.

Turkle, S., *Life on the Screen: Identity in the Age of Internet*, London, Weidenfeld and Nicolson, 1996.

Volosinov, V., *Marxism and the Philosophy of Language*, New York, Seminar Press, 1973.

Vygotsky, L.S., *Thought and Language*, Cambridge, MA, MIT Press, 1962.

Vygotsky, L.S., *Mind in Society: The Development of Higher Psychological Processes*, Cambridge, MA, Harvard University Press, 1978.

Vygotsky, L.S., 'Thinking and speech', in R.W. Riber and A.S. Carton (eds) *The Collected Works of L.S. Vygotsky*, volume 1: *Problems of General Psychology*, New York, Plenum, 1987.

Watson, M., 'The gender issue: is what you see what you get?', in R. Wegerif and P. Scrimshaw (eds) *Computers and Talk in the Primary Classroom*, Clevedon, Multilingual Matters, 1997.

Watson, N., 'Why we argue about virtual community: a case study of the Phish.net fan community', in S. Jones (ed.) *Virtual Culture: Identity and Communication in Cybersociety*, London, Sage, 1997.

Wegerif, R., 'Using computers to help coach exploratory talk across the curriculum', *Computers and Education*, 1996, vol. 26, no. 1–3, pp. 51–60.

Wegerif, R., 'The social dimension of asynchronous learning networks', *Journal of Asynchronous Learning Networks*, 1998, vol. 2, issue 1, pp. 34–49.

Wegerif, R., 'Two images of reason in educational theory', *The School Field*, 1999, vol. IX, no. 3/4, pp. 78–105.

Wegerif, R. and Mercer, N., 'Using computer-based text analysis to integrate quantitative and qualitative methods in the investigation of collaborative learning', *Language and Education*, 1997, vol. 11, no. 3, pp. 271–86.

Wegerif, R. and Mercer, N., 'A dialogical framework for researching peer talk', in R. Wegerif and P. Scrimshaw (eds), *Computers and Talk in the Primary Classroom*, Clevedon, Multilingual Matters, 1997.

Wegerif, R., Mercer, N. and Dawes, L., 'Software design to support discussion in the primary classroom', *Journal of Computer Assisted Learning*, 1998, vol. 14, pp. 199–211.

Wegerif, R., Mercer, N. and Dawes, L., 'From social interaction to individual reasoning: an empirical investigation of a possible socio-cultural model of cognitive development', *Learning and Instruction*, 1999, vol. 9, no. 6, pp. 493–516.

Wegerif, R., Rojas-Drummond, S. and Mercer, N., 'Language for the social construction of knowledge: comparing classroom talk in Mexican pre-schools', *Language and Education*, 1999, vol. 13, no. 2, pp. 133–50.

Wegerif, R. and Scrimshaw, P. (eds) *Computers and Talk in the Primary Classroom*, Clevedon, Multilingual Matters, 1997.

Wells, G., *Dialogic Inquiry: Towards a Sociocultural Practice and Theory of Education*, Cambridge, Cambridge University Press, 1994.

Wells, G., 'Using the tool-kit of discourse in the activity of learning and teaching', *Mind, Culture and Activity*, 1996, vol. 3, no. 2, pp. 74–101.

Wertsch, J., 'Adult–child interaction as a source of self-regulation in children', in S.R. Yussen (ed.) *The Growth of Reflection in Children*, Orlando, FL, Academic Press, 1985.

Wertsch, J.V. (ed.) *Culture, Communication and Cognition: Vygotskian Perspectives*, Cambridge, Cambridge University Press, 1985.

Wertsch, J., *Voices of the Mind: A Socio-cultural Approach to Mediated Action*, Cambridge, MA, Harvard University Press, 1991.

Wertsch, J., del Rio, P. and Alvarez, A. (eds) *Sociocultural Studies of Mind*, Cambridge, Cambridge University Press, 1995.

Wood, D., Bruner, J. and Ross, G., 'The role of tutoring in problem-solving', *Journal of Child Psychology and Child Psychiatry*, 1976, vol. 17, pp. 89–100.

Wooffitt, R., *Telling Tales of the Unexpected: The Organisation of Factual Discourse*, Hemel Hempstead, Harvester-Wheatsheaf, 1992.

Wooffitt, R., 'Rhetoric in English', in J. Maybin and N. Mercer (eds) *Using English: From Conversation to Canon*, London, Routledge with the Open University, 1996.

Yates, S.J., 'English in cyberspace', in S. Goodman and D. Graddol (eds) *Redesigning English: New Texts, New Identities*, London, Routledge with The Open University, 1996.

Index